PLOTTING POWER

PLOTTING

STRATEGY IN THE EIGHTEENTH CENTURY

POWER

JEREMY BLACK

INDIANA UNIVERSITY PRESS

This book is a publication of

INDIANA UNIVERSITY PRESS
Office of Scholarly Publishing
Herman B Wells Library 350
1320 East 10th Street
Bloomington, Indiana 47405 USA

iupress.indiana.edu

The paper used in this publication
meets the minimum requirements of
the American National Standard for
Information Sciences—Permanence
of Paper for Printed Library Materials,
ANSI Z39.48–1992.

*Manufactured in the
United States of America*

Library of Congress Cataloging-in-
Publication Data

Names: Black, Jeremy, 1955- author.
Title: Plotting power : strategy in the
    eighteenth century / Jeremy Black.
Other titles: Strategy in the eighteenth
    century
Description: 1st edition. | 1st edition. |
    Bloomington : Indiana University
    Press, [2017] | Includes
    bibliographical references and index.
Identifiers: LCCN 2017000809 (print) |
    LCCN 2017013816 (ebook) | ISBN
    9780253026798 (e-book) | ISBN
    9780253026088 (cloth : alk. paper)
Subjects: LCSH: Military history,
    Modern—18th century. | Strategy. |
    International relations—History—
    18th century. | World politics—18th
    century.
Classification: LCC D214 (ebook) |
    LCC D214 .B574 2017 (print) | DDC
    355/.033509033—dc23
LC record available at https://lccn.loc
    .gov/2017000809

ISBN 978-0-253-02608-8 (cloth)
ISBN 978-0-253-02679-8 (e-bk.)

1 2 3 4 5   22 21 20 19 18 17

For

ANDREW THOMPSON

Friend and Colleague

CONTENTS

PREFACE

STRATEGY IS A TERM MUCH DEBATED NOW. INDEED, IN THE West, helping both to provoke and to focus this debate, there is a sense that strategy is in some way a lost art and a repeated argument to that effect. This sense reflects a crisis of confidence as a result of repeated setbacks, or at least serious difficulties, for Western forces in Iraq and Afghanistan in the 2000s and 2010s, and the linked problems for Western goals. The rhetoric and associated disquiet about absent or flawed strategy rose to a hitherto unmatched height in 2015. This was specifically in response to the ISIS terrorist attack on Paris and to the more general imbroglio concerning Western policy toward Syria and indeed the Middle East as a whole.

The rhetoric and disquiet also reflected a more general concern in the West in the 2000s and 2010s about drift and drift in the case of the conception and implementation of what was variously described as policy and strategy. The confused and largely unsuccessful response to Chinese and Russian expansionism was an aspect of this disquiet. In this context of concern and the response to concern, the term *strategy* was much employed and not always in an illuminating fashion. That itself was an instructive comment on the vocabulary of strategy. So also was the extent to which commentators focused on differences and tensions arising from contrasting goals between the powers, notably Russia and the Western powers. These contrasts underlined the extent to which alliances and would-be alliances entailed commitments and possibilities in terms of goals and means that involved the pressures and problems of cooperation. To offer an account of strategy as a military activity that does not take adequate note of the international context and its consequences is evidently flawed, and this is also true for ISIS.

There is no reason why the same should not be the case for the past. Indeed, the use of the present to guide and equip questions and thoughts about the past is an integral aspect of assessing the historical dimension of strategy. Modern terms have to be employed to provide a twenty-first-century appraisal of what happened. As long as ahistorical perspectives are avoided, this is a rewarding approach and in practice, a necessary one.

This book reflects many years working on the eighteenth century, on both its military history and its international relations. It also arises from my concern that much work on the period, although very valuable, fails to engage explicitly with the issue of strategy and that despite the significance of strategic practice and related ideas.

The book proceeds from an introduction and a general chapter, through a series of case studies, to a conclusion. The case studies are contextualized in terms of shifts across the century. Much of the book will be devoted to those case studies. For each one, there will be a discussion of strategic culture and practice and, specifically, of the degree to which it is appropriate to use the terms of strategy. The case studies are chosen to illustrate the range of strategy and also to draw attention to key issues, notably the changing nature and importance of strategic culture. Chapter 4, which follows the assessment of France in chapter 3, focuses on the early use of the term *strategy* which was developed in France.

In thinking about this issue, I have benefited from teaching military history at Exeter for many years and would like to thank the students involved. While writing this book, I have profited from opportunities to give the Changing Character of War program at Oxford Annual Lecture in 2016 and to speak at the New York Historical Society, the University of North Texas, William Paterson University, and the 2016 Gunther E. Rothenberg Seminar in Military History, to the Foreign Policy Research Institute, to a Madrid conference on Spain in 1660–1724, to Hervé Drevillon's seminar at the Sorbonne, at Oundle School, and for the Royal Danish Defense Academy, and from the comments of Paola Bianchi, Stan Carpenter, Marco Cesa, Michael Clemmesen, Alan Forrest, Bernard Gainot, Richard Harding, Enrique García Hernán, Beatrice Heuser, Lothar Höbelt, Tim May, Martin Robson, Kaushik Roy, Rick Schneid,

Dennis Showalter, Don Stoker, Heiko Whenning, and an anonymous reviewer on an earlier draft. Conversations with Bob Citino, Stephen Conway, Enrique Garcia Hernán, Luigi Loreto, Oliver Letwin, Eduardo De Mesa, Paul Newton, and Harold Tanner have been most helpful. Advice from Jonathan Abel, Michael Axworthy, Anne Bandry, Michael Bregnsbo, Tony Claydon, Tony Cross, Huw Davies, Simon Dixon, Hervé Drevillon, John France, Iain Hampsher-Monk, Gregory Hanlon, Angus Hawkins, Jan Hoffenaar, Colin Jones, Andrew Lambert, Michael Leggière, Nick Lipscombe, Noel Malcolm, Alexander Mikaberidze, Roger Morris, Jeremy Noakes, Ciro Paoletti, Ryan Patterson, Robert Pocock, José Miguel Pereira Alcobio Palma Sardica, Satsuma Shinsuke, Tassapa Umavijani, and Peter Ward is also much appreciated. None of them is responsible for any mistakes. I am most grateful to Her Majesty the Queen, the Duke of Bedford, the Earl of Harrowby, Earl Waldegrave, Lady Lucas, Sir Hector Monro, and Richard Head for granting permission to consult their collections of manuscripts.

It is a great pleasure to dedicate this book to Andrew Thompson, a major scholar on the British empire, a colleague, and a sage and supportive friend.

LIST OF ABBREVIATIONS

Add. Additional Manuscripts

AE. Paris, Ministère des Relations Extérieures

AN. Paris, Archives Nationales

Ang. Angleterre

AST. Turin, Archivio di Stato

BL. London, British Library, Department of Manuscripts

Bodl. Oxford, Bodleian Library

CH. Cholmondeley Houghton papers

Chewton Chewton House, Waldegrave papers

CP. Correspondance Politique

CUL. Cambridge, University Library

Cumb. Cumberland Papers

FO. Foreign Office papers

HHStA. Vienna, Haus-, Hof- und Staatsarchiv, Staatenabteilung

Ing. Inghilterra

LM. Lettere Ministri

MD. Mémoires et Documents

NA. London, National Archives (formerly Public Record Office)

Polit. Corresp. R. Koser, ed., *Politische Correspondenz Friedrichs des Grossen* (46 vols., Berlin, 1879–1939)

RA. Windsor, Royal Archives

Sandon Sandon Hall, Harrowby papers

SP. State Papers

Speelman, ed., *Lloyd* Patrick J. Speelman, ed., *War, Society and Enlightenment. The Works of General Lloyd* (Leiden, the Netherlands: Brill, 2005)

Williamwood Williamwood, Ewart papers

PLOTTING
POWER

INTRODUCTION

STRATEGY IS A KEY CONCEPT IN WAR AND INTERNATIONAL relations, but the use of the word *strategy* to discuss the period prior to the development of the term is a matter of controversy. This book is written in the conviction that it is valuable to use terms for periods before they were employed by contemporaries, as, for example, not only with strategy but also with geopolitics, Enlightenment, logistics, or blitz-krieg.[1] This study will focus on the range of strategic cultures, thought, and practice in the last century before the term *strategy* was employed in Europe and will also cover the situation in the early decades of that employment. As such, I will link military ideas and practice, political concepts, diplomacy, and geopolitics. There will also be a consideration of the relationship between strategy in the external or international sense, in short of planning and implementing military and diplomatic policies, and strategy in the internal or domestic sense, of policies for strengthening society, the latter a significant element and notably for those rulers referred to as "enlightened despots." As such, strategy will emerge in the perspective of politics by other means, and with these politics understood in the widest of terms.

Partly because the range will be global, this is not simply a case of strategy before Clausewitz, although that dimension will be considered. Equally, it is very important, as this book shows, not to write in the shadow of Clausewitz. This is even more the case than in the past because Western-centric approaches to military matters and history no longer appear so credible on a global scale. Indeed, a major flaw in the existing literature arises precisely from this situation. It focuses almost exclusively on Europe and North America. That is understandable in that most of the scholarly work is on these areas and the surviving historical sources for them are far better. Such a concentration, however, should not lead to downplaying the remainder of the world.

To take, for example, encyclopedia entries as repositories of received wisdom, the 1963 edition of the *Encyclopaedia Britannica*, a work that proclaimed, opposite the title page, that it was "published with the editorial advice of the faculties of the University of Chicago and a committee of members of Oxford, Cambridge and London Universities," found strategy in the case of Alexander the Great, Hannibal, Caesar, and the Mongols but not "the Huns, the Moslems or the Crusaders," before going on to present Frederick II, "the Great," of Prussia, and even more, Napoleon as key innovators. Prior to the former, "strategy was essentially of limited aim and was greatly concerned with the art of siegecraft," but Frederick, according to the encyclopedia, was allegedly replaced by an overcautious obsession with maneuver. According to the entry, it was Napoleon who "completely transformed strategy" and "oriented modern military theory toward the search for underlying principles," a process discussed in the encyclopedia with reference to Clausewitz and Jomini. The remainder of the world did not feature in this entry.[2]

There is something particularly discouraging about the use of Clausewitz in this context. His work has been made to bear a burden, notably as a universal account, that it scarcely deserves, and that at a time when other reiterations of Western thought in the Enlightenment and Romantic periods have been subject to more criticism, deconstruction, and contextualization. As will emerge from this book, it is inappropriate to think of a single character of warfare in this period (or indeed for any other), and that problem is not tackled by arguing that there is an essential or inherent character to war. That so much of the subject has been framed in the past in terms of a discussion about the meanings and meaning of Clausewitz is not a helpful approach to the past or a necessary guide to current or future work. It is as if the past discussion, however, represents intellectual capital, in the shape, for example, of lectures and writings, that academics will not, or cannot, put to one side.

There are major problems with defining strategy and not simply because of the absence of the use of the term for most of history. In addition, the application of the understanding of strategy poses questions. Take the use in a recent study by a leading American scholar who is far more open than most military historians to considering the global dimensions of military history. Wayne Lee points out that most readers and authors think they intuitively know the difference between tactics, operations, and strategy, but that there are many definitions. For Lee, "Strategy refers to the deployment of resources and forces on a national scale and the identification of key objectives (territorial or otherwise) that operations are then designed to achieve." Operations are defined as "campaigns."[3] Thomas Kane and David Lonsdale describe strategy as "the process that converts military power into policy effect."[4]

This approach downplays any alternative to a distinctive military character to strategy, an approach similar to that considered in this book, but this is an issue that needs to be addressed explicitly. It is apparent that the function of strategy, if understood as the relationships between ends, ways, and means in power politics, is not necessarily military. At the same time, it is unclear why the national scale should be the key one, as opposed to an inclusion of the subnational or indeed the supranational.

Even for the just over two centuries when the term has been employed in English, French, German, and other languages and the concept applied, there is much difference, not to say controversy, over its definition, employment, application, and value. Strategy has been taken to refer to the full range of human activity and has served as adjective, noun, and verb.

Differences over definition and application extend to related concepts, notably that of strategic culture. Despite these differences,[5] the latter concept, nevertheless, is particularly important as it provides a context within which the issue of strategy can be approached and noticeably so in the absence of a relevant vocabulary or institutional culture, and practice. Strategic culture is employed to discuss the context within which military tasks were, and are, "shaped." It is therefore better for discussing context and continuity than significant changes. This concept owes much to a 1977 report by Jack Snyder for the US RAND Corporation on Soviet strategic culture. Written for a specific audience, the concept, which drew on George Kennan's analysis in his "long telegram" from Moscow of February 22, 1946,[6] provided a way to help explain the Soviet

Union, a government system and political culture for which sources were manipulated for propaganda reasons and accurate reports were few. This situation, in practice, describes that of many states in the past and some in the present. The idea of explaining and discussing a system in terms of a culture captured not only the social construction of power politics[7] but also the notion that there were relevant general beliefs, attitudes, and behavioral patterns and that these were in some way integral to the politics of power, rather than being dependent on the specific circumstances of a particular conjuncture.[8] Indeed, strategic culture has been presented as leavening a "collective memory with cumulative experience."[9] What governments do, how they understand it, and how they describe and justify it are involved in relationships of mutual feedback. In one particular light, the word *culture* takes on especial value due to the emphasis on "martial spectacle" as a purpose and form of activity, one at once strategic, purposeful, and imbued with a range of values, assumptions, and objectives.[10] Such spectacle was, and is, significant both for domestic and for international purposes and audiences.

Strategic culture continues to be the concept of choice when considering China, other states that are difficult to understand and/or for which the sources are limited, and, indeed, all states. Thus, in 2009, a pamphlet from the Strategic Studies Institute of the US Army War College claimed, "To craft any intelligent, effective policy towards China, the US national security community must have a clear contextual understanding of the historical and cultural factors that define China's strategic thinking, and that can best provide an . . . assessment of China's goals and intentions."[11] At the same time, it is possible, and indeed necessary, for historians to discern strategy, as well as strategic culture, in the case of China.[12] So also for India. There, strategy was understood in the eighteenth century in terms of the way to defeat and incorporate, and not to destroy, an enemy realm. Strategy therefore entailed politics and diplomacy as well as military matters. It equated with statecraft.

If both strategy and strategic culture involve choices and constraints, in terms of tasks and means, strategic culture presents these as, at once, ideological and cultural and as circumscribed by structural factors. Irrespective of the analysis of both strategy and strategic culture, there was, and is, also the issue of responding, or seeking to respond, to the values

and circumstances on the other side. The understanding of the prioritization of tasks and means is best set in this context. Thus, strategy is both
relative and contextual.

To some commentators, the delay in the development of the term
strategy reflects conceptual and institutional limitations affecting any
understanding of strategy in the past. However, in his study of strategy
before the term in the case of Russia, John P. LeDonne addressed the
possible criticism that he presented "nothing but 'virtual strategy,' in
which the author attributes to the Russian political élite a vision they
never had." He adds a helpful definition of what he terms "grand strategy" namely "an integrated military, geopolitical, economic, and cultural vision." That, indeed, is a definition that is applied in this book
but without any need to add the word *grand* to *strategy*, even though
the combination has long been employed.[13] Ironically, this word looks
back to the late-eighteenth-century use in France of the term *grand tactics*. This was a term usually employed to discuss what would today be
referred to as the operational level. In turn, LeDonne was criticized for,
as one reviewer put it, presenting strategy "in language which the contemporary Russian élites would certainly not have used."[14] This criticism
is ironic in that it is employed by scholars who do the same in much of
their analysis.

LeDonne is not alone in focusing on the significance of elite views.
This focus entails a welcome grounding in particular historical contexts,
and thus a rejection of any ahistorical, noncultural, nonrealist, framework for analyzing strategic choices. Instead, how an elite saw itself and
its identity and interests comprised the most important component of
strategic choice,[15] and thereby of resulting outcomes. Indeed, strategic consequences were central to an important feedback mechanism in
which elites came to reconceptualize their assumptions or did not do so.
This process is important to the evaluation of strategic assumptions. This
focus on elites has been broadened in order to discuss how nations see
their roles and objectives.[16] It is also an approach that covers the inherent
political character of strategy and strategic choice because these choices
were contested as they were shaped and reshaped.

Compared to the formal, institutional processes of strategic discussion and planning in recent decades, notably its military context as

a supposedly distinct activity, strategy in the eighteenth century was, at best, limited and ad hoc, lacking both well-developed structure and doctrine to match an empirical process of learning and ideas. In the case of Christian Europe (then the "West"), general staffs of a type, it has been claimed by Peter Wilson, emerged during the Thirty Years' War (1618–48), with the staff designed to assist the commander and maintain communications with the political center. Such staffs evolved from the personal assistants initially paid by the general himself,[17] but they generally remained very limited in numbers and method, and the term *general staff* may well be highly misleading. Wilson had not yet had the opportunity to develop his claim.

In addition to the Thirty Years' War, other episodes have attracted attention. For example, it has been argued that under the direction of Field Marshal Count Franz Moritz Lacy, Austria, during the Seven Years' War (1756–63), established what became an effective proto–general staff.[18] Such an argument necessarily puts earlier developments in the Thirty Years' War in the shade and/or implies a process of episodic development. Logistics was a key element in the planning of campaigns in both centuries.

With military education, it is again difficult to assess and date key developments. Indeed, in his perceptive *History of the Late War in Germany* (1766), Henry Lloyd, who, on the widespread contemporary pattern of fighting in the armies of other sovereigns, had served in the Seven Years' War, claimed that "It is universally agreed upon, that no art or science is more difficult, than that of war; yet, by an unaccountable contradiction of the human mind, those who embrace this profession take little or no pains to study it. They seem to think that the knowledge of a few insignificant and useless trifles, constitute a great officer. This opinion is so general, that little or nothing else is taught at present in any army whatever."[19] That account was substantially correct as far as formal education was concerned. However, Lloyd underrated the very important method of learning on the job, notably by example and experience, as was seen, for example, with British pamphlet debates after particular operations. Moreover, such learning offered much, as it still does.

The limited institutional character to military education and command practice in the eighteenth century can be seen as lessening the possibility of moving on from strategic culture to strategy. Conversely, the absence of a mechanism for the creation and dissemination of institutional wisdom on strategy may well have ensured that the body of assumptions and norms referred to as strategic culture were instead more effective, indeed more normative. This body affected both strategic thinkers and strategic actors, and in turn, they each sustained assumptions. Differentiating strategic culture from strategy in terms of firm distinctions is not overly helpful, but it captures the extent to which there are contrasts in emphasis.

The role of strategic thinkers, whether or not they, like Sun Tzu and Clausewitz, served in the military, attracts the attention of intellectuals, both military and nonmilitary, and particularly of academics who write on the military and who tend to seek intellectual assessments of war. Notably this is so for Clausewitz, as he is taken by some to help, in some way, explain and characterize subsequent Prussian, and then German, military success, as well as to provide a benchmark for effectiveness.

In practice, such thinkers might have been largely irrelevant or relevant only insofar as they captured and focused general nostrums and current orthodoxies and therefore served in some way to validate them. It is, however, instructive to note that in the case of China, the state, at that time, with the most-developed literary treatment of war, there is scant evidence of the use of texts for guidance. Indeed, the Kangxi emperor (r. 1662–1723), a ruler far more successful as a military leader than Louis XIV, let alone Napoleon, allegedly declared the military classics, such as the works of Sun Tzu, worthless, and references to these classics in Chinese military documents were rare.[20] The marginality of explicitly military thinkers can also be considered for other states, including even Clausewitz's Prussia. Alternatively, these thinkers can be presented as an instance of the rhetoric of power, an aspect of power that was as significant to contemporaries as its analysis and indeed far more so.

Strategy is usually discussed by military historians in terms of war-winning. That, however, is to misunderstand strategy or rather, to operationalize it in terms of military activity. In contrast, in practice, the key to strategy is the political purposes that are pursued in what is a "comprehensive, multifaceted" activity.[21] In short, strategy, whether military or nonmilitary and in the former case, whether or not focused on war,[22] is a process of defining interests, understanding problems, and determining goals. Strategy is not the details of the plans by which these goals are implemented by military means. The latter are the operational components of strategy to employ another, later, term.

As a result of this formulation of strategy, domestic attitudes, policies, and politicians can be as significant in the understanding of interests and the formulation and execution of strategy as their military counterparts and indeed, more so. Thus, in the "War on Terror," in the 2000s and 2010s, measures taken to try to secure the support of the bulk of the Muslim population of countries threatened by terrorism, such as Britain, are as germane as the use of force against new or suspected terrorists. Conversely, a ISIS manual, apparently written in 2014, which set out plans for a centralized, self-sufficient state, included the establishment of not only an army but also of military schools to create further generations of fighters, as well as bureaucratic planning, covering health, education, industry, propaganda, and resource management.

Treating the existence of strategy as highly problematic for a period when the term is absent mistakes the absence of an articulated school of strategic thinking for the lack of strategic awareness. This is a key point throughout the history of strategy. It is the activity, not the word, that is the basis of examination and analysis. For example, the claim that because there was no term for strategy, so imperial Rome lacked strategic thinking, fails to give sufficient weight to the lasting need to prioritize possibilities and threats and, in response, to allocate resources.[23] This is a need at all levels but one that is particularly apparent for far-flung states. In addition, the earlier, three Punic Wars between Carthage and Republican Rome (264–41 BCE, 218–201 BCE, 149–146 BCE) have been discussed in terms of what are presented as contemporary views of grand strategy, with the latter seen to depend on long-term planning and a good perception of geographical relationships.[24] Alongside a presentation of Roman strategy in terms of modern concepts of defense, has come a stress on factors such as honor and revenge.[25] That emphasis, however, does not negate the existence of strategy.

Moreover, the discussion of strategy in the classical period is longstanding. If it became with Thucydides writing on the strategy of the

Peloponnesian War (431–404 BCE) in which he participated, it has continued, as with Hans Delbrück's *Die Strategie des Perikles, erläutert durch die Strategie Friedrichs des Grossen* (*The Strategy of Pericles Clarified by the Strategy of Frederick the Great*, 1890). Alfred Thayer Mahan (1840–1914), the American theorist of command of the sea, was influenced by the German historian Theodor Mommsen (1817–1903) who, in his *Römische Geschichte* (*History of Rome*; 3 vols., 1854–56), presented Roman naval power as playing a crucial role against Carthage in the Second Punic War.

Strategy has also been discerned in the case of Byzantium, the Eastern Roman Empire, which lasted until 1453. It has been suggested that under incessant pressure from other powers, Byzantium could not afford to wage wars of attrition or seek decisive battles. Instead, it is argued that Byzantium sought to ally with tribal enemies of its current opponent, and that the tendency was to avoid battle.[26] As discussed in chapter 4, there was also a literature from Byzantium then that was discussed in the late eighteenth century when the term *strategy* was formulated.

As far as medieval Western Europe is concerned, sources are few. The standard chronicle narratives of war are of scant help because the chroniclers were outsiders and simply gave narratives of campaigns or hand-to-hand encounters. They had little grasp of the thinking and planning behind activities. Medieval Western strategy existed but has to be worked out from what commanders did and not, on the whole, from documents in which it was discussed, although there are valuable records, for example, from Pere III of Aragon (r. 1336–87). Medieval leaders knew what they wanted to do, but there was no school or forum to produce a dialectic, and each leader chose his methods, which is essentially the case today whatever the theory of strategy.

William the Conqueror isolated Anglo-Saxon England before his successful invasion in 1066, Henry I in 1124 allied with the Emperor Henry V against France, Richard I allied with the Low Countries powers against France, and John created a great coalition against France. In invading France in the 1340s and 1350s, Edward III sought to wear down his enemy by ravaging the countryside, an instance of strategy as, at least in part, the extension of tactical thinking. In addition, the practicalities of warfare, of feeding armies and making sure they could move, were dominant requirements. In the case of crusading warfare, Saladin in 1187 lured the army of the kingdom of Jerusalem into a waterless area where he could fight on his terms and destroyed his opponents at Hattin, while Richard I of England, soon after, advised a strategy of attacking Egypt (which ruled Palestine and Jerusalem) rather than going for Jerusalem, a strategy followed in the thirteenth century.[27]

Commentary on war, then and subsequently, was an aspect of thought that focused on choices as well as context.[28] In the case of Philip II of Spain (r. 1556–98), there is a valuable book-length work on his strategy. However, a treatment of the management of the war effort in his last years focuses on the absence of a coordinated strategy linking Spain's various commitments. In addition, a lack of consistency toward England has been discerned, notably whether to overthrow the dynasty or to force the English out of the war, and this was linked to a contrast between emphases on religious crusading or on pragmatic consideration. A lack of strategic vision has been associated with a reactive strategy of responding to English threats to the Spanish empire, a strategy that gave the initiative to the English. The article makes clear the number of possible uses for the word and the judgments bound up in them, including long-term strategy, grand strategy, strategic schizophrenia, and clear and coherent strategic vision.[29]

It has also been argued, more specifically for the Thirty Years' War (1618–48) in Europe, but also for the subsequent ancien régime, that the logistical problems posed by supporting armies made it difficult to pursue a strategy reflecting political war aims and thus hard to act in accordance with any overall strategy.[30] Choices in force structures and command methods in the early-modern period, that of the sixteenth and seventeenth centuries, however, repeatedly reflected the fusion of strategy and policy, as they often arose from fundamental assumptions about the methods best placed to preserve social norms as well as state integrity. This was the key nexus of society. Similar points can be made for the eighteenth century.

Different views have been advanced about the meaning and application of strategy. In 2005, Hew Strachan, then holding the major chair in military history in Britain, that at Oxford, published an article entitled "The Lost Meaning of Strategy," a piece he reprinted in 2008 and 2013.[31] Moreover, the argument has been much cited,[32] in part possibly because it provided a way for commentators to explain the crisis of Western military policy in Iraq and Afghanistan, and in part because it provided these commentators with a justification. Strachan is cited by other writers arguing that there is a failure to produce clear policy and coherent strategy.[33] Strachan argued that the understanding of the word and concept of strategy had been so stretched that it was in danger of losing its usefulness and that, in particular, it had been conflated with policy. To Strachan, the conflation of words led to incoherence, an incoherence reflecting the compromise between the ends of policy and the military means available to implement it. His contribution closed with the claim that it was necessary for the application of force to have concepts that were robust because they were precise. As a contribution to a debate, this was a valuable piece. It might also act as a clarion call for the future, although it is too easy to mistake precision about terms for analysis.

As a standard by which to assess the past, however, Strachan's argument was less than helpful, not least because the precise conceptualization that he saw as necessary was not present in, or for, the past and that despite the fact that many states had been militarily effective and across a great geographical range. Rather than thinking in terms of clearly defined systems, it is more pertinent to focus on complexes or bundles of institutional-practical ways of doing things[34] in a context of fitness for purpose. Moreover, there could be a functional strategy even if it did not have a linguistic or institutional formulation. As strategy is contextual, so are its definitions.

The 1976 *Encyclopaedia Britannica* noted "the demarcation between strategy as a purely military phenomenon and national strategy of the broader variety became blurred" in the nineteenth century and even less clear in the twentieth.[35] Indeed, the actual validity of differentiating strategy from policy was, is, and probably will be less valid and less practical than Strachan and others suggest.

A particular difficulty arises because of the issue of "ownership." The wide variation in the use of the term *strategy*, and indeed of the concept, in part arises from this very issue, alongside the more commonplace problems stemming from the definition and usage of conceptual terms and notably of ones that have differing resonances in specific cultural and national contexts. In large part, but far from exclusively, this issue of "ownership" arises from the determination by, and on behalf of, militaries to define a sphere of activity and planning that is under their understanding and control, a process that is supported by their civilian supporters among commentators. Much of the writing about strategy has been driven by military thinkers.

It is, therefore, no accident that strategy as a self-conscious and actively articulated practice was very much linked to the development of general staffs, which was particularly developed by Prussia in the nineteenth century. The Prussians established and improved a system of general staff work and of training at a general staff academy, a system which was to be given much of the credit for victory in 1866 and 1870 over Austria and France, respectively. Training of staff officers provided the Prussian army with a valuable coherence, as these officers had an assured place in a coordinated command system: officers from the general staff were expected to advise commanders, and the latter were also required to heed their chiefs of staff. This led to a system of joint responsibility in which either the commander or his first general staff officer could issue orders. Such a system, which rested on the reputation of the staff system, made predictable planning and the delegation of the execution of the strategic intent possible, thus encouraging forward planning. Moreover, from 1857, there was an emphasis in the Prussian army on preparing for a whole campaign, rather than simply for battle, and thus on war plans. Sweeping Prussian successes in 1866 and 1870, at the expense of Austria and France, respectively, gave the staff system prestige and greatly encouraged its adoption and emulation elsewhere.[36]

This Prussian system, however, both facilitated and reflected a reading of military affairs in which the views of the army came foremost. These views focused on a drive for autonomy, if not independence, from political oversight and civilian society, and a demand for resources. In part, both elements responded to the growing pressure on established roles and traditional assumptions that was perceived in societies that were changing rapidly, both in terms of industrialization and urbanization, and also with a decline of deference as new social assumptions came into play. Increasingly in the nineteenth century, alongside the challenges from liberal politicians and movements, came those from socialists and other radicals. Moreover, there were the changes stemming from new technologies and from the prospect that this process would continue, if not escalate.[37]

The challenges this dynamic situation posed to the military varied by context, notably national context, but also with reference to the professional specialty of the officers involved and to their political assumptions. A range of responses existed and were discussed, often explicitly in terms of their political consequences. These included conscription, as a way to discipline and contain the new masses (and also to raise numbers, an instance of the domestic-military overlap), as well as the military use of new technologies, and enhanced professionalism. The concept and practice of strategy was another response to the challenges of a changing situation and notably in the intensively competitive nature of international relations in the late nineteenth century and at the start of the twentieth century.

This focus on strategy served to entrench military professionalism and to lessen civilian intervention, which was presented as "less strategic." This argument scarcely defines and places strategy as a whole, but it helps explain its greater salience from the late nineteenth century. In essence, a term developed as an aspect of Enlightenment thought, notably of the classification of knowledge, became more prominent in a specific sociopolitical context and with reference to a particular stage and type of military professionalism. In short, the term was scarcely value-free, and attempts to treat it as such are mistaken.

This context remains relevant today with strategy and notably because modern militaries in many (but far from all states) continue to seek a professionalism that both limits government intervention and enables them to define their role. The Powell Doctrine in the case of the American military in the 1990s (Colin Powell was chairman of the Joint Chiefs of Staff) exemplified this point,[38] as did arguments over Anglo-American intervention in Afghanistan and Iraq in the 2000s and 2010s. Alongside areas generally left to the competence of military leaders, notably training, tactics, and doctrine, came the determination to maintain a key role in procurement, operations, and policy. Annexing the last in terms of what is defined as strategy and limiting government to a more anodyne and general field termed policy serves this goal. Strachan's work can be seen against this background. To detach his work from his strong personal and professional links with the British army, and what he refers to as "moral obligation,"[39] is possible but also has limitations.

More positively, military leaders who insist on clarity of roles, terms, missions, and responsibilities are in part motivated by a suspicion that the political leaders do not truly understand what they want or what they want done. As a result, this insistence is an effort to force the political leaders to articulate their goals. Sometimes this process is cynical on the part of the military, but it can also be motivated by a sense of professional duty and sometimes arises because the political leaders are incompetent in devising policy. Political leaders have frequently already made the decision before they consult the experts, and consultation is often intended to help justify the decision or simply serves as an aspect of implementation.[40]

The argument on behalf of military independence can be queried, however, in both specifics and in general. Much depends on an understanding of contexts and of institutional cultures, but the argument is as worthy of attention in terms of this subject as the commonplace division between policy and strategy. In July 1929, Basil Liddell Hart, the would-be leading British military commentator of the interwar years, addressed this issue in the political context of the 1920s. This was a situation in which democratization, notably accountability, and unpredictability were more pronounced across Western society as a whole than prior to World War I. In the *Quarterly Review*, a periodical published in London, he wrote:

> Perhaps only an absolute ruler, firmly in the saddle, can hope to maintain unswervingly the military ideal of the "armed forces" objective, although even he will be wise to adjust it to the realities of the situation and to weigh well the prospects of fulfilling it. But the strategist who is the servant of a democratic government has less rein. Dependent on the support and confidence of his employers, he has to work within a narrower margin of time and cost than the "absolute" strategist, and is more pressed for quick profits. Whatever the ultimate prospects he cannot afford to postpone dividends too long. Hence it may be necessary for him to swerve aside temporarily from his objective or at least to give it a new guise by changing his line of operations. Faced with these inevitable handicaps it is apt for us to ask whether military theory should not be more ready to reconcile its ideals with the inconvenient reality that its military effort rests on a

popular foundation—that for the supply of men and munitions, and even for the chance of continuing the fight at all, it depends on the consent of the "man in the street." He who pays the piper calls the tune, and strategists might be better paid in kind if they attuned their strategy, so far as is rightly possible, to the popular ear.[41]

As another instance of accountability, there is the question of whether reliance on the argument of military independence is an aspect, indeed very much a self-serving aspect, of what, in 2015, General Nicholas Houghton, the chief of the (British) general staff, referred to as "military conservatism." He employed this term twice in a discussion about the need to respond to changing tasks and the restrictions thereto.[42] The attempt to separate out strategy from policy is, in some respects, not only a question of apparent terminological precision but also an aspect of this conservatism, as well as being an attempt to give a distinctive military voice in the situation and to ensure that this voice has coherence and weight. An instance of a comparable qualification to the distinction between strategy and policy is that between public and private in the organization of war.[43] As a different but related point as far as the military are concerned, it is important to note that civilians often directed the military repression of popular movements.[44]

Clearly, even if a means-versus-ends distinction is to be advanced when discussing strategy and policy and the relations between them, ends are in large part set in relation with, and to, means, while means are conceived of, and planned, in terms of ends. For example, the location of Chinese garrisons was a reflection of strategic, political, and cultural factors, in so far as they could be distinguished. Under the Manchu emperors (r. 1644–1912), the bannermen, who were regarded as more reliable, were stationed in northern China, around the center of authority, Beijing, and down to the River Yangzi, and the garrisons lived in segregated walled compounds. In contrast, the more numerous Han Chinese Green Standard troops, who focused on dealing with rebellions, were stationed all over the country but with many in the south, where the first permanent banner garrison was not established until 1718.

In addition, strategy was, and is, conceptualized in terms of views on both world affairs and domestic political culture, with these views proving a key feature of the belief systems of policymakers. To separate out these factors is not only unhelpful as an account of the past but also puts an emphasis on a precision that is ahistorical as a description of the past, as well as being only an aspiration for present and future.

Strachan, in his "lost meaning of strategy" piece, cited recent American and British policy as mistaken in its understanding of strategy, an approach that served apparently to discredit imprecision as this policy. This approach was directly linked to failure in Iraq. That failure, however, was not due to imprecision but, instead, to a total misreading of the situation there, both political and military, before, during, and after the campaign, a misreading that exemplified Clausewitz's point that understanding the nature of the war is crucially necessary.

Separately, aside from the argument that a lack of coherence in strategy was in fact an appropriate response to complexity,[45] the (separate) imprecision in the understanding and practice of strategy is, in part, a reflection of the variety of environments in which policy is pursued. In addition, Strachan's argument that "strategy is designed to make war useable by the state, so that it can, if need be, use force to fulfil its political objectives,"[46] begged a whole range of issues, not only the distinction between the use of force and political objectives but also the role of nonstate actors and the very diversity of state forms and cultures. There are no "ur" (original and essential) form and dynamic of the state, just as there are none for war. Far from there being any fixed relationship between war and politics, it is the flexible nature of the links that helps explain the importance of each to the other. For example, military activity greatly altered the contours and parameters of the politics that helped cause it, and sometimes of the states involved in conflict. In some cases, military activity had a comparable impact on social structures. The centrality of war as a basis of change, however, does not mean that there was a consistent pattern of cause or effect.

The debate is still active. It is to the struggle for power that we now turn. That is valuable in itself and pertinent because of its capacity to offer insights that are instructive for the situation today. For example, an important aspect of the strategic context in the eighteenth century was the need to confront societies and militaries that operated in different ways to the state in question. This was variously the case for China in Xinjiang, for Russia on its southern borderlands, for Britain in India, and for the new American state confronting Native American opponents. The resulting confrontations and conflicts could provide opportunities for a government that was more authoritarian and less encumbered by traditional institutions[47]—for example, compared to those affecting conflict within Europe—but at any rate, also posed strategical requirements that were different to those raised by symmetrical warfare. Moreover, these requirements prefigured elements of recent and current conflict, notably between Western powers and opponents in the Islamic world.

In the case of India, the British East India Company "faced a growing major grand strategic challenge" as a result of increased participation in Indian politics. The challenge was not that of military operations, however difficult these might be, but rather, "to understand and exploit the dynamics and culture of Indian politics and war-making."[48] That was the key element of strategy. Aside from this task, the character of the "grand strategic 'mission' or 'purpose'" at the time was complex, including, as it did, a company with financial rationale and a government seeking strategic assets in pursuit of its power politics.[49]

Again, modern parallels are striking. It may be the case that the lack of comparable institutional structures affected the efficiency of devising "optimum grand strategies."[50] However, the existence of such an optimum is very much open to debate, as is the respective quality of decision making suggested by such a comparison. It is more pertinent to consider parallels across time without assuming any automatic process of improvement with time and thanks to modernization. The latter is a strategy of academic exposition that is coherent and much repeated but also unfounded. Indeed, modernization theory has created many analytical illusions for historians seeking a theoretical underpinning and pursuing and finding coherence in a developmental fashion, one that apparently links past to present.

NOTES

1. D. W. Engels, *Alexander the Great and the Logistics of the Macedonian Army* (Berkeley, CA, 1978); R. M. Citino, *Quest for Decisive Victory: From* *Stalemate to Blitzkrieg in Europe, 1899–1940* (Lawrence, KS, 2002); J. Black, *Geopolitics and the Quest for Dominance* (Bloomington, IN, 2015).

2. *Encyclopaedia Britannica*, vol. 21 (London, 1963): 453–453B.

3. W. E. Lee, *Waging War. Conflict, Culture, and Innovation in World History* (Oxford, 2016): 407.

4. T. Kane and D. Lonsdale, *Understanding Contemporary Strategy* (Abingdon, UK, 2012): 26.

5. L. Sondhaus, *Strategic Culture and Ways of War* (London, 2006). For the question of a separate definition and role for "grand strategy," see P. D. Miller, "On Strategy, Grand and Mundane," *Orbis* 60 (2016): 237–47.

6. T. H. Etzold and J. L. Gaddis, eds., *Containment: Documents on American Policy and Strategy, 1945–1950* (New York, 1978): 84–90; Gaddis, *The United States and the Origins of the Cold War, 1941–1947* (New York, 1972) and *George F. Kennan: An American Life* (New York, 2011).

7. A. Wendt, "Anarchy Is What States Make of It: The Social Construction of Power Politics," *International Organization* 46 (1992): 391–425.

8. K. Booth, *Strategy and Ethnocentrism* (London, 1979); C. G. Reynolds, "Reconsidering American Strategic History and Doctrines," in *History of the Sea: Essays on Maritime Strategies* (Columbia, SC, 1989); C. S. Gray, "Strategic Culture as Context: The First Generation of Theory Strikes Back," *Review of International Studies* 25 (1999): 49–70; L. Sondhaus, *Strategic Culture and Ways of War* (London, 2006).

9. R. W. Barnett, *Navy Strategic Culture: Why the Navy Thinks Differently* (Annapolis, MD, 2009): 130.

10. D. M. Robinson, *Martial Spectacles of the Ming Court* (Cambridge, MA, 2013).

11. K. D. Johnson, *China's Strategic Culture: A Perspective for the United States* (Carlisle, PA, 2009): 15.

12. K. Swope, "Manifesting Awe: Grand Strategy and Imperial Leadership in the Ming Dynasty," *Journal of Military History* 79 (2015): 597–634.

13. J. P. LeDonne, *The Grand Strategy of the Russian Empire, 1650–1831* (New York, 2004): vii–viii.

14. Robert Frost, *English Historical Review* 121 (2006): 850.

15. A. Johnston, "Thinking about Strategic Culture," *International Security* 19 (1995): 35.

16. W. Martel, *Grand Strategy in Theory and Practice: The Need for an Effective American Foreign Policy* (Cambridge, UK, 2015).

17. P. H. Wilson, "Strategy and the Conduct of War," in *Ashgate Research Companion to the Thirty Years' War* (Farnham, UK, 2013): 269–83, 277.

18. E. Lund, *War for the Every Day: Generals, Knowledge, and Warfare in Early Modern Europe, 1680–1740* (Westport, CT, 1999). T. C. W. Blanning, *Frederick the Great* (London, 2015): 226, more bluntly writes "a general staff was created."

19. Speelman, ed., *Lloyd*: 13.

20. K. M. Swope, "Manifesting Awe: Grand Strategy and Imperial Leadership in the Ming Dynasty," *Journal of Military History* 79 (2015): 605.

21. LeDonne, *Grand Strategy*, 219. See also E. Luttwak, *Strategy: The Logic of War and Peace* (Cambridge, MA, 1987).

22. Deterrence is an aspect of peacetime strategy.

23. The classic work, E. Luttwak's *The Grand Strategy of the Roman Empire* (Baltimore, 1976), is criticized in B.

Isaac, *The Limits of Empire: The Roman Army in the East* (2nd ed., Oxford, 1992): 372–418, and conversely, taken forward by E. L. Wheeler, "Methodological Limits and the Mirage of Roman Strategy" and "Rome's Dacian Wars: Domitian, Trajan, and Strategy on the Danube," *Journal of Military History* 57 (1993): 7–41, 215–40; 74 (2010): 1185–227; and 75 (2011): 191–219, and K. Kagan, "Redefining Roman Grand Strategy," *Journal of Military History* 70 (2006): 333–62. See more recently, Y. Le Bohec, *La guerre romaine: 58 avant J.-C.-235 après J.-C.* (Paris, 2014) and G. Traina, "La tête et la main droite de Crassus. Quelques remarques supplémentaires," in A. Allély, ed., *Corps au supplice et violences de guerre dans l'Antiquité* (Bordeaux, France, 2014): 95–98.

24. L. Loreto, *La grande strategia di Roma nell'età della prima guerra punic (BCE 273-229). L'inizio di un paradosso* (Naples, Italy, 2007). For the earlier situation in the Greek world, see P. A. Brunt, "The Aims of Alexander," *Greece and Rome* 12 (1965): 205–15 and "Spartan Policy and Strategy in the Archidamian War," *Phoenix* 19, no. 4 (1965): 255–80; J. K. Anderson, *Military Theory and Practices in the Age of Xenophon* (Berkeley, CA, 1970).

25. S. P. Mattern, *Rome and Enemy: Imperial Strategy in the Principate* (Berkeley, CA, 1999).

26. E. Luttwak, *The Grand Strategy of the Byzantine Empire* (Cambridge, MA, 2009).

27. P. Contamine, *War in the Middle Ages* (Oxford, 1984); M. Prestwich, *Armies and Warfare in the Middle Ages: The English Experience* (New Haven,

CT, 1996); F. Garcia Fitz, "¿Hube estratégia en la adad media? A propósito de las relaciones castellano-musulmanas durante la segunda mitad del siglo XIII," *Revista da Faculdade de Letras. História*, ser. 2, 15 no. 2 (1998): 837–54: this is published by the University of Porto; C. J. Rogers, *War, Cruel and Sharp: English Strategy under Edward III, 1327-1360* (Woodbridge, UK, 2000); J.-W. Honig, "Reappraising Late Medieval Strategy: The Example of the 1415 Agincourt Campaign," *War in History* 19 (2012): 123–51. On Pere, J. Black, *Geopolitics and the Quest for Dominance* (Bloomington, IN, 2016): 38–39.

28. B. Heuser, *The Strategy Makers: Thoughts on War and Society from Machiavelli to Clausewitz* (Westport, CT, 2010) and *The Evolution of Strategy* (Cambridge, UK, 2010).

29. G. Parker, *The Grand Strategy of Philip II* (New Haven, CT, 1998); E. Tenace, "A Strategy of Reaction: The Armadas of 1596 and 1597 and the Spanish Struggle for European Hegemony," *English Historical Review* 118 (2003): 855–82. See also E. Ringmar, *Identity, Interest and Action: A Cultural Explanation of Sweden's Intervention in the Thirty Years War* (Cambridge, UK, 1996).

30. G. Perjes, "Army Provisioning, Logistics and Strategy in the Second Half of the Seventeenth Century," *Acta Historica Academiae Scientiarum Hungaricae* 16 (1970): 1–52; D. A. Parrott, "Strategy and Tactics in the Thirty Years' War: The 'Military Revolution,'" in C. J. Rogers, ed., *The Military Revolution Debate. Readings on the Military Transformation of Early Modern Europe* (Boulder, CO, 1995): 242–46; J. Luh,

"'Strategie und Taktike' im Ancien Régime," *Militargeschichtiche Zeitschrift* 64 (2005): 101–31 and *Ancien Régime Warfare and the Military Revolution: A Study* (Groningen, the Netherlands, 2000): 178.

31. H. Strachan, "The Lost Meaning of Strategy," *Survival* 47 (2005): 33–54, reprinted in T. G. Mahnken and J. A. Maiolo, eds., *Strategic Studies: A Reader* (Abingdon, UK, 2008) and Strachan, *The Direction of War: Contemporary Strategy in Historical Perspective* (Cambridge, UK, 2013).

32. See, e.g., P. Porter, review of L. Freedman, *Strategy: A History* (Oxford, 2013) in *RUSI Journal* 159, no. 4 (2014): 117.

33. J. Gaskarth, "Strategy in a Complex World," *RUSI Journal* 160, no. 6 (2015): 4–11; P. Porter, "Why Britain Doesn't Do Grand Strategy," *RUSI Journal* 155, no. 4 (2010): 6–12.

34. J. Haldon, review of M. C. Bartusis, *The Late Byzantine Army: Arms and Society, 1204–1453* (Philadelphia, 1992), in *War in History* 1 (1994): 235.

35. *The New Encyclopaedia Britannica* XIX (Chicago, 1976): 558.

36. D. T. Zabecki, *Chief of Staff: The Principal Staff Officers behind History's Great Commands* (Annapolis, MD, 2008).

37. J.-J. Langendorf, *La pensée militaire prussienne: Etudes de Frédéric le Grand à Schlieffen* (Paris, 2012).

38. R. F. Weigley, "The American Military and the Principle of Civilian Control from McClellan to Powell," *Journal of Military History* 57 (1993) and "The Soldier, the Statesman and the Military Historian," *Journal of Military History* 63 (1999); R. H. Kohn, "Out of Control: The Crisis in Civil-Military Relations," *National Interest* 35 (1994).

39. Strachan, *Direction of War*: xii.

40. On the problems of evaluation and implementation, see M. D. Cohen, J. G. March, and J. P. Olsen, "A Garbage Can Model of Organizational Choice," *Administrative Science Quarterly* 17 (1972): 1–25.

41. *Quarterly Review* (July 1929): 127; Liddell Hart papers, King's College London, 10.5/1929/1.

42. Houghton, "Response to the Toast to the Guests," Livery Dinner of the Worshipful Company of Armourers and Brasiers, London, November 19, 2015.

43. J. Fynn-Paul, ed., *War, Entrepreneurs and the State in Europe and the Mediterranean, 1300–1800* (Leiden, the Netherlands, 2014); J. Black, *War in Europe: 1450 to the Present* (London, 2016): 1–10.

44. J. M. House, *Controlling Paris: Armed Forces and Counter-Revolution, 1789–1848* (New York, 2014).

45. P. Cornish and A. M. Dorman, "Smart Muddling Through: Rethinking UK National Security beyond Afghanistan," *International Affairs* 88 (2012): 213–22 and "Complex Security and Strategic Latency: The UK Strategic Defence and Security Review 2015," *International Affairs* 91 (2015): 351–70.

46. Strachan, "Lost Meaning": 50.

47. K. J. Banks, *Chasing Empire across the Sea: Communications and the State in the French Atlantic, 1713–1763* (Montreal, 2002): 218.

48. G. J. Bryant, *The Emergence of British Power in India 1600–1784: A Grand Strategic Interpretation* (Woodbridge, UK, 2013): 321.

49. Bryant, *Emergence of British Power*: 328.

50. Bryant, *Emergence of British Power*: xin3.

ONE

THE STRUGGLE FOR POWER

STRATEGY IS THE WAYS BY WHICH NATIONS, STATES, RULERS, elites, and others seek to shape their situation, producing international and domestic systems that provide security and that safeguard and pursue interests. The key element is the contest for power, but power takes different forms, has varied uses, and is not understood in a uniform fashion. In assessing strategy and strategic culture, it is necessary to consider how states, or rather their elites and leaderships, seeking to maintain and increase power, pursue internal as well as external agendas, and do so knowing that it will make them better able to wage war. The relationship between the two agendas is crucial and also affects both. Linked to this were (and are) the perennial questions of who directed strategy and to what ends.

Across the world, most strategy in the eighteenth century occurred in a monarchical context and was made by the rulers themselves. This situation scarcely produced any uniformity, not least to the diversity of contexts and the inherent differences between rulers. Nevertheless, there were common elements in terms of the rationales of dynasties and the inherent dynamics of royal courts. The two combined to produce strategic cultures focused in particular on dynastic aggrandizement and *gloire*. The alternative means of shaping the situation are worth considering, notably republics and elective monarchies, such as Poland, but the monarchs of the latter also had dynastic agendas.

A moral tone, one that picked up long-standing religious and political themes, was offered by the *Monitor*, then the most influential London newspaper, in its issue of April 5, 1760, which appeared in the midst of a major European war. The anonymous article argued that aggressive wars

> arise from the heart of the mighty; who envious of another's glory,
> covetous of another's riches or country, or aspiring to universal empire;
> seek all occasions to quarrel, to oppress, to ruin, to subdue that object of
> their envoy, covetousness and ambition; and never consents to a cessation
> of arms, except he finds himself unable to accomplish his destructive
> intentions, and in need of further time and leisure to recruit, and to carry
> his project more effectually into execution.

Unpredictability was also a major element. In September 1733, William Cayley, the British consul in Cádiz, commenting on Spanish naval preparations in the developing international crisis, preparations on which he provided intelligence information, wrote:

> the season of the year is now so far advanced, that one would naturally
> imagine, form the least further delay, they would find it too late to go upon
> any enterprise of consequence. Though it is certain, at the same time,
> that no judgment can be formed of the conduct which may be held by this
> Court, or of what they may or may not undertake from the common rules
> of reason and prudence by which other people generally act, there being, as
> your Grace is very sensible, nothing so wild, extravagant or destructive to
> the real interests of the kingdom, that they are not capable of, when it will
> afford the least gratification to the passions of the Queen.[1]

The significance of rulers was captured by the Marquis de Silva, a Sardinian (Piedmontese), in his *Pensées sur la tactique, et la strategique ou la vrais principes de la science militaire* (1778), a work in which he sought to locate politics and the military:

> Le plan general de la guerre renferme deux sortes d'objets. Les uns qui
> sont du resort de la politique, et les autres qui dependent immédiement
> et totalement de la science militaire. Lorsqu'un Souverain est lui même le
> Général de ses armées . . . il embrasse et combine tous ces différens objets.
> La machine n'a pour lors qu'un seul principe de movement, et ce movement
> n'est bien plus parfait.[2]

An emphasis on rulers as conservative figures obsessed with *gloire* leads to the assumption that a developing interest in strategy from the late eighteenth century in some respect reflected a new and different public age linked to more intensive conflict, in short was an aspect and product of a modernization of war. However, alongside this approach can come a very different location of the eighteenth-century discussion of war-making. In this location, it can be argued that in the pre-Revolutionary West (i.e., the West prior to the French Revolution), there was less stress than hitherto on the themes and idioms of sacral monarchy and more on the monarch as a governing ruler characterized by competence and open to advice accordingly.

This contrast in emphasis, which was not one that suddenly emerged but, instead, one that can be long traced, can be related, for the eighteenth century, to a shift in sensibility, one from the attitudes, themes, and tropes summarized as Baroque to those summarized as Neoclassical. Such a shift took a number of forms, and there were a number of separate chronologies at stake. These included developments in international relations and in attitudes toward them. For example, concern about the supposed threat of universal monarchy, a threat attributed to the Habsburgs in the sixteenth and early seventeenth centuries and to Louis XIV of France in the late seventeenth century, was seen in 1733 as an "old prejudice"[3] but was to be revived in response to Napoleon's expansionism.

The development from the Baroque sensibility to the Neoclassical was present from the outset of the eighteenth century[4] but gathered pace in the period of enlightened despotism, the term generally employed to describe many of the Western monarchies in the second half of the century. The Enlightenment impulse in government was linked to this turn from sacral to utilitarian and instrumentalist functions of government, a development that was especially pertinent as new territories were brought under control. The organization of ministries became more bureaucratic and specialized, and information played a key role in the conduct of government, international relations, and war.[5] However, by later standards, there was a general lack of administrative support for the rulers and ministers who balanced demands and assessed resources, albeit often not planning individual operations.[6] Significantly, the image of Western monarchs and ministers changed in the second half of the century and notably with the final abandonment of Baroque themes. An emphasis on information and rationality was suggested with their depiction as indicating maps.[7]

The focus on ruling individuals and groups helps explain why the later matrix of strategy, that of general staffs, a matrix that helped drive the process of defining strategy, is not, however, readily or sensibly applicable to the earlier period. A focus on the court context of the earlier period ironically, however, also directs renewed attention to strategy during the last quarter millennium as a whole, the period when the word has been used. In particular, the leaders of the last quarter millennium frequently operated in a fashion that would not have been out of character or, indeed, context for their predecessors. Thus, there are elements of decision making under Napoleon or Hitler that would not have been totally out of place for Louis XIV and, in many cases, the comparison was closer or deliberately sought, as with Mussolini and his attempt to strike a resonance using reference to the Roman emperor Augustus. This continuity is more especially the case if the focus is on strategic culture or strategic process, rather than strategic content or broader international context.

In particular, there is the question of how far *gloire*, the search for prestige and the use of the resulting reputation to secure international and domestic goals, are particularly attractive and important in monarchical systems, indeed providing them with their prime strategic purpose, tone, and drive. This approach understandably works in a diachronic fashion—in other words, across time. An emphasis on the value of prestige and reputation adopts a cultural functionalism that is linked to a psychological approach to image and competition. In part, a competition for prestige can enhance all the powers involved. More commonly, however, the competition was necessarily at the expense of other powers, and was very much desired and affirmed in these terms. Dynastic rivalry, whether of Habsburgs and Bourbons or of Ottomans and Safavids, can be approached in these terms. In part, this was because of the wide-ranging dynamics of prestige and space involved in dynastic considerations.[8]

It has been argued that dynasticism functioned as a moderating norm by limited claims, containing stakes, and requiring the regulation of shifts in sovereignty.[9] As such, it was an aspect of a rule-based system, one that could be described in terms of "the law of nations and the usages commonly acknowledged and practised among all nations in Europe."[10] Moreover, this system was capable of development and expansion, as with the idea for maritime leagues to protect neutral trade from blockades, a measure designed to counter Britain's dominant position at sea.[11]

However, such systems did not cope well with relations between different cultures and did not usually work well within an individual culture. Indeed, the dynastic drive was generally competitive and also, as with Austria in the 1690s–1730s, could take precedence over other elements.[12] Dynastic politics set very difficult tasks for strategy. The protection of Hanover for Britain after the accession of the Hanoverian dynasty in 1714 was one of the striking examples, but even more so was the Austrian attempt to incorporate the Spanish empire. Wars of succession of one sort or another were the outcome of strategic marriage alliances but with a greater element of chance involved than for many nineteenth-century expansionist schemes.

In addition to competition among the dynasties of different states, the search for status within dynasties, as rulers confronted the reputation of their predecessors, and also between successive dynasties ruling the same state can be approached in part in terms of a necessary drive for *gloire*. This search was very much set by the emphasis on the value of reputation and by the focus on the glory of predecessors. Thus, the rulers of Sardinia struggled with making themselves worthy of the reputation and example of Victor Amadeus II (r. 1675–1730), the victor of the dramatic and decisive battle of Turin in 1706, and those of Prussia with that of Frederick William I, the "Great Elector" (r. 1640–88). Visual images of past success were to the fore. Frederick William commissioned Andreas Schlüter to design an equestrian statue depicting him as a commander in armor and holding a field marshal's baton.[13] Philip V of Spain (r. 1700–46) spent time in his palace in Seville where tapestries that are still in place depicted the success of the expeditions of Charles V (Charles I of Spain) in the early sixteenth century. Philip himself was with the army that invaded Portugal in 1704. Louis XV and Louis XVI struggled with the need to match themselves with the image created by Louis XIV, although Louis XV did campaign in the mid-1740s: at the siege of Freiburg in 1744 and the battle of Fontenoy in 1745. Louis XVI never did so. France helped the Thirteen Colonies win independence from Britain, but this brought no benefit to Louis XVI in terms of personal prestige. The strong association between monarchical prestige and military success was demonstrated by the Qianlong emperor in his treatise *Yuzhi shiquan ji* (*In Commemoration of the Ten Complete Military Victories*), composed in 1792, a treatise that claimed the Chinese failures against Myanmar and Vietnam as successes.

That rulers tended, when they could, to command forces in battle, an integration of political and military leadership that could help ensure decisiveness, contributed greatly to this competition with one another and with the past. This was not only the case in the first half of the century where it was seen, for example, with George II of Britain at Dettingen in 1743. In 1788, the emperor (ruler of Austria) Joseph II rejected advice from his chancellor, Count Kaunitz, that he not lead his forces in person. The direct interest and personal commitment of rulers was highly significant to the strategic culture, as was the idea of trial by battle in a form of almost-ritualized conflict.[14]

Royal splendor served, moreover, as the basis of noble splendor. The cult of valorous conflict helped define honor and fame, whether individual, family, or collective. A stress on these themes directs attention away from the idea of bureaucratization. In 1734, Philip V, the surviving grandson of Louis XIV, claimed that war was necessary for the political stability of the French monarchy.[15] This was a critical comment on Cardinal Fleury, France's leading minister from 1726 to 1743, an elderly cleric who lacked commitment to war.[16]

Cultural values were significant. Personal honor and reputation were crucial for commanders, and the related cultural conditioning that made the cult of honor dynamic was central to civil-military relations, limiting bureaucratic processes.[17] The recently restored Winter Palace in Vienna of the great Austrian general Prince Eugene includes a hall with paintings of battle scenes as well as stucco reliefs with military themes.[18] Martial values for the elite could be advocated even in states such as Britain that had a more commercial ethos: "our young nobility: most of their honors are derived from the sword; and they should be more particularly devoted for their sovereign and their country."[19] In 1760, the head of the Hanoverian ministry observed that governments were run by the passions and by cabals.[20]

Cultural values were related not only to strategic goals but also to tactical methods. For infantry, cavalry, and siegecraft, there was a consistent tension between firepower and shock tactics. The choices reflected circumstances, experience, the views of particular generals, and wider assumptions in military society; and these choices were not dictated by technology. The focus on attack represented a cultural imperative in the face of the growing strength of firepower; but in practice, this strength did not preclude advantages for attacking forces. As a reminder of the variety of factors involved at all levels, and strategically as well as tactically and operationally, the prestige of the attack, rather than a reliance on ideas and practices of deliberate siegecraft, could, for example, encourage attempts to storm fortresses. However, so too could a need for speed, both in order to press on to achieve results and so as to deal with logistical problems that were greatly exacerbated by lengthy sieges.[21]

As an aspect of *gloire*, the notion of a place in history is still very much seen today, which, again, serves as a reminder of continuities in strategy and of its historicized character. So, too, with the holding forth of the past in the form of what are treated as discrete episodes with clear lessons, as warnings, and also as strategic building blocks. Today, this is the case most notably with "Munich," "Suez," "Vietnam," and now also "Iraq" and "Afghanistan." There were obviously equivalents for earlier periods, and they helped guide strategic thought and discussion, although they have not attracted comparable attention in recent work.

To consider Britain in the eighteenth century, there were many references to earlier eras, notably Elizabeth I's struggle with Spain,[22] while the legacy of the events of the period 1688–1714, proved significant in subsequent decades. For example, the Treaty of Utrecht (1713) played a major role in subsequent political contention and strategic dialogue within Britain, as did the Treaty of Aix-la-Chapelle (1748) and the Peace of Paris (1763). In the House of Lords in November 1739, John, Lord Carteret, a former diplomat and secretary of state then in opposition, both pressed for a strategic focus on gains in the West Indies and argued that William III had understood the logic of this policy.[23] In 1758, the term *doctrine* was employed in discussing whether Britain was maintaining William's emphasis on keeping the Low Countries out of French control.[24]

This process is readily easy to follow for Britain as there was an extensive debate in print and public about foreign policy, one that reflected the
relatively liberal nature of British public culture and the role of Parliament. The situation was similar in the United Provinces (Netherlands,
Dutch Republic) but very different in most states. That, however, does
not mean that there was not in all states both a governmental and a public
process of learning from the past or, at least, of employing a reading of
the past in the discussion of policy.

How best to assess such elements is of considerable interest. The
weight of the past could be highly selective, but it focused in particular
on battles and challenges. Thus, for Prussia, the relatively minor victory
of Fehrbellin (1675) was played up,[25] in part because it was a triumph won
by Prussian forces alone and in part because it was won at the expense of
Sweden, a state that had dominated northern Germany from the successful invasion by Gustavus Adolphus in 1630. For the Dutch, the formative
struggle for independence against Spain in the sixteenth century was
succeeded by the survival from a major and initially successful French
assault in 1672. Such episodes proved important in narratives and analyses about domestic and international politics and concerning political
and military strategies.

Consideration of governmental and public processes of discussion and response is, to a degree, related to the subsequent distinction
between strategic thinkers and actors. The distinction, however, is in part
questionable, as all actors are thinkers and, therefore, is better phrased as
strategic writers and actors. A major problem is posed by the suggestion
that thought is measured by writing. That approach reflects positivist
approaches to evidence as well as intellectual bias, but it is unhelpful.
Indeed, a strategic landscape, such as that presented in the iconography
of a royal palace and garden[26] or conversations during a hunt or other
elite gathering, represents thought and expression that were more central to the policymakers than the strategic treatises that tend to attract
modern attention. By its nature, that is a claim that is impossible to prove,
but that does not make it any less significant. It is particularly important
not to abstract royal views from the court ideologies and cultures that
influenced them and that set the context for their life. Strategy was seen
in the enaction of power for identified ends, as in art and literature.

It is also important not to assume monocausal explanations. For example, in 1719, when Britain was at war with Spain, albeit allied with France, Charles Delafaye, undersecretary in the Northern Department, commented on the plan for an attack on St. Augustine, the most important Spanish base in Florida, that it would "do real service" but also "perhaps allay" the "clamour" in Britain over colonial vulnerability.[27]

These circumstances pertained not simply for major powers but also for their lesser counterparts. The latter found it harder to influence greatly their political environment unless they could work with more potent powers. Their strategies dictated by their circumstances,[28] the lesser states, such as Bavaria, Denmark, Savoy-Piedmont (Sardinia), and Saxony were often therefore obliged to conduct their strategy in a very deceitful manner, seeking to play off their powerful neighbors. Rivalries could be exploited, for example, by Savoy-Piedmont, but it was common for major states to sacrifice the interests of their weaker allies. Partly as a result, the latter found it difficult to move into the rank of great powers,[29] and if Prussia succeeded in doing so in midcentury, it only did so with great difficulty.

Accepting continuities in court culture and geopolitics, there is no reason to anticipate that the situation was unchanging. For example, in the West, the degree to which the spatial dimension of strategy was affected by developments in mapping, both cartographical production and cartoliteracy, is at best suggestive, as evidence on the point is limited and mostly indirect. However, the evidence is still striking. There was indeed an important increase in such production as well as improvements in the ability of maps to reflect geographical realities on the ground. Advances in the depiction of longitude proved particularly important. These advances ensured that the graticule or grid within which positions were located was more accurate and notably an improvement on the previous situation at sea. The number of maps and the extent to which the land surface was covered in detail both also increased. The accumulation of cartographic information and the production of maps owed much to the work of the military. This reflected not only their relevant skill base and the extent to which armies and navies were institutions under the control of the central government but also the need of both armies and navies for cartographic information if they were to plan and record their moves. The survival of maps and cartographic references in military archives is indicative, although there is not the basis at present for a statistical survey in part because there has been no systematic trawl of the available sources. Alongside a more fixed understanding of space, the creation of more reliable and portable watches helped in creating a sense of mastering time.

The availability of maps was linked to greater cartoliteracy in the West, cartoliteracy that was also seen in the publication of maps in newspapers and other publications. This information aided a public grasp of strategy in so far as there was a growing public engagement with the world of print and a greater willingness to publish material accordingly. So, too, with publications on recent and current conflicts.

This was but one aspect of a dynamic character to strategy, a character that added the possibility that the situation changed (or did not change) in particular strategic cultures. That question will be a theme in the case studies that follow, although evidence on the point is largely suggestive and can be patchy in the extreme. At the same time, alongside this dynamic character, there was a fundamental continuity in military affairs arising from the reliance on men alone as soldiers and the impact in the military of social hierarchies and practices, as well as the largely constant nature of economic and environmental contexts and their consequences for military activity and planning. The limited productivity of economic activities was a key element.

In addition, the role of climate, weather, and seasons both in the safety of voyages[30] and the availability of fodder was significant. Fodder was necessary for cavalry and for the draught animals that were crucial for artillery and logistics. Indeed, grass growing at the side of roads was a crucial resource and a comment on the logistical capability. This factor did not prevent winter campaigns, but it made these operations more difficult and thus lessened the chance of a strategy of constant pressure. This was especially so if the winter was combined with bad weather, and the latter was held as an indicator that there would be no campaigning.[31] The springtime start of most campaigns was due not only to grass growing but also to river levels falling as snowmelt ceased and to the ground no longer being frozen. Road surfaces were greatly affected by the weather. In the summer and autumn, the need for action before the winter was a frequent theme.

Seasonality was also a factor that varied across the world, creating constraints that were especially important for foreign forces that were unfamiliar with them. Monsoon conditions were a major issue, particularly in India where they encouraged winter campaigning and determined maritime power projection. Thus, in 1760, after the Marathas drove the Afghan garrison from Delhi in July, campaigning stopped in the monsoon season while inconclusive negotiations took place, only for the Marathas to advance anew in October. The storming of the Siamese capital, Ayuthia, by Myanmar (Burmese) forces in 1767 was possible only because the lengthy campaign against the city had persisted through two rainy seasons, the soldiers growing their own rice so that the army did not fade away in the meanwhile.

The dependence of wind-powered wooden ships on the weather and their vulnerability to storms[32] was also a key factor linked to the weather. Indeed, dependence on the weather rendered strategic concepts such as control of the sea inappropriate. It was possible to evade blockades, as in 1708, 1719, 1745, and 1798 when invasion attempts were launched on the British Isles.[33] There were also fears about the invasion of Britain on other occasions,[34] while powers considered the viability of naval moves by their allies in light of the weather and, therefore, the advancing season.[35] The possibility of mounting an invasion thus became a key strategic factor.

It was not only military figures who were aware of these factors. Indeed, the role of both climate and weather were particularly easy to understand. In October 1739, Dudley Ryder, the British attorney general, met Sir Robert Walpole, the prime minister, while the latter was hunting deer, as he often liked to do. Walpole told him that the French had not yet agreed to assist Spain against Britain:

> That, however, they would have a squadron of 20 men of war at Brest [France's Atlantic naval base] in a month's time, which, though it would not act offensively against us at present, could not be neglected. That, by this means, they will put us to the expense of a war and the running away with our trade.[36]

Thus, two senior governmental figures, neither with a military background, were able to discuss strategy. Walpole himself also took part in the key Cabinet Councils on military matters, such as that on June 4, 1739. What the diary also demonstrates is the significance of such sources for understanding the world of strategic discussion. Ryder was fairly unusual due to his social background. The son of a nonconformist tradesman (his father was a mercer), he worked his way up through the law. As an example of the openness of the British elite, Ryder's son became a peer and his grandson an earl. Most government figures did not keep diaries, but the discussion still took place.

These problems were accentuated by the absence of reliable surveillance, which was limited to the telescope, while messages were passed from ship to ship by flags flying at mastheads. French invasion attempts on Britain were wrecked by the weather in 1744 and by disease in 1779. At the same time, the weather was still a major constraint for the invasion of Normandy in 1944 and for the British reconquest of the Falklands in 1982.

The difficulties of naval operations affected the potential for an amphibious strategy. The lack of powered landing craft was an element, not least because it lessened the opportunities for evacuation. In 1758, Holdernesse also commented on the need:

> to hit upon some place, where, if we have the good fortune to succeed, we
> may be able to maintain ourselves even against a superior enemy; the very
> nature of the undertaking proves the difficulty of it, as the same reasons
> which would enable us to keep our ground, will operate against us in
> an attempt to seize some post of consequence, unless we have the good
> fortune to hit upon a spot where the enemy are ill-provided, and may be
> surprised.... As to any attempt upon the coast of Flanders, it would be
> next to impossible to succeed in it, considering the time that is necessary
> for disembarking a large body of men and that the enemy would be able to
> send a superior force to drive us back, before it would be possible to throw
> up any entrenchment to secure our stores and provisions, not to mention
> the hazard of reimbarking in the face of a superior enemy.[37]

Experience, in the shape of the friction of operational difficulties, vindicated these concerns. A month later, Holdernesse explained the failure of hopes, noting that the British commander, Charles, 3rd Duke of Marlborough

> found that the place could not be carried without a regular siege; that roads
> must have been made in a most impracticable country for the artillery; and

consequently that the undertaking would have taken up too much time, as the enemy would have been able to assemble a superior corps . . . and as the transport vessels could lie no nearer than Cancalle, His Grace might have run the risk of having his retreat cut off; which induced him to reimbark the troops.[38]

Comparisons with the consideration and planning for amphibious operations during the two world wars are instructive. Planning and speculation were also affected by the major difficulties in maintaining an army by sea alone.[39]

Despite the many limitations, only some of which have been noted, there were marked improvements in military capability during the eighteenth century that provided enhanced strategic and operational opportunities. New and more effective administrative structures were important. They were seen throughout the century, most prominently with the rulers of ca. 1740–ca. 1790 known as the enlightened despots, such as Frederick II, the Great, of Prussia (r. 1740–86), Charles III of Spain (r. 1759–88), Catherine II, the Great, of Russia (r. 1762–96), and Joseph II of Austria (r. 1780–90), but also both earlier in the century and indeed during the Revolutionary period in the 1790s. In ca. 1700–ca. 1740, the principal drivers were not only the competitiveness of war but also postwar attempts at repair, reform, revival, and preparation, each of which was also highly competitive. Thus, Peter the Great of Russia (r. 1689–1725) established a Russian navy on the Baltic, totally reorganized the army, and offered a different level of direction to that of his predecessors with the foundation of a War College (ministry) in 1718–19. Conscription systems were introduced in Denmark in 1701, Spain in 1704, and Russia in 1705. In Prussia, a cantonal system was established between 1727 and 1735 with every regiment assigned a permanent catchment area around its peacetime garrison town, from which it drew the draftees allowed by the system established in 1693.

Such systems enhanced control. For example, in 1734, Philip V of Spain (r. 1700–46) ordered the establishment of thirty-three new provincial militia regiments to provide a reserve of twenty-three thousand men. This militia, which, however, did not cover regions with strong traditions of autonomy, freed Spanish regular troops for service in Italy in the War of the Polish Succession (1733–35), and subsequently served to recruit for the forces operating there. As a result, there was less of a need to rely on hiring foreigners to serve in the army, which had, hitherto, been an effective restriction because of the cost entailed. The establishment of the militia involved issues of cost and reliability as well as the creation of a less conditional military. Moreover, on the French model, the Spanish army benefited from a network of *intendentes* of the army (officials in the regions), who were answerable to a secretary of state for war, and thus responsible for implementing his instructions.

More generally, despite their many deficiencies in practice, administrative form and bureaucratic regularity were important to the ability to organize and sustain mass and activity. Without this form and regularity, standing forces were difficult to maintain other than by adopting ad hoc remedies to ensure support. Enhanced capability was seen in larger and better-supported armies and navies. These created a capacity to act effectively in more than one sphere simultaneously. Moreover, the development of naval strength enhanced the capacity for amphibious operations, and this capacity was increased as long-range, including transoceanic, operations became more practical. As a result, uncertainty from the point of view of other powers continued, if not increased. This was especially so with reference to naval operations. For example, when Spain prepared an expedition at Cádiz in 1738, it was unclear at first whether the expedition was designed to act in the Mediterranean against Barbary pirates or in the Caribbean against the Dutch.[40] It subsequently became clear that the target was Britain. So, too, with Spanish preparations on other occasions: for example, in 1719, 1732, 1733, and 1741.

Directed by the Imperial Council of War, the Austrian army (the army of the Austrian Habsburgs) rose to wartime peaks of 137,000 in 1714, 205,700 in 1735, 203,600 in 1745, 201,300 in 1760–61, and 497,700 in 1789–90. These, and similar rates of increase elsewhere, were the product of two related, but different, sociopolitical currents. The first was the Crown-aristocracy realignment of the late seventeenth century in Europe, a factor that demonstrated the significance of social underpinning and the politics bound up in that. This realignment was, simultaneously, the foundation of the ancien régime military and the factor that kept it working.[41] The crucial relationship was that of central government and ruling elite. Members of the elite owned and controlled much of the land and were the local notables, enjoying social prestige and effective governmental control of the localities.

In contrast, central government lacked the mechanisms to intervene effectively and consistently in the localities, unless with the cooperation of the local elite. Central government meant, in most countries, the monarch and a small group of advisers and officials, and the notion that they were capable of creating the basis of a modern state is misleading. Lacking the reach of modern governments, those of the early-modern period relied on other bodies. In addition, in what was, in very large part, a prestatistical age, the central government of any large area was unable to produce coherent plans for domestic policies based on the premise of change and development. Without reliable, or often any, information concerning population, revenues, economic activity, or land ownership and lacking land surveys and reliable and detailed maps, governments operated in what was, by modern standards, an information void.

Due to these factors, the improvement in relations between governments and elites was important. In Hungary, part of the Habsburg dominions and an area where royal authority had frequently been challenged, especially in the 1700s, wars had revealed the inadequacy of traditional means of raising and organizing armies, notably the general levy of the nobility, the basis of its tax exemption. In response to this, and to the end of the rebellion, the Diet of 1715 saw the king and the estates cooperate to establish a permanent army. This was to be paid for by taxes, while the obligation on the nobility to obey the ruler's call for a general levy continued. In 1741, the estates promised Maria Theresa, the embattled new ruler, four million guilders in war taxes, as well as the nobility's general levy, sixty thousand recruits, and food and forage for the army, in return for promises of autonomy. The Hungarian forces served to help overrun Bavaria, a French ally, in 1741–42 and, in particular, offered a cavalry that Austria could not provide.

At the same time, there was no necessary strategic outcome to enhanced capability whether, for Austria, in the shape of improved artillery or of Hungarian cavalry. Instead, the varied political contexts— for example, the geopolitical dimension—were crucial. Maria Theresa enunciated a clear and consistent strategy with her focus, as in May 1756, on the defense of the Habsburg hereditary lands, notably Austria, and not on what she termed the "remote parts of her dominions," such as the Austrian Netherlands (Belgium).[42]

Second, and as an aspect of the Crown-aristocracy alignment that was crucial to military strength[43] but one with the potential for a very different outcome, the development of conscription systems by a number of states, notably Russia and Prussia, was very important. These systems rested on, and represented, the successful realignment of Crown and aristocracy, and a related model of state-army identity, as well as, to at least a degree, the raising of information about numbers and location of people. Conscription and censuses were a government project in the eighteenth century that proved less effective than in the twentieth century but more so than the means of raising troops in the early seventeenth century.

Conscription systems and military professionalism were not coterminous, but the former encouraged an emphasis on the directing role of the state. This emphasis challenged the implicit, but often uneasy, partnership between Crown and aristocracy. So, too, to a degree, did professionalism, for, while many aristocrats sought the prestige of command, not all of them wanted the chore of service, and notably so in Western Europe. Hierarchies in command that did not match the hierarchy of social rank were potentially highly disruptive. While much of this challenge was latent, and most training for commanders continued to be limited, on the job, and without any real doctrinal consideration, especially of other types of conflict, nevertheless there was already an important change in tone. Knowledge was applied at the operational level, while there was a proliferation of textbooks and military academies that schooled cadets in military engineering and artillery. An emphasis on commanders with technical professional skills encouraged a demand for intellectual accomplishment and technical skill. The latter was particularly significant for the command of ships, as navigation required a knowledge of astronomy and calculation and an ability to apply this knowledge. Technical skill was also important for artillery officers, such as Napoleon. These were systems to teach skills as opposed to strategic education, and the same was the case at sea.

At the same time, the model and practice of state control and direction had to face the realities of what has been termed moral economy and of the contractor state. In the first case, soldiers were committed to a customary framework of rights and obligations and very much understood their service in contractual terms.[44] In the second case, these, in practice delegated military systems, saw very many functions in effect subcontracted. This was done in a variety of ways and with variable effectiveness, but the overall effect both increased the number of stakeholders in the state and yet also weakened what was to be understood, in the prism of later utilitarian bureaucracy, as control and direction. The ancien régime military and the system it rested on were therefore affected by a range of internal tensions, although that is also true of modern militaries, not least with subcontracting. Such subcontracting was not only the case in Western states, although there has been far less work on the situation outside the West.

Alongside the strategies, capability, and dynamics of the military systems came those of opponents within states. Indeed, the extent to which insurgencies were characterized by strategies is one that does not have to wait for discussion of the American Revolution that broke out in 1775. There is generally only limited material available for considering insurgent strategies, and much of that material comes from the governments being opposed. Nevertheless, it is possible, as well as necessary, to integrate this dimension to strategy. A key divide was between insurgent groups that essentially wished to keep the central government and its forces away—for example, the Jinchuan of western Sichuan, who resisted the Chinese in 1747–49 and 1770–76 and proved very difficult to overcome—and on the other hand, insurgent groups that sought to operate more widely, including overthrowing the government itself. The latter generally required the seizure of the capital and the defeat of government forces, whereas the first type of insurgency essentially rested on repelling, deterring, or avoiding attack. In the latter case, there was also the hope, often justified at least in the short term, that the government would be deterred by other commitments.[45]

From a very different direction, the eighteenth-century military was also to be challenged by intellectual speculation and radical politics, at least in the West. The first, associated in particular with the influential intellectual movement of the mid- and late eighteenth century known as the Enlightenment[46] but in practice, far more widespread in its causes

and course, asked questions about practicality and challenged established methods and more particularly, forms of prestige. This was a matter not only of fame derived from war but also of the automatic reverence
for social rank. Enlightenment tendencies were potentially subversive
in that they raised important questions about professionalism and the
need for it as opposed to rank. Enlightenment writers also made highly
critical remarks about the value of war. This was particularly apparent
with the philosophes in France and was an important aspect of their
midcentury criticism of Louis XV. Voltaire proved an especially sardonic
critic of war as pointless and destructive, and notably of the Seven Years'
War (1756–63).

The questioning associated with the Enlightenment gave renewed
energy to the discussion about methods of conflict that became more
active from the 1720s. This discussion was notably apparent in France
but was also seen more widely, including in the German lands and in
Britain. As a result, military development from the eighteenth century,
and particularly from the 1760s, very much took place in a context of
debate, including public debate, a situation that continues to the present. This debate was different in scale and character to the more episodic
discussion in print that had been seen from the European Renaissance
of the fifteenth century.

Military history was an important aspect of this discussion and took
on considerable relevance in this context. This discussion went back
to the Classics, but there was also consideration of recent and current
conflicts. Thus, the supposed lessons of the American War of Independence (1775–83) were debated, especially in Britain and France. Partly as
a result of these factors, the French Revolution did not take place against
a conservative or static background and notably not so in military affairs,
both in terms of thought and practice.

There are specific problems with much of the evidence about military
thought and practice. In part, this was because the theory of authority
was frequently different to the realities of power. Even when the monarch
was able and active, many affairs were handled without his or her direct
oversight or even, in practice, any oversight. Furthermore, there were
periods when, due to ill-health, absence, or inattention, the ruler was not
able to handle important business. However, permanent mechanisms

to cope with this situation, and thus to produce a regular archival trail, were not well developed.

The term *mechanism* is ironic as one of the major ideas of the period, that of the balance of power, an idea applicable to international as well as domestic politics, and frequently employed in diplomatic correspondence, indeed being an "old beaten topic,"[47] in practice lacked precision. However, this lack helped make the idea of the balance so easy to discuss and readily applicable. The same was the case for the related point about restricting supposedly hegemonic powers. To a considerable extent, the same point about the value of the imprecise is pertinent for modern use of the term *strategy*.

As a separate, but linked, issue, there is the problem of mistaking effect for cause in ideas about international relations, as with the subsequent discussion of military matters with reference to strategy. In particular, it is necessary to consider the extent to which the language employed represented a rationalization of the situation or, indeed, a political and/or rhetorical device for influencing and/or explaining policy. For example, although the balance of power was often cited, its application was contentious,[48] while in practice, the desire for primacy can be seen as a more potent drive.[49] It is also very necessary not to mistake events for consequences. In 1769, the historian William Robertson discerned, in his *History of the Reign of the Emperor Charles V*, one of the more successful historical works of the period:

> That great secret in modern policy, the preservation of a proper
> distribution of power among all the members of the system into which
> the states are formed. . . . From this era we can trace the progress of that
> intercourse between nations which had linked the powers of Europe so
> closely together; and can discern the operations of that provident policy,
> which, during peace, guards against remote and contingent dangers;
> which, in war, hath prevented rapid and destructive conquests.[50]

In practice, that was a highly complacent view of a much more complex dynamic, both in terms of ethos and with regard to contingent outcomes. The dynamism extended to the permutations of power relationships as they spread in practice and consideration. Thus, rivalry between Russia and Turkey was seen as helpful to France while, conversely, the ability to end it was regarded as detrimental to France.[51]

In 1739, the British government thought that peace between Russia and Turkey would thwart the Swedish plan to regain losses from Russia, but at the same time, the secretary of state added a reference to the supposed pressures from domestic opinion on the Swedish ministers:

> they may find it absolutely requisite, for the sake of gratifying the present martial humor of the public and keeping up their own credit with the nation, to substitute some other enterprise in the room of it.[52]

Correspondingly, the French government argued that it was still in Turkey's interest to keep Sweden in a state to attack Russia.[53] Conversely, when France was allied to Russia's ally Austria, then rivalry between Russia and Turkey was seen as very unwelcome to France, as during the Seven Years' War and in 1787 during the Dutch Crisis as such rivalry would make it less likely that Russia could exert pressure on Prussia which was, at once, Austria's enemy and Britain's ally.

There are significant analytical comparisons, in the modern discussion of strategy, to the mechanistic interests and approaches of the past. For example, the recent claim that "the strategic function simply insists that ends, ways, and means should be mutually supportive" rests on concepts of the mathematical optimum.[54] These concepts are in practice highly problematic but served to replace the concept of God as the director of developments, a concept that had acted as a salve for fears of the uncertainty of the world. In 1781, in one of his perceptive works on the character of warfare, works in large part presented as military history, General Henry Lloyd (ca. 1729–83) presented war as "a state of action," at once moving into a mechanical discussion:

> An army is the instrument with which every species of military action is performed: like all other machines it is composed of various parts, and its perfection will depend, first, on that of its several parts; and second, on the manner in which they are arranged; so that the whole may have the following properties, viz. strength, agility, and universality; if these are properly combined, the machine is perfect.[55]

In practice, and at every level, the situation was not one characterized by perfection. Instead, variety and compromise, in intentions and outcomes, were both integral. For example, war encouraged strategic reach by leading powers anxious to seek assistance from the rivals of their opponents or pursuing diversionary activity, and thus a degree of inherent escalation. This was seen, for example, with the extension of English/British naval power into the Mediterranean, which represented a significant geopolitical shift. This development reflected the extent to which warfare was not a struggle in the abstract, nor simply an expression of powerful sociocultural drives, important as they indeed were, but instead, a carefully honed process in which particular goals were pursued. These objectives varied by state and conflict. Trade was certainly an element. The naval protection of trade made the English/British commercial system more efficient by creating a clear distinction between mercantile and military shipping, thereby cutting the cost of the former by reducing the need for defense and thus increasing the appeal of investing in trade. That the discussion of policy, notably in public, frequently involved commercial issues made them more important in strategy and as a way of judging the appropriateness and success of strategy. In December 1758, *Owen's Weekly Chronicle* announced:

> Perhaps nothing can so much prove the importance of the Cape Breton [Louisbourg] expedition, as the case of insuring; for since the reduction [capture] of that place, insurance to America etc has fallen from 25 and even 30 per cent to no more than 12; with this remarkable advantage, that our enemies insurance has risen in proportion to the falling of ours.[56]

The ideological dimensions to strategy were many and complex, both for context and for content. They were also highly significant as they helped establish measures and equations of success and failure. Aside from assessing impact, there are also the problems of working out how the situation changed. In particular, there is the question of whether religion was a dated and minor factor or one that was by no means anachronistic and, indeed, that translated well to the world of public discussion. The *Monitor*, Britain's most influential newspaper at the time, in its April 22, 1758 issue, presented the Seven Years' War as "a religious war" by France and Austria, to extirpate Protestantism on the Continent prior to turning against Britain. Providence was presented as helping, both by leading Britain to alliance with Prussia and in the results of particular battles.[57]

Strategic elements tended, however, to focus on power politics. England/Britain, for example, was drawn into the Mediterranean not through any particular interest in Mediterranean or Italian affairs or in pursuit of anti-Catholicism but in order to obstruct the expansionist schemes of Louis XIV's France. Demonstrating the salience of domestic political elements and the extent to which strategic culture could change, the Glorious Revolution of 1688–89 ensured that England was regarded, within Britain and more generally, as France's key strategic and ideological opponent. Moreover, this was to a degree that neither France nor Spain had generally been earlier during the seventeenth century. Spanish weakness under Carlos II (r. 1665–1700) helped produce a power vacuum in Italy and the western Mediterranean, one that the impending end of the Spanish Habsburg line appeared to make more serious. As part of an anti-French alignment, William III (r. 1689–1702) developed an alliance with another royal general, Victor Amadeus II, ruler of Savoy-Piedmont (r. 1675–1730), that was signed in 1690. William also encouraged English naval forces to deploy in the Mediterranean's western basin. Both these elements were maintained after Carlos's and William's deaths. The English fleet's entry into the Mediterranean in 1703 encouraged Victor Amadeus to abandon Louis XIV anew and indicated a key strategic aspect of naval power—that of displaying strength. In addition, England paid the bulk of the foreign subsidies that helped Victor Amadeus to finance his war effort against France, although the role of subsidies should not be exaggerated either in terms of Victor Amadeus's finances or in guaranteeing strategic action and results.

This context helps in the assessment of individual battles in strategic terms. For example, the French navy made one major attempt to challenge English naval predominance in the western Mediterranean during the War of the Spanish Succession but was checked at the battle of Málaga in 1704. Although no ships were sunk in the battle, which is considered tactically and operationally indecisive, Málaga was strategically decisive because it helped limit the French fleet from taking any major action in the region. This example underlines the need to assess strategic goals when discussing success or failure. Thereafter, Britain was the major naval power in the region until 1756, a situation helped by it generally being the power focused on the maintenance of the status quo.

The understanding and application of the concept of decisiveness requires an understanding of strategic and operational goals and capabilities. Victory could be so hard won that the strategic goals of the defeated side were obtained, as with the French victory over William III at Steenkirk in 1692: William withdrew from the field, but the French abandoned plans for attacking the major fortress of Liège.[58] A successful defensive victory, such as that of Peter the Great over Charles XII of Sweden at Poltava in 1709, was followed by a strategic offensive. Frederick the Great was wont to cite Charles's strategy as an instance of the danger of strategic overextension. Another instance of a hard-won victory was one that would show the victorious side that success would be too costly.

There were different interests in the anti-French coalition during the War of the Spanish Succession (as in other conflicts), and they greatly affected strategic goals. In 1705, for example, when the British considered naval operations against Toulon, France's leading Mediterranean naval port, Victor Amadeus, instead, pressed for their help in regaining his principal port, Nice, from the French. In 1707, when the British sought an invasion of the Provence region of southern France, the Austrians were more interested in consolidating their hold on Italy and driving the Spaniards from Naples (a situation that recurred in 1746–47). In addition, once the French had been driven from northern Italy in 1707, then the alliance with Victor Amadeus could only be of strategic use for Britain and help divert French forces from other areas, if his territory of Savoy could serve as the base for an advance into France. Victor Amadeus's attitude to such a policy was ambivalent. He had only joined the anti-French coalition because he had been promised sections of the Milanese (Lombardy), but the Austrians, who sought this as part of the Habsburg inheritance, were unhappy about this condition. In contrast, the prospect of Victor Amadeus obtaining permanent territorial gains from France was minimal. Thus, the strategic plans of the alliance were operating contrary to Victor Amadeus's schemes for territorial expansion. Moreover, British ministers regarded Italian campaigns as primarily a means of diverting French troops and money from those areas where British troops were operating: Flanders and Spain. The British had no wish to see France dominate Italy, but they were more concerned about the French threat to Flanders.

Strategy was also for peacetime. The war saw Britain and Victor Amadeus develop a key strategic relationship that led to vital postwar

British support for the House of Savoy, which the British viewed as a crucial counter to French ambitions and to the united weight of the House of Bourbon, rulers of France and Spain. Britain, moreover, proved a keen supporter for Victor Amadeus in the peace negotiations. In 1711, the French proposed that he be given the Milanese, a step directed against Austria. Instead, with British support, he received Sicily as a kingdom, thus lessening the Spanish inheritance of Philip V. British naval assistance was vital in establishing this new order. A British squadron took Victor Amadeus to Sicily in 1713. Furthermore, a British squadron tried to maintain his power there in 1718 while he faced a Spanish invasion and, ultimately, the more heavily gunned British destroyed a Spanish fleet off Cape Passaro, with seventeen ships captured and eight burned. Encouraged by this victory, such a deployment continued to be an issue in power politics.[59]

Planning was part of the equations of politics and force at the international level, and contemporaries referred to plans as an aspect of the questions of options and of assessing resources. Planning entailed an understanding of the possibilities of action and the precise organization of resources toward an intended end. Thus, in July 1719, the Lords Justices, who were governing Britain for the absent George I, then in Hanover, reported:

> as for tumults at home, they are of opinion that when there is an impossibility of assistance from abroad, they are by no means to be apprehended; but should all the ships we have go to the Baltic [against Peter the Great of Russia], it is certain we cannot get any more ships to defend our own coast or insult that of Spain, which is esteemed to be the same thing, and we shall be open to any attempt of the Cardinal's [Alberoni, leading Spanish minister] without a possibility of defending ourselves, who I am afraid is but too exactly and too constantly informed of our circumstances and conditions.[60]

In 1725–27, competing European alliance systems led to planning for war by many states. This planning involved a host of strategic issues including the respective strength of land and sea forces. For example, in May 1726, Frederick William I of Prussia received Charles Du Bourgay, the British envoy as well as an army officer, and told him that unless Prussia, then allied to Britain and France under the Treaty of Hanover, was secured against the Russian threat, which would be a formidable task, he would abandon his allies and accept Russian and Austrian approaches for an alliance. Frederick William stressed the role of force:

> Your people in England imagine that they can bring about what they please with their pen, but the only way to prevent the ill designs of our enemies is to be ready with your swords—as to your fleet it is of no manner of service to me.

Emphasizing the need to protect Prussia, Frederick William insisted on the readying of the Hanoverian troops and wanted their British counterparts prepared for embarkation.[61] In response, the British government offered a strategic conspectus that played to Britain's naval strength and made more sense of its hopes. Charles, 2nd Viscount Townshend, the key minister for foreign affairs, presented practicality in terms of British views when referring to Prussian fears of a Russian advance through Prussia to Sleswig (a dominion ruled by the king of Denmark) as

> a design that will be attended with such difficulties that it is impossible any cool head in Muscovy can think of it, especially at this time when the King [George I of Britain] has so strong a fleet in the Baltic that will employ the Czarina's [Catherine I] thoughts another way.

On land, Townshend referred to the Hanoverian, Hessian, and Danish forces that would help, "not to mention the great armies that France can pour into those parts on any occasion."[62]

Townshend was secretary of state for the Northern Department and, in effect, foreign minister, and not a minister with formal responsibility for military administration or conduct. However, planning for the use of the army owed more to the nexus of Crown and secretaries of state than to the army leadership. In contrast, the lords of the admiralty provided a degree more of cohesion to the direction of the navy. The consistent presence of the first lord of the admiralty on the council helped ensure that the council could act as an effective vehicle for discussing strategy, as in June 1739 as war with Spain was planned.[63]

In 1726, Prussia's move to the side of Austria soon after the correspondence above put Hanover in the front line against attack and thus accentuated the strategic crisis. Worry about a possible attack on Hanover by Austria, Prussia, and/or Russia led to greater need for the support of Hesse-Cassel and to British pressure on the Danes accordingly to hold troops in readiness in Holstein and on the Swedes to move troops to Swedish western Pomerania. It also increased concern over the French willingness to act, and the deployment of French troops to and across the Rhine was seen as the major support for Hanover and its ally Hesse-Cassel against attack.

This situation underlined the politics of strategy, namely the extent to which Hanover was a strategic incubus for Britain, with all the military, diplomatic, governmental, and political problems this led to. Composite states, like alliances, entailed such problems of strategic burden. There was the separate problem of naval capability. Naval power offered Britain protection against invasion and provided power projection, but it did not bring consent abroad. The idea in 1726 that the dispatch of a fleet to the Mediterranean would deter Austrian action elsewhere, for example in 1725–31,[64] was regarded by others as fanciful as well as vulnerable in domestic political terms,[65] although it was possible to suggest that naval power would allow Britain to guarantee Sicily to Victor Amadeus II if he became an ally.[66]

The planning for coalition conflicts left particular evidence of strategic thought. This can be seen, for example, not only in 1725–27, but also with the British attempt to put together a coalition to act against Russia in 1720 and with the planning in 1730 by Britain, France, and Spain for war against Austria. Each posed the issue of how best to get an alliance to work. As a result, this was a key aspect of strategic planning. This was clear with the coalition attempt to impose its terms, agreed by the Treaty of Seville of November 1729, of an introduction of Spanish garrisons into Parma and Tuscany on an unwilling Austria. In Britain in late 1729, there were hopes that Austria would respond to bullying, but the emperor, Charles VI, refused. The allies, however, continued until summer 1730 to hope that the Austrians would change their mind if the terms offered were slightly improved, or if they were frightened by the allies' preparations. Negotiations by the allies with the Austrians continued, but largely under pressure from the British and the Spaniards, an attempt was made to devise a plan of operations against Austria. Conferences were held at Fontainebleau, and several different schemes were proposed.

The major issue discussed was whether operations in Italy should be matched by others north of the Alps. The French were very interested in an invasion of the Austrian Netherlands [Belgium], a scheme that, as the Austrians had predicted, was opposed by the British and the Dutch. Fear of the expansion of their French ally played a role, as did concern about the Austrian response and that of its allies Prussia and Russia. Britain and the Dutch were anxious about the security of Hanover and the Dutch Republic and wanted the deployment of a French army specifically designed for their protection. However, the Dutch wished to confine offensive operations to Italy, and the British tended to concur with this view.[67] There was less disagreement over plans for campaigning in Italy. It was generally accepted that if the Tuscan ports—where there were many Austrian troops—were closed to the Spaniards, Sicily—an Austrian possession since 1720—should be invaded, while the French would seek to gain the support of Savoy-Piedmont (Victor Amadeus II, now king of Sardinia) and invade the Milanese overland.[68] They were to do so, in a very different international context, in 1733, underlining the extent to which strategic significance owed more to this context than to the operational practicalities of particular military moves.

In 1730, there was a dispute between the allies over the timing of the intended invasion of Sicily and over the French demand that no offensive moves should be undertaken until agreement had been reached both on war aims and on the extent and nature of the territorial changes which should be sought in the war. This was referred to as a treaty of equilibrium. It had been specified, in the event of war, in the Treaty of Seville that had established the alliance, but the French demand angered Britain and Spain: they regarded the issue as an indication of French unwillingness to fight. Furthermore, Spain, anxious to regain its former Italian possessions now held by Austria, did not wish to see its potential gains confined by treaty. Rather than wanting the simple introduction of their garrisons, the Spanish government, and in particular the influential queen, Elisabeth Farnese (second wife of Philip V), wanted a war that would provide opportunities for Italian conquests. A member of an Italian princely dynasty, Elisabeth sought such conquests for her sons, as Spain would be inherited by a son of Philip's first marriage.[69]

The British ministry was worried by these delays and suspicions of its allies. Aware of Spanish impetuosity, the ministry was especially concerned with the delays caused by the French insistence on the need to concert a treaty of equilibrium. It feared that it would cause Spain to doubt the commitment of its allies to the introduction of Spanish garrisons, and that this might lead Spain to renounce the alliance and resume negotiations with Austria, which would be disastrous for the British government, both diplomatically and for domestic political reasons. The French were criticized for delay and for seeking to embitter Anglo-Spanish relations.[70]

British domestic politics played a major role in the strategy of the crisis. One of the factors encouraging the Austrians in their opposition was the conviction that the British ministry would be defeated in the 1730 parliamentary session, and the British ministry was intensely, and rightly, suspicious of links between the opposition and foreign envoys. The ministry survived the session, including a major attack on the alliance with France, but the opposition claim that the nation would not accept an endlessly uncertain diplomatic situation and a dangerous and expensive alliance system had come close to fruition.[71]

Separately, the continuation of negotiations with the Austrians created tension between the allies. Furthermore, the disagreements at Fontainebleau became worse as the summer progressed. The British were convinced that the French did not want war but were seeking to shift the blame for inaction on them and that if the French did decide to fight, they would insist on doing so in areas where the British were opposed to French gains. The Austrian rejection of a proposed expedient to ensure a settlement led the British to press their allies for an immediate attack upon Sicily. The British hastened their military preparations for such an expedition, but that summer, the French insistence on the prior settlement of a treaty of equilibrium thwarted the British plan.

Timing was, as so often, a key element of strategy. The British had wanted to see hostilities begin in 1730 in order to prevent Spain turning to Austria. The French, in contrast, claimed that it was better to settle plans in 1730 for a general war in 1731. Before hostilities were commenced, they argued that efforts should be made to win the alliance of the Wittelsbachs. In particular, it was claimed that cooperation with the elector of Bavaria would put pressure on Austria. The French also stressed that operations in Italy required the help of Savoy-Piedmont. This approach can be ascribed to a political disinclination to force the issue in order to ensure that negotiations could continue, but there were also reasonable military considerations. The military effort demanded of the French was large, for they were expected not only to invade Italy but also to protect Hanover and the Dutch.[72] Britain, Spain, and the Dutch were not called upon to make a comparable effort.

The French view of the desired equilibrium was an ambitious one. On August 7, 1730, at a conference of British, Dutch, and French representatives held at Compiègne, Germain-Louis de Chauvelin, the bold French foreign minister, "explained himself more clearly. . . . Upon the Equilibre than ever I had heard him. His discourse tended to divest the Emperor of all the dominions he had in Italy." The British were unwilling to accept such a plan and Chauvelin complained that they would only accept a scheme that did not harm the emperor. In turn, on August 2, the British representatives in Paris had noted that "it never was His Majesty's intention to new model the possessions of Europe, and to make a new distribution of dominions and territories for pleasing the Queen of Spain."[73]

British strategic planning therefore was subject, by summer 1730, to pressure from France, Britain's leading ally, to ensure a possible recasting of the European system. The abasement of Austria was to become a matter of planning and action, and not of speculation. Moreover, there would be major commitments, for example, to win over Savoy-Piedmont, a "reward . . . out of the Emperor's Dominions in the Milanese . . . or great subsidies."[74] It was scarcely surprising that the British decided to approach Austria in order to negotiate the settlement eventually achieved in March 1731. On other occasions also, the alliance context of strategic planning has left plentiful material in the archives, both in official records and in personal papers.[75]

The question of Italy or transalpine Europe as the focus for operations in 1730–31 was a key strategic issue. It was located not so much in the sphere of military practicality as both areas were possible but rather, in those of international relations. In these, the central questions were those of desired and anticipated allies and enemies, an issue at once

subjective and objective. Thus, in 1733, as Europe moved into the War
of the Polish Succession, Thomas, Duke of Newcastle, the secretary of
state for the Southern Department, suggested that if the French won the
alliance of Spain,

> they will rather turn their arms against Italy, where they may be in hopes
> of making very great and considerable conquests; than send their army
> into Germany, where unless they attack the Empire [Holy Roman Empire],
> and by that means bring the whole Empire upon them, they must content
> themselves at least for the present with taking two or three towns from the
> Emperor, which will be of no very great advantage to them.[76]

There was frequently an assumption of inevitable outcomes that
was based on a failure to distinguish adequately between output and
outcomes, and/or on a misleading appreciation of capability. In 1735,
Brigadier-General James, 2nd Lord Tyrawly, a veteran of the War of
the Spanish Succession, who was Britain's bumptious envoy in Lisbon,
reported on the deficiencies of the Portuguese and Spanish armies, then
apparently close to war (it did not occur), adding: "I am confident ten
thousand good dragoons drawn up on the frontiers between the two
countries might take their choice which metropolis [Lisbon or Madrid]
they would march to, or perhaps a much smaller body."[77]

This was the kind of argument that those confident of the effectiveness of their forces frequently resorted to, as when Colonel John Hely-
Hutchinson claimed in 1806 that Egypt could be easily conquered by
Britain,[78] a claim disproved the following year and for the British in South
America in 1806–7; and they still do. Ignorant of political context and consequences, such an approach was also flawed on a military basis, as Napoleon's forces were to discover in Spain in 1808. Understanding the enemy
is a perennial problem of strategists and a key aspect of strategic culture.

Speculation about military options frequently related to inherent issues of the respective capabilities of land and sea power. In 1756,
Andrew Mitchell, the perceptive British envoy in Berlin, reported the
view of Frederick the Great of Prussia that France might attack vulnerable Hanover the following year, Frederick adding:

> especially if the attempts she [France] is now making in America and in
> Minorca should fail, or if their fleet should be beaten at sea, for it will then
> be the only card France has to play, and even this he thinks they may be

disappointed of, if a timely concert is entered into . . . and he is willing to
offer plans to His Majesty for that purpose, in which however the thirty
thousand Russians make an essential part.[79]

Thus, Frederick argued that the prospects of Anglo-Prussian cooperation depended on the maintenance of Britain's alliance with Russia, as
it would free Prussia from the fear of Russian attack and provide troops
to assist the two powers. In reality, Russia abandoned its links with Britain because of its anger with Britain's new alliance with Prussia, and
this helped explain why Frederick did not send the promised help to
Hanover when it was indeed attacked by the French in 1757. This attack
was intended to lead to a neutrality for Hanover that would compromise the Anglo-Prussian alliance and thereby make each power more
vulnerable.

As this, and other, episodes indicated, the prospects for, and of,
alliances frequently encouraged strategic speculation as an aspect of
alliance building. This process can be seen, for example, with the pam-
phleteers and advice writers setting out plans for large-scale and wide-
ranging action against the Ottoman (Turkish) empire, for example,
in the sixteenth century. There was no special conceptual vocabulary
involved, but this in no way lessened the impact of such suggestions.[80]
Alongside such speculation, there was the continual flow of news, report,
and rumor,[81] much of it inaccurate. A basic theme was that of preparations for conflict, and given that a key role of strategy was defense and
deterrence, these reports led to pressure for verification. Diplomats,
military observers, and spies frequently had to comment, as in 1739–40
when Edmund Allen, the British consul in Naples, denied speculation
that support would be provided by Naples for Spain.[82] Scenario planning
was a key aspect of strategy, as it remains.

These points return us to the question of who was assessing goals,
feasibility, practicality, and why. The "accuracy" of their assessment is
difficult to distinguish from the question of why strategy and particular
strategies were being pursued and, in addition, what the ends meant.
The contemporary understanding of the international situation did not
always rest on an assumption that direction was necessarily from the
center. For example, in 1756, commenting on Austrian military preparations at a time of confrontation with Prussia, a confrontation that swiftly

led to war in the shape of Frederick ordering an attack, Robert Keith, an experienced British diplomat, reported:

> it is to be feared, that when so great armies are so near one another, with a good deal of bad humour and animosity subsisting between the two courts, some unlucky accident, or other, may happen, which may kindle a fire that will not be easily extinguished.[83]

Indeed, two years earlier, the actions of local commanders on the frontiers of empire in North America had led to conflict between Britain and France, conflict the consequences of which that helped drive escalating decisions made in London and Versailles. Nevertheless, in general, a top-down analysis is pertinent for military and diplomatic policy and was offered by contemporary commentators. Moreover, local commanders and officials did tend to consult with the center, as in 1739 when James Oglethorpe, the British commander in chief in South Carolina and Georgia, in the absence of a declaration of war, wrote to Walpole, the prime minister, that he thought "the best measures here would be only to turn the Indians loose,"[84] which would be a means to apply pressure on the Spaniards in Florida.

Frequent references in the sources to how military policy developed were set alongside more general reflections on the nature of war. These preceded the first use of the term *strategy* and the later writings of Clausewitz. For example, it is instructive to consider the ideas of General Henry Lloyd (ca. 1729–83), who developed a critical approach to military thinking and whose publications indicate enough public interest in the topic to sustain the appearance of a number of books. Lloyd served under Marshal Saxe in the Low Countries, at his victory in the battle of Fontenoy (1745), and was at the successful storming of the major Dutch fortress of Bergen-op-Zoom (1747), thus providing (as did Joly de Maïzeroy, who is discussed in chapter 4), a link between that key French general and thinker of the first half of the century and developing work on war in the second half. Having gone on to serve in the armies of Austria (1758–61) and Brunswick, Lloyd became a Russian major-general (1772) who helped plan the key campaign into the Balkans in 1774, an offensive that led to the victorious end to the war with the Ottomans (Turks) and to the Russian ability to concentrate forces against the Pugachev

rebellion within Russia. Prefiguring Clausewitz, Lloyd emphasized the
political context of warfare, as well as the role of "passion" in the shape
of psychological and moral factors. The extent to which Clausewitz
presented anew themes that had recently been advanced would repay
detailed attention. That is a habitual issue, not least for historians, but
one that cannot be countered by referring to particular individuals as
seminal thinkers.

As a separate strand that underlines the range of factors involved, the
financial context was also highly important and central to strategy. That
remark does not simply relate to a context for strategy but also shows the
degree to which there was a financial strategy for war, including for protecting the credit network on which logistics and war finance depended.
Thus, in 1759, Newcastle, then first lord of the treasury in Britain, wrote
to his colleague John, 4th Duke of Bedford, the lord lieutenant of Ireland,
who, as another former secretary of state (in his case in 1748–51), had in
part then been responsible for foreign policy, about his concern about a
run on two Irish banks. Expressing his pleasure that the Irish Parliament
had set up an association to address the issue, Newcastle added:

> The want of specie [coin, as opposed to paper money] is the complaint
> both here and in Ireland, and was severely felt by us in the last year . . . it
> is something better now from the coming in of the fleets. The height of
> our credit from the great and surprising successes of this last year, and
> lately from the happy circumstance of the exportation of our corn . . . but
> as immense sums must necessarily go out of the kingdom as long as the
> war lasts, for the support of our fleets and armies in the several parts of
> the world, I am afraid we shall not be able to promise much specie from
> hence.[85]

Thus, an integrated strategy rested on far more than military factors.
Financial considerations also played a role in more detailed military
planning, and this was crucial for Britain due to its way of fighting. Considering how best to respond to French invasion plans, Bedford wrote
that year:

> I hold myself in constant readiness to take the field [take command of
> troops] on the very first notice of the enemy's appearing upon any of these
> coasts, and I have so posted some advance parties, without any danger
> of their being cut off from the main army (which in this case I intend to

assemble at Clonmell), as possibly to make their landing difficult, should they attempt it, either in the counties of Cork or Kerry, both of which are counties full of strong posts and defiles, or, should that be impossible, to impede them in their march, and thereby gain time to march with the main army to prevent their taking possession of Cork, which is a place of the utmost consequence to defend, as well, on the one hand, on account of the revenue it constantly brings in to His Majesty, as, on the other, the great utility a city and port of that consequence would be to the enemy.[86]

The structural factors were readily apparent to treasure contemporaries. Drawing attention to what was to be the basis of British subsidy policy over the century, an anonymous British pamphleteer claimed in 1719:

No superiority in the field could be a match for their superiority of treasure; for money being the basis of the war, in the modern way of carrying such things on in the world, it has since been a received maxim in the case of war, that the longest purse, not the longest sword, would be sure to conquer at last.[87]

Bedford's correspondence underlines the extent to which most states operated in an acutely threatening international order. This was not the case for isolationist Japan, which did not take part in any foreign war during the century, but was for both established political systems and also for new regimes and for would-be states. Defining interests in this context was inherently dynamic, a situation that became more so from 1776 as colonies broke away and formed independent states. The degree of unpredictability in international relations and in strategy led to insistent questions about how best to prepare for conflict and to manage risk. What might be called "antistrategy," or preventative strategy, was important, as the easiest forms of prevention were military strength and deterrent alliances.

There was also the strategy provided by a reliance on fortifications. This strategy involved repeated choices and priorities not only relating to the costs of construction, maintenance, and improvement, but also to the garrisons that could, as a result, not be readily used for other purposes, a key instance of the problems of deterrence and deferred benefit. Those fortifications near Susa designed to protect Piedmont from invasion from the Alps along the valley of the Dora Riparia were estimated in 1764 to require a garrison of "near 4000 men" to defend them.[88] Such forces could act as an operational reserve, but more commonly, garrison forces lacked mobility, flexibility, and even combat effectiveness.

Fortification systems were also regarded as elements in international relations. Thus, in 1754, Newcastle argued that it was pointless to propose an alliance with Austria unless the latter made an effort to improve the fortifications of the Austrian Netherlands (Belgium) so as to be able to block a French conquest of the Low Countries.[89] This proved a long-standing matter of dispute between Britain and Austria.

The pursuit of security was not simply an external process. There was also the question of how best to control military forces. This question involved the specific issue of loyalty, with the political consequences that might arise, and the more general one of the long-term political and social impact of these forces. Security and strategy were very much domestic as well as international, and this book will consider both.

Throughout, a key element for strategy was set by the willingness of rulers, commanders, and combatants not only to kill large numbers but also to accept heavy casualties, which could have a major effect on the economy. Preserving the army was a key strategic priority, an end as well as a means, but there was a greater willingness to take casualties than with much, although by no means all,[90] modern warfare. A functional explanation of this contrast can be noted, one that focuses on the cost of training modern troops and their relative rarity.

However, social, cultural, and ideological factors are, and were, more significant and contributed to the strategic culture already mentioned. There was a marked contrast between modern individualism and hedonism and, on the other hand, earlier concepts of duty and fatalism in a much harsher working environment. The acceptance of casualties was crucial to the bellicosity of the age and to the means of furthering aims—in other words, the strategy of the age. Although dependent on the ability to replace manpower, this element was more significant than any automatic response to tactical and technological issues, constraints, and opportunities. Enlightenment individuals in the West, and other moralizing commentators of the period, might criticize all, or much, of this belligerence, presenting it as a pointless and, indeed, dishonorable bloodlust, but these views had scant impact on the goals and means of waging conflict. Instead, the continued normative character of resorting to warfare was more notable and across the world. Wars were believed to be not only necessary but also, in at least some respects, desirable. The belief in necessity affected the attitude to civilians.

NOTES

1. Cayley to Thomas, Duke of Newcastle, Secretary of State for the Southern Department, September 22, 1733, NA. SP. 94/220.

2. Silva, *Pensées*: 303–4.

3. Chetardie, French envoy in Berlin, to Germain-Louis de Chauvelin, French Foreign Minister, August 26, 1733, AE. CP. Prusse 95 fol. 85.

4. J. C. Rule and B. S. Trotter, *A World of Paper: Louis XIV, Colbert de Torcy, and the Rise of the Information State* (Montreal, 2014).

5. G. Paquette, *Enlightenment, Governance, and Reform in Spain and Its Empire, 1759–1808* (Basingstoke, UK, 2011).

6. R. J. B. Muir and C. J. Esdaile, "Strategic Planning in a Time of Small Government: The Wars against Revolutionary and Napoleonic France, 1793–1815," *Wellington Studies* I (1996): 26–27.

7. C. Iglesias, ed., *Historia militar de España. Edad moderna. III. Los Borbones* (Madrid, 2014): 431–33.

8. C. Noelle-Karimi, "Afghan Polities and the Indo-Persian Literary Realm. The Durrani Rulers and Their Portrayal in Eighteenth-Century Historiography," in N. Green, ed., *Afghan History through Afghan Eyes* (London, 2015): 77.

9. J. Shovlin, "War and Peace. Trade, International Competition, and Political Economy," in P. J. Stern and C. Wennerlind, eds., *Mercantilism Reimagined: Political Economy in Early Modern Britain and Its Empire* (Oxford, 2014): 315.

10. George, 2nd Earl of Bristol, British envoy in Madrid, to William Pitt the Elder, September 24, 1759, NA. SP. 94/160 fols. 133–34.

11. Choiseul, French Foreign Minister, to Ossun, November 24, 1759, AE. CP. Espagne 526 fols. 74–76.

12. L. Höbelt, "From Slankamen to Zenta: The Austrian War Effort in the East during the 1690s," unpublished piece. I would like to thank Lothar Höbelt for sending me a copy of this; J. Black, *Why Wars Happen* (London, 1998).

13. K. Friedrich and S. Smart, eds., *The Cultivation of Monarchy and the Rise of Berlin: Brandenburg-Prussia 1700* (Farnham, UK, 2010): 57.

14. J. Q. Witman, *The Verdict of Battle: The Law of Victory and the Making of Modern War* (Cambridge, MA, 2012).

15. AE. CP. Espagne 419 fol. 67.

16. Solaro, Sardinian envoy in Paris, to Charles Emmanuel III, March 10, March 20, 1734, AST. LM. Francia 170.

17. Muir and Esdaile, "Strategic Planning": 80.

18. See illustrations in A. Husslein-Arco, ed., *Prince Eugene's Winter Palace* (Vienna, 2013): esp. 41, 59, 77–84.

19. *Owen's Weekly Chronicle,* June 3, 1758.

20. Gerlach Adolf von Münch-hausen to Newcastle, March 10, 1760, Hanover, Niedersächsisches Hauptsta-atsarchiv, Des. 91, von Münchhausen, I Nr. 69 fol. 6.

21. J. Ostwald, *Vauban under Siege: Engineering Efficiency and Martial Vigor in the War of the Spanish Succession* (Leiden, the Netherlands, 2007).

22. *Monitor*, April 22, July 15, 1758.

23. W. Cobbett, ed., *Parliamentary History of England* (36 vols., London, 1806–20), XI, 16.

24. Joseph Yorke, British envoy in Berlin, to Robert, 4th Earl of Holder-nesse, Secretary of State for the North-ern Department, April 12, 1758, NA. SP. 90/71.

25. D. McKay, *The Great Elector* (London, 2001): 220–24.

26. C. Pencemaille, "La guerre de Hollande dans le programme iconographique de la grande galleries de Versailles," *Histoire, Economie et Société*, 4 (1985): 313–33; C. Mukerji, *Territorial Ambitions and the Gardens of Versailles* (Cambridge, UK, 1997).

27. Delafaye to James, Earl Stan-hope, Secretary of State for the North-ern Department, September 29, 1719, NA. SP. 43/63.

28. Arnaud, French envoy in Turin, to Bernis, French Foreign Minister, June 3, 1758, AE. CP. Sardaigne 229 fols. 2–3.

29. B. Kroener, "Von der bewaff-neten Neutralität zur militärischen Kooperation Frankreich und Bayern im europäischen Mächtekonzert 1648–1745," *Wehrwissenschaftliche Rundschau* 6 (1980): 180–87.

30. Re: impact of bad weather on Spanish expedition, James Craggs,

Secretary of State for the Southern Department, to John, 2nd Earl Stair, envoy in Paris, April 2, 9, 1719, NA. SP. 104/30, and for impact of wind on Brit-ish naval expedition, cf. September 10, 14, 1719.

31. George Cressener, British agent in Liège, to Sir Everard Fawkener, Secretary to William, Duke of Cumber-land, December 26, 1747, RA. Cumb. P. 30/221.

32. Benjamin Keene, British envoy in Spain, to Newcastle, September 7, 1733, NA. SP. 94/117.

33. For a warning of this danger, Colonel Adam Williamson, Acting Governor of the Tower of London, to Sir Robert Walpole, July 31, 1739, CUL. CH. Corresp. 2899.

34. J. Black and A. Reese, "Die Panik von 1731," in J. Kunisch, ed., *Expansion und Gleichgewicht. Studien zur europäischen Mächtepolitik des ancien régime* (Berlin, 1986): 69–95.

35. Assessing Spanish preparations, Maurepas, French Secretary of State for the Marine, to Lastre, French consular official, September 26, 1733, Paris, AN. Archives de la Marine, B⁷ 145.

36. Ryder diary, October 6, 1739, Sandon.

37. Holdernesse to Yorke, May 3, 1758, NA. SP. 90/71.

38. Holdernesse to Andrew Mitch-ell, envoy in Berlin, June 27, 1758, NA. SP. 90/71.

39. Count Maffei, Sardinian envoy in Paris, to Victor Amadeus II, January 23, 1730, AST. LM. Francia 165.

40. Carpene, Sardinian envoy in Madrid, to Solaro di Breglio, Sardinian envoy in Paris, March 10, 1738, AST.

LM. Francia 176. Re: the pressure created by uncertainty about opposing naval moves, J. Pritchard, "French Strategy and the American Revolution. A Reappraisal," in D. Stoker, K. J. Hagan, and M. T. McMaster, eds., *Strategy in the American War of Independence. A Global Approach* (London, 2010): 51.

41. T. M. Barker, *Army, Aristocracy, Monarchy: Essays on War, Society, and Government in Austria, 1618–1780* (Boulder, CO, 1982); J. A. Lynn, *Giant of the Grand Siècle: The French Army, 1610–1715* (Cambridge, UK, 1997).

42. Keith to Holdernesse, NA. SP. 80/197 fols. 104–24.

43. E. G. Hernán, "War and Society in Spain. New Perspectives on the Military History of the Early Modern Period," *International Bibliography of Military History* 35 (2015): 35.

44. S. Conway, "Moral Economy, Contract, and Negotiated Authority in American, British, and German Militaries, ca. 1740–1783," *Journal of Modern History* 88 (2016): 34–59.

45. J. Black, *Insurgency and Counterinsurgency: A Global History* (Lanham, MD, 2016): 57–86.

46. R. Porter and M. Teich, eds., *The Enlightenment in National Context* (Cambridge, UK, 1981).

47. Charles Emmanuel III of Sardinia to Cardinal Fleury, the leading French minister, July 18, 1733, AST. LM. Francia 168, James, 2nd Lord Tyrawly, British envoy in Lisbon, to Charles Delafaye, Undersecretary in the Southern Department, January 15, 1734, NA. SP. 89/37 fol. 272.

48. Chavigny, French envoy in London, to Chauvelin, French Foreign Minister, October 5, 1733, AE. CP. Ang. 382 fol. 22.

49. J. R. Sofka, "The Eighteenth Century International System: Parity or Primacy?," *Review of International Studies* 27 (2001): 147–63.

50. W. Robertson, *Charles V* (3 vols., London, 1769), I, 134–35.

51. Holdernesse to Yorke, September 13, 1754, NA. SP. 84/467.

52. Harrington to John Burnaby, Secretary in Stockholm, October 2, 1739, NA. SP. 95/87.

53. Amelot, French Foreign Minister, to Villeneuve, French envoy in Constantinople, November 4, 1739; W. Holst, *Carl Gustaf Tessin* (Lund, 1931): 357.

54. C. S. Gray, "Conclusion," in J. A. Olsen and C. S. Gray, eds., *The Practice of Strategy: From Alexander the Great to the Present* (Oxford, 2011): 286.

55. Speelman, *Lloyd*: 385.

56. Re: West Indies' sugar, see also the issue of December 23.

57. See also *Monitor*, November 24, 1759, and for "Providence," Holdernesse to Mitchell, December 9, 1759, NA. SP. 90/74.

58. D. Chandler, "Fluctuations in the Strength of Forces in English Pay Sent to Flanders during the Nine Years' War, 1688–1697," *War and Society* 1 (1981): 11.

59. C. Baudi di Vesme, "L'influenza del potere marittimo nella Guerra di successione d'Austria," *Nuova Rivista Storica* 37 (1953): 19–43.

60. James Craggs, Secretary of State for the Southern Department, to James, Earl Stanhope, the Secretary of State for the Northern, July 7, 1719, NA. SP. 44/269A.

61. Du Bourgay to Charles, 2nd Viscount Townshend, Secretary of State for the Northern Department, May 17, 1726, NA. SP. 90/20.

62. Townshend to Du Bourgay, May 31, 1726, NA. SP. 90/20.

63. For ministers conferring with Anson on the state of the navy and its plans, Count Viry, Sardinian envoy in London, to Charles Emmanuel III of Sardinia, February 29, 1760, AST. LM. Ing. 65.

64. Townshend to Du Bourgay, June 7, 1726, NA. SP. 90/20.

65. Horatio Walpole to Newcastle, June 26, 1726, BL. Add. 32746 fols. 296–97.

66. Aix, Sardinian envoy in London to Victor Amadeus II, April 1726, Canberra, National Library of Australia, Department of Manuscripts, Townshend papers, 10/2/3.

67. Stephen Poyntz to Benjamin Keene, March 6, William, Lord Harrington and Poyntz to Newcastle, March 25, April 12, 1730, BL. Add. 32765–6; A. Baudrillart, *Philippe V et la cour de France* (5 vols., Paris, 1890–1901), IV, 35–60.

68. Maffei to Victor Amadeus II, January 23, April 24, 1730, AST. LM. Francia 165.

69. Keene to Poyntz and Harrington, envoys in Paris, March 16, 24, Poyntz to Newcastle, February 1, March 10, Harrington and Poyntz to Keene, April 1, 16, Harrington and Poyntz to Newcastle, April 12, 27, 1730, BL. Add. 32765–6; Philip, 4th Earl of Chesterfield to Harrington, August 25, "Short Abstract of What Has Passed about the Treaty of Equilibre," anon. memorandum, summer 1730, NA. SP. 84/307, 103/113.

70. Harrington and Poyntz to Newcastle, April 12, 1730, BL. Add. 32766.

71. J. Black, *British Politics and Foreign Policy, 1727–44* (Farnham, UK, 2014).

72. Thomas Pelham to Robinson, August 24, Horatio Walpole and Poyntz to Newcastle, June 25, Chauvelin to Broglie, French envoy in London, May 9, 1730, BL. Add. 23780, 32767, Eg. 3124; A. M. Wilson, *French Foreign Policy during the Administration of Cardinal Fleury, 1726–1743* (Cambridge, MA, 1936): 221–22.

73. Waldegrave journal, August 7, 1730, Chewton; Chauvelin to Chammorel, Chargé des Affaires in London, August 20, 1730, AE. CP. Ang. Sup. 8; Horatio Walpole, Waldegrave, and Poyntz to Keene, August 2, 1730, BL. Add. 32770.

74. Poyntz to Charles Holzendorf, Secretary to the British envoy in The Hague, February 12, 1730, BL. Add. 32765.

75. For projects for 1748 campaign, RA. Cumb. P. 31/120–3.

76. Newcastle to William, 3rd Earl of Essex, draft September—1733, BL. Add. 32782 fol. 305.

77. Tyrawly to Newcastle, May 19, 1735, NA. SP. 89/38 fol. 33.

78. Hutchinson, memorandum, November 22, 1806, BL. Add. 59282 fols. 76–81.

79. Mitchell to Holdernesse, May 27, 1756, NA. SP. 90/65.

80. N. Malcolm, *Agents of Empire: Knights, Corsairs, Jesuits and Spies in the Sixteenth-Century Mediterranean World* (New York, 2015): 406–7.

81. A. Pettegree, *The Invention of News: How the World Came to Know about Itself* (New Haven, CT, 2014).

82. Allen to Newcastle, October 13, November 24, 1739, February 2, 1740, NA. SP. 93/10 fols. 26, 32, 60.

83. Keith to Holdernesse, July 9, 1756, NA. SP. 80/197.

84. Oglethorpe to Sir Robert Walpole, October 8, 1739, CUL. CH. Corresp. 2926.

85. Newcastle to Bedford, November 18, 1759, *Bedford Papers*, II, 397.

86. Bedford to William Pitt the Elder, Secretary of State for the Southern Department, November 1, 1759, *Bedford Papers*, II, 391. For his concern about the risk of invasion, see also Bedford to Pitt, August 29, 1759, Woburn Abbey, Bedford papers.

87. Anon., *The Chimera: Or the French Way of Paying National Debts, Laid Open* (London, 1719), cited in J. Macdonald, *A Free Nation Deep in Debt: The Financial Roots of Democracy* (Princeton, NJ, 2003): 205.

88. BL. Add. 61979A fol. 40.

89. Reporting remarks by Newcastle, Perron, Sardinian envoy, to Charles Emmanuel III, August 15, 1754, AST. LM. Ing. 58.

90. John, 2nd Duke of Argyll, Commander-in-Chief of British Forces in Spain, to Major-General Thomas Whetham, November 24, 1711, CUL. Add. 6570 fol. 59; Newcastle to Cumberland, April 5, 1748, RA. Cumb. P. 33/273.

TWO

THE REACH FOR WORLD
EMPIRE: BRITAIN, 1700–83

INTRODUCTION

It is particularly pertinent to discuss strategy in the case of Britain
because the century was very much that of the rise of its power and significance, both in Europe and on the global scale. Furthermore, with Britain
having an especially active public politics, centered on Parliament and
the press, and an accompanying strategic dialogue, a consideration of the
nature of strategy there becomes a good way to assess the importance of
that particular context. Indeed, the growth of public politics in Britain,
notably from the 1690s, played a major role in the evolving discussion of
strategy. This point underlines the mistake of treating the latter solely, or
largely, in terms of the actions and thought of government, or of a branch
of government. Instead, there was strategy as a sphere for, and means of,
public debate, a factor that is also significant today.

This situation existed generally in the eighteenth-century world,
even if such debate was usually constrained by ideas and habits of secrecy.
The debate was more significant where there were ideas and practices of
public accountability and where these took constitutional and political
form. All of these characteristics were particularly the case with Britain.[1]

A discussion of British strategy in the eighteenth century entails, as
for other states, the question of the validity of employing the concept of
strategy for which the language then was different or absent, and also
the issue of shaping, into a false coherence, the often disparate discussion, limited planning, and bitty and frequently indirect pointers of evidence, that exist. These problems underline the additional difficulties of

aligning the situation in one state in one period with that in other states, in the same or other periods. This is always a task for which historians lack the enthusiasm of social scientists and, separately, brings to the fore the problems entailed in the search for what might be termed a "unified theory of strategy." A key element in eighteenth-century Britain, as elsewhere, was the lack of any unpacking of strategy and policy. This lack reflected the absence of any institutional body specifically for strategic planning and execution, and also the repeated tendency, in politics, government, and political discussion, to see what could subsequently be differentiated as strategy and policy as, in fact, one, and necessarily so.

As a consequence of these factors, the development of strategy during the eighteenth century had two very different courses. On the one hand, there was the process by which the government and the military discussed and planned, and on the other, that of the public. The pivot was the ministry, more particularly the ministers who explained strategy in Parliament and who played a central role in formulating and implementing it, not that the two groups were necessarily coterminous. However, in the persons of the secretaries of state, notably for the Northern and Southern Departments, there was an overlap, with these individuals always responsible for such a defense, although when they both sat in the House of Lords, the defense of policy in the Commons rested on colleagues who held other posts. The secretaries of state shared the responsibility for foreign policy, ensuring that this aspect of strategy was the leading factor in political discussion. There was no comparable role for leading military figures. In many respects, strategy was the key element of political debate and at a time when government did not deal to the degree seen today with economic and social policy. That senior ministers also electioneered and otherwise sought to bolster political support was part of the political equation.[2] The need to sell strategy was linked by ministers and others to the value of receiving parliamentary support.[3]

In part, strategy was a matter of stating the blandest of nostrums about national security and the safety of trade and the constitution, but strategy also involved an established litany of priorities and slogans, both of which were encoded in the partisan history of the period. "Blue water" and continental strategies were the basic building blocks in both litany and partisanship, although, as with other strategic concepts across time—for example, "containment" during the Cold War—each had a variety of meanings and associations. Moreover, the context changed in accordance with international and domestic political developments. For example, then at war with France, the British had to respond at once to the Austro-French alliance of 1756, an alliance that posed a fundamental challenge to British assumptions about the international system as it brought Britain's hitherto leading ally to a pact with the French.

These assumptions should not be separated from whatever is understood by the term *strategy*. The public and governmental debates over strategy in Britain were followed abroad, not least due to the extent to which reports of parliamentary debates and newspapers were collected by foreign governments. Thus, in 1748, the French Ministry of the Marine, which was responsible for the colonies, received a copy of the *Westminster Journal* of February 6. This opposition newspaper argued that the British navy provided security for Britain from invasion but did not protect the North American colonies:

> Whatever the creed of some persons may be, mine, that of the British Americans . . . is that to people and secure New Scotland [Nova Scotia], to reduce Canada, and open a communication betwixt our settlements in Hudson's Bay and those on the ocean, should be one of the principal objects in view in a war against France. Let us turn out these bad neighbours while we have power and lawful authority, lest they in time cause us to remove. It is of much more concern to us than who had the possession of Italy.[4]

This bold prospectus was to be fulfilled in the next war, but some newspaper strategizing took political partisanship and military speculation too far. Opposed to the dispatch of British forces to join the army under Ferdinand, Crown Prince of Brunswick, an army that it presented as designed for Hanoverian goals, the *Monitor*, in its issue of August 12, 1758, suggested, instead, that British forces should have invaded France in order to link up with Ferdinand. The paper added, overoptimistically:

> The difficulty of our carrying the war into the heart of France, at the time when their main army was totally routed and dispirited, and their best troops were engaged at the distance of Bohemia; and when the allies, flushed with victory, had nothing to fear, could they have made good their junction with an English army, depended entirely on its landing upon the

coast of France; which, experience convinces, is practicable on almost any part, under the cover of our fleets.

THE CHARACTER OF STRATEGY

Strategic planning existed but with a very different context, structure, and doctrine to more recent times, the last understood both from the perspective of the present day and from that of the eighteenth century as the political and governmental system had changed greatly as a consequence of the Glorious Revolution of 1688–89. Despite repeated experience of war, especially for Britain, for most of the years between 1652 and 1674, 1689 and 1720, and 1739 and 1763, as well as in 1775–83 and from 1793 to 1815, and continued concerns that war might recur (e.g., in 1677, 1721–35, 1770–1, 1787, and 1790–1), there were serious deficiencies in the administration of the British war effort (e.g., the separate administration of the Ordnance), let alone in military planning.[5] These deficiencies focused on structures, not least the lack of a general staff. In 1782, at a time of war, Charles, 3rd Duke of Richmond, the effective master-general of the Ordnance, wrote with reference to the threat of a French attack on the major naval base of Plymouth, a threat that a planned Franco-Spanish invasion in 1779 had made more pertinent:

> the many real difficulties that exist and prevent one's doing business with that dispatch that could be wished. I have many delays to surmount in my own office, but depending also upon others, upon the Commander in Chief who has his hands completely full, and then upon a numerous Cabinet which is not the more expeditious for consisting of eleven persons who have each their own business to attend to.[6]

However, it is worth noting that the most significant structural problem, that of army-navy coordination, both strategic and operational,[7] remained the case recently, notably, for Britain, with the Falklands War of 1982 and for the United States of the Iran rescue mission in 1980 and the invasion of Grenada in 1983. Moreover, whatever the theory, modern joint structures and doctrines face the reality of continued hostility, or at least difference, between the services, as seen with the history of air power. The problem of coordination also occurred with other states. It was an aspect of practical problems, notably of communications and power sources, but also of culture: "jointery" is aspiration and a mind-set.

As a naval power, Britain had particular strategic requirements, issues, and opportunities. Prioritization was a recurrent theme. For example, the need for planning, and the experience of it, can be seen with the detachment of naval squadrons from home waters, notably for the Baltic and the Mediterranean. This issue remained a recurrent feature in naval planning and, with a different geographical span, is still pertinent today. Moreover, a strategy of naval commercial interdiction played a role in operations against the Dutch in the late seventeenth century and, including a powerful transoceanic dimension, in conflict or confrontation with France and Spain. Thus, it was seen in the Anglo-Spanish crisis of 1725–27, in war with Spain in 1739–48 and 1762–63, and in wars against France, and successfully so, including in 1747–48. In 1748, Newcastle argued that if the war unavoidably continued, the key element would be "the operations of our fleet, for the destruction of the commerce and marine of France." He saw this as a way to gain better peace terms, which was the key strategic goal at that point.[8] The calibration of force, on land and sea, and of goals was appropriate but exposed to the friction of the events of the forthcoming campaigning season.[9]

The French government was certainly exposed to the fiscal and economic costs of conflict, and this exposure affected continued support for war.[10] A linkage of war, trade, and popular views was commonplace among envoys. Thus, in 1758, George, 2nd Earl of Bristol, British envoy in Turin, reported of France: "their commerce is entirely ruined in the Mediterranean, their manufactures are at a stand, and no money circulates in the southern provinces. The general cry is for peace."[11] His successor, James Mackenzie, proposed to increase the pressure by using British warships to intercept grain shipments from Italy to France.[12] Commercial warfare as a component of British strategy had many facets, some quite bold. *Lloyd's Evening Post* argued on January 10, 1759, that the only way to drive France to peace was to make it poor and that, to that end, it was necessary to block neutral trade, especially that of the Dutch.[13] This became a major theme in economic warfare. Grain shipments were of particular significance as shortages and price rises in urban centers could cause disorder, as in Paris in 1789.

The planned use of naval power by Britain in international crises, as in 1730, 1731, 1735, 1770, 1787, and 1790, can be regarded as wide-ranging and reasonably sophisticated given serious contemporary limitations with communications and institutional support. The navy could be readily employed to blockade France, as in 1748 when it sought to prevent grain shipments thither. The navy and Ordnance, however, posed issues of management that were greater than those of the peacetime army,[14] and the navy was particularly expensive. The extent and range of discussion about the use of naval power is such that the claim that "political-strategic dimensions" were absent and that only tactical issues were covered is unfounded.[15] In practice, the political ends of naval warfare were much considered and notably so in public discussion, for example, in Parliament and the press. So also with the strategic potential caused by naval bases and the consequent discussion of securing them or inhibiting their use. This discussion was especially pronounced in the case of British ministers and commentators, discussing, for example, the state of the French base at Dunkirk.

Others also took a role, as in 1748 when the Austrian envoy in Turin, the envoy of one British ally to another ally, pressed the need for Britain to prevent France establishing itself in Corsica, and argued that this had strategic implications for both Italy and for the Mediterranean.[16] Broader contextual issues played a role. In 1768, when France bought Corsica from Genoa, Austria was allied with France.

Planned operations on land were also varied, with options such as interventionism, in turn involving further choices over where to send troops and what to do with them, as in 1742.[17] On land, there was a degree of greater complexity because such operations frequently involved coalition warfare and all the strains to which this gave rise. There was an intertwining of military planning and diplomatic exigencies, and whatever is meant by strategy cannot be separated from coalition diplomacy. Each, indeed, were aspects of the other, a situation that is more generally true. This intertwining can be seen with the Third Anglo-Dutch War of 1672–74, the Nine Years' War, and the War of the Spanish Succession, in which Britain was involved from 1689 to 1697 and 1702 to 1713, respectively, and again in the War of the Austrian Succession, in which Britain was involved as a combatant from 1743 to 1748, although war with France was not declared until 1744. In 1755, George II argued that Robert, 4th Earl of Holdernesse, one of the two secretaries of state and a former diplomat, should meet a Dutch general in Brussels "in order to settle some sketch of a plan in case of any immediate attack upon the Low Countries [modern Belgium and Netherlands]."[18] Holdernesse was referring to the risk of French attack but also indicated the linkage of alliance politics and military planning, each key factors in strategy.

Therefore, an important background to the issue of strategic culture during the Seven Years' War (1756–63) and the War of American Independence (1775–83) is to appreciate that strategy existed as a concept, even if the word was not used in English until about 1800 when (after earlier use in translation) it was borrowed from the French where, as chapter four will indicate, a usage had developed from the 1760s. The earliest citation in the *Oxford English Dictionary* is from Charles James's *Military Dictionary* of 1810.

IDEAS OF POWER

If that is one context for the subject, a second is provided by an understanding of strategy in a widest sense—namely, to relate to the health and strength of the country as a whole. From this perspective, the British role in the Seven Years' War (1756–63) was a symptom, albeit a very significant one, of a wider anxiety about the condition and future of the country and its people, and, indeed, more clearly so than in recent wars.[19] This point may seem far removed from the habitual consideration of this or, indeed, any conflict. Nevertheless, the idea of a wider anxiety repays attention because it helps explain the contours of contemporary public political concern, as well as the extent to which policy and strategy were not distinguished. These elements, in turn, helped drive the politics of conflict and of preparedness for war.

The anxiety referred to reflected the extent to which organic theories of the state were important, theories that anticipated, in some of their implications, the Social Darwinism of the late nineteenth century. There is a tendency, in contrast, when considering the eighteenth century, to emphasize mechanistic themes, not least because of the strong intellectual thrall then of Newtonian physics, and the extent to which notions of balancing power were regarded as of importance, and notably so in Britain and the United States. This importance was the case both for international relations and for domestic constitutional, political, and social issues. As far as international relations were concerned, states were regarded as sovereign but as linked, as if within a machine. This system was considered self-contained and as part of a static and well-ordered (and thereby benign) world. The concept was based on the model of the machine which, in turn, was treated as well ordered and as enabling its parts to conduct activities only in accordance with its own construction. The mechanistic concept of the system of states was well suited to the wider currents of thought, specifically Cartesian rationalism and mathematics, as well as their successors.

A classic instance of the application of these ideas was provided in the United States with the Ordinance of 1784 for the government of the Western Territory. The product of a congressional committee chaired by Thomas Jefferson (later president), this Ordinance proposed that all new American states in the new country have boundaries based on the precision of mathematics, rather than the variations of topography. This idea was taken further in the Land Ordinance of 1785 which proposed a grid system for the allocation of land.

These currents of thought provided not only an analytical framework but also a moral context for international relations. For example, to take balance-of-power politics, which, as generally presented from the period of the French Revolution (1789) on, appear as selfishly pragmatic, as bereft of any overarching rules, and as lacking any ethical theoretical foundations; in practice, however, the situation was somewhat different. There was a widely expressed theory of the balance of power, and rules for its politics, outlined in tracts, pamphlets, doctoral dissertations, and explanations of the reasons for the resort to war. In 1759, in response to the British capture of Quebec from France, a victory that spelled the end for French Canada once the attempt to reverse it in 1760 failed, Spain pressed Britain about the need to maintain the balance established in North America by the Peace of Utrecht of 1713, only for the British government to respond that there was no question of such a balance and no reason why France should not suffer from defeat, as it had done well when successful.[20]

The relationship between such theoretization and rules, on the one hand, and decision-making processes, on the other, is obscure. This relationship clearly varied by ruler and minister. At the same time, such discussion set and/or reflected normative standards that helped shape strategies and responses.[21]

Strategy, in short, drew on widely diffused concepts of how power could, should, indeed must, operate—concepts that, in part, reflected the perception of what occurred. This element of political placing and cultural conditioning was, and is, crucial, not least as the application of ideas were contested. For example, the *Craftsman*, an opposition London newspaper, in its issue of September 15, 1739, drew on the well-established opposition and popular hostility to a large army, arguing that "whilst there is an equal division of power amongst the Princes of Europe, there will be no occasion for a numerous standing [permanent] army." A very different view from that autumn emerged from the diary of Dudley Ryder, a government minister, which showed the highly experienced prime minister, Sir Robert Walpole, employing the idea of an attacking military strategy to plan domestic politics: "He told me the true way in Parliament to oppose these people's violent measures was not to act on the defensive so much as to carry the war among the enemy and attack them."[22]

Without denying a central role for the notions bound up in the balance of power, it is necessary to complement them with an awareness of organic assumptions. These were important not so much at the level of the international system (until the nineteenth century), but at that of individual states. Moreover, these assumptions helped provide a dynamic component that is generally lacking with the more structural nature of the mechanistic themes. This dynamic component was vitalist in intention. In particular, there was a sense of a state as the expression of a nation, of the latter as linked in a national character, and of this character as capable of change and as prone to decay and collapse. This supposed trajectory looked in large part to long-standing cyclical accounts of the rise and fall of empires. These accounts drew much of their authority from the commanding role of classical Rome in the historicized political thought of the period and also reflected religious arguments.

There was also a strong input from ideas of health. Thus, a traditional sense of the nation as akin to a family or a person remained important and affected notions of development and attitudes toward divisions. This sense greatly influenced the metaphors of politics and the consideration of strategy. This idea also translated into the international sphere with a view of nations as competitive and as under threat from challenges that were foreign as well as domestic in their causation and mechanism.

Looked at in one respect, the importance of these issues, and the very value of terms such as balance of power, overreach, limits, revolution or enlightenment, is a product of their varied applicability and conceptual flexibility; this is also true for strategy as understood since. Considered differently, the very flexibility in the use of terms makes the contemporary conceptualization of only limited value because it was imprecise. Aside from the problem of assessment, there is also the contrast, often strong contrast, between the use of a concept in a descriptive or in a prescriptive fashion. This was a contrast more generally seen as strategic assessment was, and is, translated into strategic planning, and particularly as attempts were made to understand the likely moves of opposing powers.

STRATEGY AND LIMITS

Notions of balance encouraged action on the part of a Britain that, in the Atlantic world, was opposed to the would-be hegemonic power, France, for most of the period, and at war with it for much of it. Yet these notions of balance also acted as a restraint, not least because of anxieties about the possible domestic consequences of such action in terms of an overmighty state and an overexpanded army. Indeed, an antiarmy ideology that drew on a reading of politics, as well as of the current international situation, was significant in Britain. However, in normative as well as prudential terms, in so far as the two were possible to separate readily, war and imperial expansion appeared practical, successful, and necessary in Britain for most of the period up to 1945. Winston Churchill pursued colonial gains for Britain as late as World War II (1939–45), at the expense, he hoped, both of the Italian colony of Libya and of Thailand.

Within Europe, states in the eighteenth century sought simultaneously to consolidate authority and to gain territory, in Europe, or overseas, or both. They each were goals that involved normative and prudential valuations. To opt out would not have seemed sensible or even practical. With its stress on honor and dynastic responsibility, and its concern with *gloire* and the normative values of combat, the dominant political culture of continental Europe was scarcely cautious or pacific. This was the case irrespective of the more general commitment to territorial expansion, although much of that was presented in terms of advancing dynastic claims.

Due to domestic circumstances, as well as its island position, Britain (although not, from their accession in 1714, its Hanoverian rulers) was different as far as European expansion was concerned. However, the analysis and depiction of this difference has to be handled with care, for it was more the case of the area of territorial concern than of any lack of bellicosity. At one extreme, for Britain not to have resisted the American Revolution (1775–83) would have appeared as bizarre as for Philip II of Spain not to have opposed the Dutch Revolt two centuries earlier. More generally, as far as expansion was involved, a prudent defense of interests was an issue for all powers, and not a case to be simply stigmatized in terms of overreach or, indeed, elite ambition. This distinction was true whether the case was advancing Spanish goals in Italy (from the 1490s to the 1740s), or China seeking to conquer the Zunghars, or Britain pursuing objectives in the Ohio Valley region in the early 1750s.

For Spain under Philip II, China with regard to the Zunghars, or Britain in the long eighteenth century (1688–1815), to respond to rivals by trying to avoid conflict and, instead, defining mutually acceptable spheres of influence, was a difficult, if not impracticable, diplomatic strategy, and, again, the parallel with the modern United States may be considered. Such a policy would have been politically and ideologically problematic. It would also have been a serious signaling of weakness. Last, for Spain, as far as the Ottomans, France, or the Dutch were concerned in 1500–1700, or for China for the Zunghars in the 1690s–1750s, for the Mughals as far as the Marathas were concerned, or for Britain in 1689–1815 as far as France was the case, there seems little reason to believe that compromise could have been reached and sustained short of large-scale conflict. A similar point can be made at the military level when discussing the practicalities solely of defensive operations.

In part, therefore, strategic reach and ambition could only be defined as part of, and yet also in response to, what others might see as over-reach. Indeed, far from being alternatives, reach and overreach were part of the same process. Moreover, the very success of Spain, China, and Britain makes it clear that overreach is a difficult, although still useful, concept. The conquest, by relatively small Spanish and British forces in the sixteenth and eighteenth centuries, respectively, of large areas, and the successful laying of claim to others, did not demonstrate the value of limits, and nor did eventual Chinese success in destroying the Zung-hars. Indeed, a desire to avoid risk would have prevented Britain from responding to French expansionism in 1754–55 and 1792–93, and to fears of further expansionism, or have kept the Spaniards in the Caribbean offshore the American mainland in the early sixteenth century. Neither of these options would have appeared prudent in hindsight; and in the British case, such a course would have been politically impossible.

Furthermore, the element of perception central to the apparently objective notion of strategic overreach also reflects the ideological and cultural assumptions of the perceiver, assumptions that are frequently subliminal but nonetheless very significant. This situation is the case for all powers, and Britain and Spain can be fruitfully compared in this con-text. For Spain, there is a long-standing perception that can be described as Whiggish or liberal. This perception, which was seen among both con-temporaries and historians, reflected, and still reflects, critical views on Catholicism and, correspondingly, the customary association of prog-ress with Protestantism. Aside from being anachronistic, the Spanish Empire emerges, in this account, as something that had to be defeated in order to usher in the future as understood by the British. Given this perception, part of the "strategic culture" of the subject, it is not surpris-ing that the idea of overreach was, and is, applied to Spain, and that its strategy is judged accordingly. Moreover, these views help shape the response to both the partition of the Spanish Empire in 1700–14 and to the subsequent attempts to revive it. Each attempt proved highly impor-tant to the geopolitics of the Western world, and each reflected not only power politics but also assumptions about its political structure and culture. A similar point can be made about the struggle between Britain and France, but with the key difference being the sense that France, although authoritarian and Catholic, was more effective than Spain.

STRATEGY AND DYNASTICISM

Comparison with Britain can be instructive.[23] First, it is important to stress the role of contingency and, thereby, apparently imminent limits on Britain during the period 1700–83, and, more generally, that of 1688–1815. If Spain experienced rebellions during the period 1566–1714, so too did Britain in 1688–1798 and indeed China, notably in the 1640s, 1670s, and 1790s. Moreover, in Britain there was, from 1689 with the Jacobites (or exiled main branch of the Stuarts), a rival dynasty, with all the issues that situation posed to stability and loyalty. This situation did not occur in Spain until the 1700s and, then again, in 1808–13, or in France, after the 1590s, until the crisis of the monarchy in the early 1790s. In contrast, dynasties were overthrown in China in the 1640s and Persia in the 1720s.

Britain, moreover, faced a threat that Spain did not confront in 1560–1660 or China in the eighteenth century: that of a large-scale foreign invasion. Indeed, in 1688–89, the male line of the Stuart dynasty was overthrown by William III of Orange as an invasion met with domestic support alongside an indecisive and poor response by James II, William's uncle and father-in-law. Subsequently, invasion attempts on behalf of the Jacobites were mounted on a number of occasions, including 1692, 1708, 1719, 1744, 1745, and 1759. Each was backed by France, apart from the 1719 attempt, which was supported by Spain. Thereafter, invasion attempts were mounted by France in its wars with Britain, including in 1779, 1798, and 1805. Nothing comparable could be launched by Britain against France, which was a fundamental strategic asymmetry reflecting the size of the respective armies. The frequency of the French attempts, and the even more insistent level of threat, brings forward the question of appropriate strategy, both for the state and, more problematically, for the dynasty. Differentiating between the two became a major element in public debate—a debate that had to be taken into account when considering strategy.

The challenge posed by foreign support for the Stuarts was such that a key strategic element became that of displaying the domestic stability of Britain. Arthur Villettes, the British envoy in Turin, suggested in 1739 to a fellow envoy that

> A quiet [parliamentary] session with the appearance of a little more unanimity, would be of more effect towards disappointing the schemes of our enemies and bringing the Spaniards to terms, than all our fleets and our armies, and would soon convince those who are misled, how much the difficulties our country is now brought under are owing to our own dissensions.[24]

The Jacobite challenge was very much an eighteenth-century version of total war and regime change.

The question of strategic grasp and overreach can be reconceptualized to ask whether rule of Britain represented overreach for the Orange and Hanoverian dynasties. This approach draws attention to dynastic strategies, which included, in particular, marriage strategies. In the former case, the reign of William III was short (1689–1702), and he was already in opposition to Louis XIV of France. If becoming ruler of Britain opened up another military front for William and tied up Dutch and allied troops that might otherwise have been deployed against France on the Continent in 1688–90, it did so in a way that also weakened France. The British war became a major source of military and naval commitment for Louis, and after that situation had ceased when James's supporters were driven from Ireland in 1692, William benefited greatly from British resources, both in the war with France that continued until 1697 and in the subsequent postwar negotiations.

British financial resources were significant as well as their military counterparts. Indeed, there was an instructive contrast between William's failure to sustain a strong alliance able to limit Louis after the Dutch War ended in 1678, when he did not have the support of Britain, and the greater success shown by him after 1697. The latter was seen in negotiating a European settlement with France, with the Partition Treaties of 1698 and 1700. This success was also seen after the partition of the Spanish Empire was rejected by Louis in 1700 in favor of his backing for the inheritance of the whole by his younger grandson, Philip, Duke of Anjou, who became Philip V of Spain (r. 1700–46). William's preparations for a Grand Alliance for the forthcoming war, that of the Spanish Succession, which Britain entered in 1702, entailed strategic planning.

The question of shared strategic interests is more problematic as far as the Hanoverian dynasty was concerned. Initially, the British connection, which began with the accession of George I in 1714, appeared a way to advance Hanoverian dynastic claims to territory and status, notably in the partition of the Swedish Empire as a result of the Great Northern War (1700–21). Sweden's serious defeat by Russia at Poltava in 1709 opened up the possibility of a territorial reworking of northern Europe, and that possibility in turn helped direct military operations, as in 1716 when Denmark moved against supporting a Russian invasion of Sweden. British naval moves were part of the equation then as they were designed to further Hanoverian territorial interests.

George II (r. 1727–60) continued this policy, with hopes of gains for Hanover in Germany, especially, but not only, the neighboring territories of Hildesheim, Osnabrück, and East Friesland. Yet these hopes were not realized despite major efforts. Instead, the vulnerability of Hanover was repeatedly demonstrated, whether by the threat of Prussian (1726, 1729, 1753, 1801, and 1805) or of French (1741, 1757, 1803, and 1806) attack. The electorate was seriously devastated by the occupying French forces in 1757 and Hanover's participation in the Seven Years' War (1756–63) proved very costly. As another instance of strategic prioritization, Frederick II was, quite naturally, unwilling to heed British pressure to help resist the French conquest of Hanover in 1757 preferring, instead, to focus on retaining Silesia.[25] Hanoverian ministers speculated about ending the dynastic link with Britain. This situation indirectly looked toward Hanoverian neutrality in 1795–1804 in the face of French power and Prussian neutrality.[26] The British commitment could be regarded as the cause of Hanover's plight in 1757, not least as George II, under pressure from his British ministers, rejected the option of neutrality that his Hanoverian ministers favored.[27]

Conversely, strategic limits can be seen in another aspect of the relationship, because the attempt to pursue what could be presented as shared Anglo-Hanoverian interests in Europe ran up against such hindrances as the dynastic rivalry of the ruling houses of Hanover and

Prussia; second, the Austrian defense of the authority of the Holy Roman Emperor and the interests of Catholic Church against Protestant rulers such as Hanover; and third, the expansionist schemes of Russia, particularly in northern Europe.[28] The result was repeated Anglo-Hanoverian failure, albeit a failure overshadowed by transoceanic British expansion. The contrast between the two elements, specifically between the backers and the success of the two elements, was important to the politics of strategy. Britain was moving from being a European power with overseas interests to a transoceanic imperial power.

STRATEGY AND THE LIMITS OF IMPERIAL POWER

As with Spain in 1560–1660, or indeed the eighteenth century, this point opens up the question of where emphasis should be placed in strategic analysis, and again, whose emphasis? It might be suggested that this is a simple question of contrasting contemporary with modern values, but neither is that clear cut. For example, there is an important debate about the extent to which eighteenth-century Britons were committed to transoceanic goals,[29] the dominant view in the literature of the 1990s or rather, European ones, an argument increasingly prominent in more recent years and one complicated by questions of indirect benefit, notably doing well in the transoceanic sphere as a consequence of intervention in continental Europe.[30] Similar debate attaches to Britain at the present moment. Such debate underlines the highly problematic nature of the thesis that interests are clear, indeed that national interests can serve for more than rhetoric, a point that needs stressing when there is discussion of strategy. This very discussion about strategy is largely a matter of the debate over interests, however defined: national, state, dynastic, class, and so on. This point makes the debate more, not less, important. This, moreover, is the case for all states.

There is the parallel between the American Revolution (1775–83) and that against Philip II in the Netherlands from the 1560s, and the question how far the two indicate limits of strategic capability. Here, limits can be seen as much, if not more, in terms of policy as of the geography of strategy. Indeed, a focus on the latter may appear to represent a militarization of strategy and of the question of limits that is disproportionately important in the literature. In contrast to this militarization of issues of policy and strategy, other policies would certainly have led to very different situations, affecting the possibility of rebellion, the likelihood of support within the areas that rebelled, and the prospect for a reconciliation short of conflict, let alone revolution. This issue reconceptualizes the question of strategic effectiveness because it removes this question from the realm of mechanistic theories of the state/empire. These theories take the form of thus far is appropriate, but more ambition and activity causes a reaction whether military, diplomatic, or domestic, or all three—rather like a machine cutting out, or a rubber band losing its stretch.

Instead, it is the very drive of the system that is at question when policies and the pressures for obedience and order are considered. Partly for this reason, there is a need to include domestic policy as a key aspect of strategy. Indeed, as earlier with limits, the value of a flexible definition for strategy emerges. It is conventional to restrict the term to the military, but this practice is not terribly helpful from the perspective of the pursuit and limits of power. This is because strategy emerges as primarily political in background, goal, and indeed means, with the use of force simply an aspect of the means and frequently one that is only to be employed as a substitute for political failure. Thus, strategy should be understood in terms of a process of policy formation, execution, and evaluation, a process to which military purposes are frequently secondary. The language of strategy is very much employed in such a sense at present. So also with the tendency to treat strategy as akin to an adjective, as in describing a process to confront a dangerous issue, a process involving serious consideration and difficult planning. David Cameron's account in 2015 of his drawing up a strategy for tackling hate language is a prime instance.

In part, the definition and discussion, in recent decades, and notably in the West from the 1980s, of an operational dimension to war, a dimension that is clearly military, provides, as a consequence, a key opportunity for reconceptualizing strategy, away from its usual military location and, instead, toward an understanding of the concept that is more centrally political. That is a point that should not be thrown away in a sentence, for it reminds us of the extent to which modern conceptualization affects earlier "modern" evaluations of previous situations. The use of the term *strategy* offers a classic instance. If the operational level is to be considered and applied widely, then the room for a military understanding of strategy is lessened and altered. Separately, this process also reflects the understanding of strategy in terms of "grand strategy," a development with a longer gestation.

In any event, even at the operational and tactical levels, political considerations play a major role. Indeed, they can be seen as aspects of the political character of warfare, notably again the sense of limits in means and methods as well as goals, with this sense well represented in modern military doctrine. This point is not a semantic play on the notion of limited war, instructive as that is in this context, or indeed, a reference to Clausewitz's discussion of politics. Instead, the emphasis here is on the extent to which war-making inherently involved limits or their absence—for example in the treatment of prisoners and civilians—or the imposition and extent of scorched earth policies, as well as in the attitude to casualties. Moreover, there were differences between conflict designed to retain and/or incorporate territory (or at sea to retain or gain access) and warfare more focused on battle and the defeat of opposing forces.

To turn to the naval dimension, which was highly important for Britain, and indeed remains so, the British navy had a role in preventing the interruption of trade routes that was not matched elsewhere in the eighteenth century. Such interruption posed a fundamental problem for the operation of the French and Spanish economic systems. Indeed, French vulnerability highlighted the political significance in 1748 of whether Britain would ban grain exports to France, a measure that divided domestic views as such exports brought prosperity to farmers.

However, there was nothing to match the British dependence, in terms of its economy (of credit and public finances), on overseas trade. This situation posed a fundamental challenge to the British navy because trade protection, like the sea denial called for in invasion prevention, was fundamentally reactive. It was necessary to block or react to the sailing of hostile warships and privateers: under circumstances in which intelligence (especially prior intelligence) was limited and communications about any such sailing were slow and not readily subject to confirmation.

However, active sea denial could deter the development of an invasion strategy by a hostile force, such that invasion became a last resort, as for the French in 1759.

Toward the close of the period, there was a degree of improvement in communications with the introduction of semaphores, notably between London and the main naval base at Portsmouth, yet their impact was restricted. More serious was the extent to which balloons did not offer the capacity for aerial surveillance that later developments in powered flight were to provide. Thus, the British navy focused on tasks that forced it into a reactive operational stance. However, this stance also formed the basis of effective sea projection as it caused attrition and deterrence to enemies and provided Britain with strategic flexibility in the middle and long term. In contrast, the French Atlantic fleet was largely cooped up in Brest. A reactive stance is not the picture that generally emerges from popular accounts of naval operations, let alone battles. In practice, many battles arose as a result of blockades, as in 1759 and 1778, and thus were indicative of the essentially reactive strategy central to the use of British naval power. France and Spain preferred to employ their fleets for specific strategic missions, as in the unsuccessful plans to invade Britain in 1692, 1744, and 1779 and Jamaica in 1782.

The contemporary British conception of British naval power was also very different. It was proactive, not reactive, and that assumption posed a different form of challenge, one, moreover, that was accentuated by the nature of British public politics. The call to action was frequent, both in peacetime and during war, and there was scant sense of any limits on what the navy could achieve. In 1739, the government was urged not to attack the Spanish coast or bombard Cádiz, which were presented as useless, but instead, to follow a strategy of amphibious operations, seizing Sicily and Spanish America.[31] Failure repeatedly led to savage criticism, with the press very ready to condemn naval strategy and operations. Ultimately, however, it was possible to absorb specific defeats, notably the loss of Minorca in 1756, as long as capability was maintained in the Channel.

There was also pressure for action by allies. Thus, allied to Britain against France, Portugal, in 1705, also sought British help in Indian waters against Omani and other attacks.[32] In practice, the British focus then was on the Mediterranean. During the Seven Years' War, Frederick II's pressure on behalf of a British Baltic commitment was unavailing. The British government, in response, emphasized the value to Prussia of the operations against the French coast, adding

> The distant operations, in America, are of, at least, as much consequence to what ought to be, and, I am persuaded, is, the King of Prussia's ultimate end . . . it is the result of the great struggle, between England and France, which will determine the conditions of the future peace.[33]

Indeed, British naval victories in 1692, 1718, 1747, and 1759 were strategically decisive.

The national politics of naval strategy is a topic that has received only patchy attention for the (long) eighteenth century,[34] in part because of a focus, instead, on the politics of naval command. Moreover, there has been a preference for focusing on strategy in operational terms, especially the location of fleets, as in the discussion of the strategic grasp of John, 4th Earl of Sandwich, the first lord of the Admiralty during the War of American Independence.[35] This, however, does not exhaust the issue of strategy, and not least that of the wider politics of naval tasking and the rating of naval requirements within British public culture and government. For Britain, not losing and staying in the war constituted a strategic success as Britain thereby was able to benefit from long-haul financial attrition and to secure a say in the peace negotiations.

As an instance of the challenges posed by the requirements of government, the Glorious Revolution of 1688–89 led to the replacement of a monarch, James II, with a deep personal commitment to the navy by the first in a series with no such commitment. Although William III (r. 1689–1702) came to Britain by sea, he was very much a general. This was even truer of George I (r. 1714–27) and George II (r. 1727–60). As young men, they had gained important military experience but on land and not at sea. Moreover, both men had a powerful commitment to their native Electorate of Hanover, which was not a naval power and would not become one. This attitude on the part of the Crown was taken further by the powerful and long-standing commitment to the army by royal princes, especially William, Duke of Cumberland, and Frederick, Duke of York, the favorite sons of George II and George III, respectively.

Royal attitudes were not central to the political position of the navy but an element in the complex circumstances under which it had to operate. Parliament could prove more intrusive, not least when things went wrong, as they tended to in the early stages of most wars. The resulting controversies were in part an aspect of the problems stemming from an assumption of success. This assumption became more insistent because the Wars of the Spanish Succession (1702–13) and Quadruple Alliance (1718–20) did not leave any strong legacy of perceived failure, or at least, one that could apparently not be accounted for by political mistake and/or malice.

As a result, the concerns of 1744–46, 1756, 1759, and 1779 about projected or possible French invasions appeared unacceptable to many and in fact, the product of political and/or naval neglect. This situation underlined the political and thus strategic problems stemming from a reactive operational posture. The need to plan to fend off an attempted invasion was not necessarily a result of failure, however much that might have seemed the case to elements in British public politics. In turn, these political issues created the context for military preferences in terms of force structure. Indeed, the nature of the cooperation on which military systems rested was very much part of this political context.

THE TONE OF STRATEGY

As far as Britain and other states were concerned, there was (and is) a major problem in assessing strategy arising from the extent to which territorial expansion was pursued from the center or, alternatively, largely by colonial lobbies and proconsular generals and officials and, in part, in response to commercial interests.[36] This was not only a functional question of how government worked but also a contentious political question. Each could be directly germane to the question of the appropriateness of the use of armed force in particular junctures and, as a linked point, the extent to which limits on expansion were a matter of debate and nuance, and certainly not clear cut. This was also the case with such "ethnic violence" as the contentious expulsion of the Acadians (French Canadians) from Nova Scotia in the 1750s, or indeed the contested policies followed toward Native Americans. Limits in tone thus overlap with limits in

policy, the two influencing and also expressing each other. Variations
in tone bring up key cultural elements in strategy. For example, religion
was important to the various aspects of the character of British imperialism.[37] The concept of the tone of strategy is, in one respect, a way to
consider or apply strategic culture and, notably, without the somewhat
determinist character the latter may seem to have. More positively, the
concept of the tone of strategy opens up other ways to consider the subject, not least in terms of overlap with other aspects of political culture
and social ethos. So also with the idea of the style of strategy.

Tone, significantly, was a matter of form as well as content. Thus,
with a parliamentary democracy of sorts in Britain and certainly in contemporary terms, there was a need to explain strategy to the king and
Parliament (and in the press) in a manner more relevant than in France.
There was also a degree of accountability and exposure to popularity[38]
not seen there, as well as a use of the domestic political response as a
comment on strategic choices—for example, the extent of Prussian support in 1758 for the army protecting Hanover under Crown-Prince Ferdinand of Brunswick.[39] Tension occurred with allies as a result. Thus, in
spring 1760 when Frederick II, under great pressure himself, recalled the
cavalry he had provided to the British-financed army in Westphalia, this
troubled the British ministry as it made it harder to justify the subsidy
to Prussia. Andrew Mitchell, the British envoy, told Frederick that he
feared the effect

> upon the minds of the People of England, who were accustomed to reason,
> and to judge upon appearances. . . . The King of Prussia replied with some
> vivacity that though he was accountable to no Parliament, yet he owed
> protection to his subjects, whom he was obliged to defend with his whole
> force,

and that he did not wish to face popular reproach.[40] Such factors had
specific consequences, some of which are easy to scrutinize, but also less
specific and less readily accessible consequences.

SEVEN YEARS' WAR

Religious factors were readily apparent as elements in the tone of strategy. As far as the Seven Years' War (1756–63) was concerned, British

anti-Catholicism was not only a matter of anger with, and suspicion toward, France[41] but also important in affecting British attitudes.[42] This dynamic encouraged a belief that the struggle must be sustained even in the face of news that was very negative, which was the case in the early days of the war.[43] Anti-Catholicism, indeed, led to a sense of existentialist and metahistorical struggle, and of a struggle that could be traced back to the Reformation. Episodes such as the Spanish Armada of 1588 provided a clear sense of long-term challenge and were presented in that light. Thus, policy and strategy rested on a clear ideological commitment, and one in which international and domestic goals and means were both important and overlapped. Similarly, Catholic powers referred to the need to stand firm against "heretics."[44]

A clear ideological commitment was particularly important due to the development in Britain, as a consequence of the overthrow of the autocratic James II of England (and James VII of Scotland) in the Glorious Revolution of 1688–89, of a new "domestic space" for strategy. This process was brought to fruition with the Seven Years' War. The constitutional, ideological, political, social, and economic changes bound up in the Glorious Revolution and its consequences, the so-called Revolution Settlement, ensured the rise of public discussion and of a political accountability through Parliament that, to a degree, resonated with public themes. A repeated consideration of strategy in parliamentary debates, pamphlets, and newspapers was an especially noteworthy feature and contrasted with the situation in most other states in the world.

British war-making in the Seven Years' War was greatly affected by the possibilities and exigencies of alliance politics, as indeed had been the case throughout the years of war with France from 1689, and many, but not all, earlier conflicts, for example, the Third Anglo-Dutch War of 1672–74. Britain alone could hold off attack, although only one invasion attempt needed to succeed, as William of Orange showed in 1688. As an instance of the creation of public myths, William's takeover is not generally seen as an invasion.

The *Monitor*, a London newspaper that supported Pitt, asked on January 13, 1759:

> What has exalted Britain to its present power and glory? Its naval strength duly employed. What has humbled France? The British power by sea,

levelled against her shipping, her coast, and her settlements. What has
made this nation respectable to the rest of Europe? Her formidable fleets,
and wise ministry. What multiplies our riches at home? The care that is
taken of our navigation.

"Blue water" exponents focused on naval strength and colonial expansion.[45] However, eighteenth-century Britain could not overthrow its
opponents, particularly France but also Spain and Russia. This was a
lasting problem in British strategic culture. Britain had to rely upon
diplomacy (in order to lessen the buildup of an opposing coalition),
intelligence (in order to ascertain what its opponents would do), and a
strong navy.

In the Seven Years' War, Britain's ally, Frederick II, the Great, of Prussia, possessed the resources (just) and skill to put up a good resistance to
Austria, France, Russia, Sweden, and many of the German principalities.
In turn, Britain was able to defeat France (and Spain when they fought
in 1762) in the sense of capturing colonies and sinking warships (and
blocking the French campaigns in Germany and the Spanish invasion of
Portugal). Whatever their indirect purposes and benefits,[46] coastal raids
on France accomplished relatively little, and the loss of Britain's Austrian
and Dutch alliances in 1756 ensured that there was no operations in the
Low Countries, as had been the case in the Nine Years' War, the War of
the Spanish Succession, and the War of the Austrian Succession. These
operations could enable each side to put pressure on the other. For 1748,
Newcastle had feared a French attack on Breda, Maastricht, or both,[47]
and there had been major disillusionment with the Dutch inability to
field the promised forces, a disillusionment that owed much to the hopes
focused on the overthrow of the previous Dutch government in 1747.[48]
In 1753, Joseph Yorke, both a diplomat and an army officer, saw French
preparations to attack Austria and the Dutch as the obvious deterrent to
prevent Britain from using its navy.[49]

As with earlier struggles,[50] the strategy of the Seven Years' War was a
complex mixture of taking initiatives and responding to those of Britain's
enemies: France and, from 1762, Spain by this means. There was also the
impact of Britain's indirect enemies, Austria and Russia, which fought
Prussia, but not Britain. The relationship of the two tasks was framed
in the contexts of domestic and international politics. These contexts,

and the events linked to them, took precedence over the actual conduct of the war. The key questions arose from the impact of two events in 1756: the entry into senior office of William Pitt the Elder and the alliance with Frederick II. The former led to an emphasis on transoceanic operations and, within Europe, on coastal operations against France. This was a consequence of Pitt's linkage with (Whig) Patriot and Tory political groupings and themes and of his determination to maintain these while in office, notably in order to give himself an independent policy and political position, one not dependent on the "Old Corps" Whigs.[51] As such, the alternative policies advocated in 1757 by William, Duke of Cumberland, George II's surviving son and the head of the army unsuccessfully protecting Hanover, were pushed to one side.

Pitt had had experience as a peacetime cavalry cornet but had no real view on the conduct of war other than that he wanted it to be vigorous and successful. This was itself a key point as far as strategy was concerned for tone, as much as content, was the keen theme for Pitt and indeed for Parliament.[52] Thus, in operating in North America, Pitt pressed for the defense of the British colonies and the conquest of Canada from France. However, despite sometimes highly specific instructions, as by Pitt for the siege of Louisbourg in 1758, the extent to which these priorities entailed battles or sieges was generally up to the commanders on the ground and to circumstances, notably the French response. The same was true of naval operations. Britain, British trade, and British overseas operations had to be protected from attack, but it was difficult to force battle on opponents unless they left harbor, and therefore the watch on France's ports came foremost.

As far as British policymakers were concerned, the war had been forced on Britain by French aggression in the Ohio Valley region in the early 1750s, and the extent to which the conflict was intended to yield territorial gains was only clear with success. Prior to that, it was probable that the war would end, as the War of the Austrian Succession had done in 1748, with the exchange of territorial captures. The latter was the norm and was not, therefore, the basis for any aspirations or strategy focused on conquest. Indeed, during this war, it was only in 1758 that Britain made major territorial gains, notably Louisbourg on Cape Breton Island, the major French position on the Atlantic seaboard of North America.

However, such an exchange of gains had been highly contentious in 1748, a peace settlement that led Britain to restore Louisbourg, and the wish to avoid another such domestic political storm was a key point for the wartime ministry. In the event, there was to be a controversy in 1762–63 over the peace terms. For all powers, strategy in part was a matter of securing advantageous peace terms, and was seen in that light, as with reports in 1760 that France would seize Hanover to that end.[53]

Alongside European and North American strategies for Britain, there was a naval one. The main aspect of British naval strategy was commanding the Channel approaches through the use of the Western Squadron to block up French trade and fleets in European waters,[54] thereby allowing the exercise of maritime power. This was far from easy, as Admiral Rodney, blockading the French Channel port of Le Havre in autumn 1759, pointed out.[55] In turn, the situation changed when Spain entered the war in 1762 and the main British deployment became the Mediterranean fleet. The focus therefore for Britain was on command and exploitation for the furtherance of war aims. Frederick II's pressure for the dispatch of a fleet to the Baltic was countered by the argument that

> the whole force of France, by the measures the King has taken this winter, had been obliged to stay in Europe, and that he [Frederick] would be sensible, considering the force we had abroad, it was necessary to be upon our guard, and preserve something more than an equality near home.[56]

For France, in contrast, the object was not to command or control the sea but to achieve mission-focused objectives, as with the force assembled at Louisbourg in 1757 to deter a British attack; and the same could be said for 1794 and the protection of the incoming grain convoy. This contrast serves as a reminder of the strategic asymmetries arising from contrasting capabilities (military and diplomatic) and goals and the difficulties these asymmetries posed when trying to assess how best to translate the ability to engage in, and win, battles into the outcome of decisive success. The French success in 1757 in deterring an attack on Louisbourg, which the British expedition commanders themselves thought too hazardous, demonstrated the extent to which strategic implementation was "very uncertain."[57]

Strategic choices for all powers in part rested on assumptions about how these choices would affect the policies of opponents, although arguments were expressed in terms of what was expedient in political terms, both domestic and international. In April 1758, Frederick II pressed hard for British attacks on the French coast:

> because he said he was convinced if we made them towards Dunkirk, that it would oblige the Comte de Clermont to detach that way, and that might perhaps give a fair opening to the King's army to pass the Rhine[58]

in order to attack France. In turn, the British repeatedly pressed for Prussia to send troops to help fight the French further west in Germany, and thus to protect Hanover.[59]

The Seven Years' War is more generally instructive for the consideration of strategy as sources survive to a degree that is greater than any previous war. In part, this was due to a change in the character of European rulership, one that can be characterized as a move away from the Baroque style of show and, instead, a focus on a more bureaucratic style of kingship, one associated with what was later described as Enlightened Despotism. In terms of accessible sources, there was certainly a contrast between Frederick II (the Great) of Prussia (r. 1740–86) and his father, Frederick William I (r. 1713–40). So also with the move from the rule of the Emperor Charles VI of Austria (r. 1711–40) and from Elizabeth of Russia (r. 1741–62) to Catherine II, the Great (r. 1762–96).

This transition was a question of more than individuals, although they were very important. There was also the somewhat intangible issue of the mood of policymakers and, in particular, the willingness to think of international relations in terms of a system in which the views of others had validity and in which alliances were pursued accordingly. At the same time, sensitivity to other views was very much subordinate to the drive of fulfilling specific goals focused on the understanding of particular interests. The notable shift was not at the international level so much as the changing conceptualization and presentation of interests at the state level and, notably, the greater emphasis on national themes.

The latter encouraged a degree of prioritization. This was particularly apparent in the discussion of alliances. The *Herald*, a London newspaper, warned on December 22, 1757, that Frederick II had different interests to Britain, adding:

> German affairs are indeed become, from the circumstances of things, essentially collateral to our interests, but far from being direct and entire

to them. The victories effectually to serve us must be achieved either
in America or on the ocean. Prussia may be prosperous while Britain is
undone.

The Seven Years' War drove forward a global reach to British strategy
and speculation. Cause and effect is complex. There was long-standing
discussion of some ideas, such as expeditions into the Pacific, but the
capture of Manila in 1762 acted as a major spur for such activity. In campaigning against the Caribs of St. Vincent in 1772–73, the British moved
troops from North America and from elsewhere in the West Indies. At
the same time, the Seven Years' War and its aftermath revealed the capacity of "imaging an imperial order which was entirely at odds with the
realities of power on the ground."[60] The role for political imagination in
strategic formulation and evaluation is a crucial one.

WAR OF AMERICAN INDEPENDENCE

In contrast to the Seven Years' War, the political context, both domestic
and international, was very different in the War of American Independence (1775–83). This point underlines the extent to which, while any
focus on war-winning involves understanding strategy, or rather, opera-
tionalizing it, in terms of military activity, in fact, the key to strategy is
the political purposes that are pursued. In short, strategy is a process of
understanding problems and determining goals, and not the details of
the plans by which these goals are implemented by military means. There
was a need on the part of Britain to respond to American strategy, a strategy that is considered in chapter seven, but the prime requirement was
an attempt to impose on it such that there was no basis for an American
strategy. To employ modern terms, counterinsurgency was designed to
ensure that there was no prospect for insurgency.

British strategy in the War of Independence has to be understood in
this light because this strategy was very different to that during the Seven
Years' War. Indeed, the difference, which reflected the different type of
conflict, very much established the significance of politics. In the latter
case, the British focus had been on conquest in North America from
France and not on pacification there. The latter was clearly subservient
to the former, although different policies were pursued for the purpose of

pacification. These included an eighteenth-century equivalent of ethnic cleansing in the expulsion of the Acadians from Nova Scotia, as well as the very different postconquest accommodation of the Catholics of Quebec, which looked toward the Quebec Act of 1774. This accommodation proved highly successful, unlike the policies followed in the case of the British colonies farther south. Indeed, the difficulties the government encountered in the latter made it more necessary to press for the accommodation of Quebec.

In the War of Independence, pacification was the British strategy, and the question was how best to secure it. The purpose of the war was clear—the return of the Americans to their loyalty—and the method chosen was significantly different to that taken in response to the Jacobite rebellions in Scotland and northern England in 1715–16 and 1745–46. In the latter cases, as later in the face of the Irish rebellion in 1798, the remedy had been more clearly military. However, in making that argument, it is necessary to note postwar policies for stability through reorganization, most obviously in the introduction of radically new governmental and political systems for the Scottish Highlands and Ireland.

In the case of America, there was not this sequencing but instead, a willingness to consider not only pacification alongside conflict but also new political systems as an aspect of this pacification. Indeed, in one sense, pacification began at the outset in 1775, with the misconceived and mishandled British attempt to seize arms in New England. It continued with the unsuccessful attempt to overawe resistance at Bunker Hill, for the display of British forces there in preparation for their attack had an intimidating character. The most prominent instances of pacification were the instructions to the Howe brothers, the commanders appointed in 1776, to negotiate as well as fight, and even more clearly, the dispatch of the Carlisle Commission in 1778, again with instructions to negotiate, each of which were approaches rejected by the Americans. Moreover, the restoration of colonial government in the South was a concrete step indicating, during the war, what the British were seeking to achieve.

Alongside that, and more insistently, were the practices of British commanders. Although the Americans were traitors, they were treated with great leniency, and suggestions of harsher treatment were generally ignored. This point underlines the extent to which conduct in the field both reflects strategy and also affects the development of strategic culture. In most cases during the century, rebels were treated far more harshly. So also, eventually, with the treatment of Confederate citizens and Southern society in the American Civil War of 1861–65, as opposed to that of 1775–83 which is not generally presented as a civil war. In practice, there was no comparable move in the War of Independence toward the "hard" approach seen in Union conduct in the American Civil War.

This focus on pacification provides an essential continuity to British strategy, but there were of course differences in emphasis. An attempt at overall evaluation faces the classic problem that history occurs forward, 1775 preceding 1776, but is analyzed from posterity, with 1775 understood in light of 1776. This approach is unhelpful, however, not least because the course of the war was affected by two key discontinuities that changed the parameters for contemporaries. The usual one given is the internationalization of the war, notably with France's formal entry in 1778 on the American side. However, prior to that, the declaration of American independence in 1776 transformed the strategic situation. Alongside these discontinuities came military unpredictabilities, such as the initially successful but eventually totally unsuccessful American invasion of Canada in 1775–76 and the British failures at Saratoga (1777) and Yorktown (1781). These events were not secondary to the military operationalization of strategy but instead, helped direct it. The wider political dimension was also greatly affected by events, both military and diplomatic.

Thus, the Southern strategy, both military and political, the focus on regaining the Southern colonies, that dominated British policy from late 1778 when a British amphibious force swiftly captured Savannah, arose in large part from the impact of formal French entry into the war earlier in the year. This entry ended the unusual situation in which Britain was at war solely in North America, and therefore able to concentrate attention and resources on it. Moreover, from French entry, Britain was essentially pushed into a bifurcated struggle involving separate strategies. A struggle for pacification continued in the Thirteen Colonies (albeit being greatly complicated by the French military presence there on land and at sea and by the prospect of a larger presence), while a straightforward military struggle with France began elsewhere, especially in the West

Indies, India, and West Africa. Again, this apparently clear distinction can be qualified by noting that Britain had political, as well as military, options to consider in both cases, as well as offensive and defensive aspects to strategy.

The general impression is of inevitable and progressive moves toward such a bifurcated war, although in practice, the political dimension again came first. This was made more complex by the need to consider the goals and moves of various powers, including unpredictable responses to the actions of others. Thus, aside from Britain's relations with the states with which it eventually came to war—France in 1778, Spain in 1779, and the Dutch in 1780—there were relations with neutral powers, both friendly and unfriendly, Russia being prominent among the latter. These relations were, in part, linked to the military operationalization of strategy, notably with the British commitment to commercial blockade as a means to employ, retain, and strengthen naval strength, and with the possibility that alliances and agreements in Europe would yield troops for North America. This was a key goal as, lacking conscription, Britain was very short of troops. Furthermore, the European crisis of 1778, which led to the War of the Bavarian Succession of 1778–79 between Prussia and France's ally Austria, created diplomatic opportunities for Britain and, indeed, was seen in this light. There has also since been scholarly discussion on the lines that a more interventionist European policy would have distracted France from taking part in the American war, with major consequences for British options there.

This point covers a fundamental aspect of British strategy in the 1770s. Britain was acting as a satisfied or status quo power, keen obviously to retain and safeguard its position, but not interested in gaining fresh territory. Representing a satisfied power, British ministers were also wary of becoming involved in continental European power politics. Here, the American war fitted into a pattern that had begun with George III's rejection of the Prussian alliance in 1761–62, a rejection that proved highly contentious in British domestic politics, both ministerial and public. This wariness had continued with a subsequent refusal to accept Russian requirements for an alliance, as well as with the rebuff of French approaches for joint action against and in response to the First Partition of Poland by Austria, Prussia, and Russia in 1772.

Thus, there was to be no recurrence, during the War of Independence, of the situation in the Seven Years' War—namely, war in alliance with a continental power. However unintentional, this situation had proved particularly potent, both in terms of domestic politics and of international relations, or had been shaped thus by William Pitt the Elder with his presentation of British policy in terms of conquering Canada in Europe. In the War of American Independence, there would be no alliance with Prussia (or anyone else) to distract France and thus, in military terms, no commitment of the British army to the Continent, as had occurred in 1758. Even more, subsidized German troops, such as those deployed in 1757 in an unsuccessful attempt to defend the Electorate of Hanover, would not be used for "German" or European power political purposes. Instead, some troops would be retained in Europe—Hanoverians, for example, being sent to serve in the Gibraltar garrison. Most, however, notably Hessians, were sent to America where, at peak strength, they comprised nearly 40 percent of the British army. Britain's fundamental strategy thus rested on a policy coherence that had military consequences; passivity in Europe combined with the preservation of status in America.

Reviewing the strategies on offer, it is reasonable to consider the what-if of Austrian or Prussian pressure on France, or the possibility of this pressure deterring the French from helping the Americans from 1778, and thus justifying a British commitment to Continental power politics. Such counterfactuals were very much to the fore in contemporary public discussion of strategy, and provided a prime means by which this discussion was conducted. Counterfactuals were also crucial in the speculation by rulers and ministers about the likely international permutations of events, permutations made important by the roles of coalition warfare and diversionary campaigning. Separately, counterfactuals also provide a means to assess both the choices made in the past and the sphere for choice. The latter is significant, as understanding strategy in large part requires appreciating the parameters established by ideas, assumptions, and issues, as well as those relating to capabilities, opportunities, and needs. This distinction is related to that between idealist and realist concepts in modern international relations theory but is not coterminous with it.

Returning to the 1770s, it is pertinent to ask whether an alliance with a continental power would have led not to benefits but instead, to a highly damaging British commitment to one side or the other in the Austro-Prussian War of the Bavarian Succession (1778–79). The Seven Years' War, in which Britain had allied with Prussia, was scarcely encouraging in this respect, as it was initially far from clear that Britain's involvement in the conflict on the Continent then would work out as favorably as, in the event, happened. Given the use made of this example, that point provides a key instance of the nature of strategic thought and culture as recovered memory and in political contention.

In addition, had Britain allied with Austria or Prussia in the War of the Bavarian Succession, then Hanover would presumably have been exposed to attack by its opponent. Hanover was vulnerable, as was repeatedly demonstrated, and had it been overrun, as had been threatened by the French in 1741 and achieved by them in 1757, then its recovery might have jeopardized the military, diplomatic, and political options of the British government. Furthermore, the War of the Bavarian Succession was restricted to two campaigning seasons—1778 and 1779—but could have been longer, like the Seven Years' War, or have been speedily resumed, as with the two Austro-Prussian conflicts of the 1740s. Either outcome, furthermore, would have posed major problems for Britain, limiting other strategic options. Each outcome was possible as far as contemporaries were concerned.

Moreover, as another critique of the interventionist argument and, in this case, specifically the claim that it could, indeed would, have deterred French action, and thus ensured British victory, the British had, prior to French entry into the war in 1778, already failed to translate victories in North America, such as the battle of Long Island and subsequent capture of New York in 1776 and the battle of Brandywine and subsequent capture of Philadelphia in 1777, into an acceptable political verdict. Thus, the issue of French strategy was less crucial to British success than might be suggested by a focus on the major French role in the Franco-American defeat of the British at Yorktown in 1781. This underlines the need to locate speculation about diplomatic and strategic options in a context of understanding strategic possibilities.

Goals also need to be borne in mind. Britain was a "satisfied" power after 1763, and as a consequence, it was difficult, if not dangerous, to try to strengthen the status quo by alliances with powers that wished to overturn it. There was also no significant domestic constituency for an interventionist strategy and notably none for any particular interventionist course of action.

Aside from the practicalities of British power, and the nature of British politics, the Western Question, the fate of Western Europe, more particularly the Low Countries, the Rhineland, and Italy, had been settled in diplomatic terms in the 1750s. In particular, an Austrian alliance with Spain and then, far more unexpectedly, with France, resolved issues, while France's willingness in 1748, as part of a peace settlement, to return recent wartime gains from the Austrian Netherlands and the United Provinces was also highly significant.

These alliances, while challenging to established British assumptions, also removed both need and opportunity for British intervention. This shift in power politics was crucial, for, in Britain, the public support for interventionism on the Continent was fragile, if not weak, unless the Bourbons (the rulers of France and Spain) were the target and, even so, then also as alternative targets were preferred. Indeed, the domestic coalition of interests and ideas upon which public backing for foreign policy rested was heavily reliant on the consistency offered by the resonance of the anti-Bourbon beat. Thus, British military strategy in the war cannot be separated from wider currents of political preference and engagement.

What British strategy appeared to entail in North America, however, varied greatly during the conflict. The initial British impression was of opposition largely only in Massachusetts, and this assessment suggested that a vigorous defense of imperial interests there would save the situation. This view led to British legislation in 1774 specific to this colony and to a concentration of Britain's forces in North America there. The initial military operationalization of strategy continued after the clashes at Concord and Lexington in 1775, both because the stress on Massachusetts appeared vindicated and because there were not enough troops for action elsewhere. This situation, specifically force profile, represented a key failure in British preparedness but was also a product of the small size of the British army.

In the event, this policy failed, both in Massachusetts and elsewhere. In the former, the military presence was unable to prevent rebellion or to contain it. Indeed, eventually, in March 1776, the British had to evacuate Boston when the harbor was threatened by American cannon. Elsewhere in North America, the lack of troops stemming from the concentration on Boston ensured that British authority was overthrown in the other twelve colonies involved in the revolution. Moreover, in 1775, the Americans were able to mount an invasion of Canada that achieved initial success, bottling up the British in Quebec.

As a result of the events of 1775–76, the second stage of the war, a stage expected and planned neither by most of the Patriots nor by the British government, led to a major British effort to regain control. This policy entailed both a formidable military effort and peace-making proposals. Here, again, it is necessary to look at the military options in terms of the political situation. The end of the rebellion/revolution could not be achieved by reconquering all of the Thirteen Colonies (and driving the Americans from Canada). Prefiguring in a way the Union's position during the Civil War (1861–65), the task was simply too great, leaving aside the issue of maintaining any such verdict. Instead, it was necessary to secure military results that achieved the political outcome of an end to rebellion in the shape of surrender. Such an outcome was likely to require both a negotiated settlement and acquiescence in the return to loyalty and in subsequently maintaining obedience. This outcome rested on a totally different politics to that of the conquest of New France (Canada) during the Seven Years' War.

What was unclear was which military results would best secure this outcome. Was the priority the defeat, indeed destruction, of the Continental Army, as it represented the Revolution, not least its unity, or was it the capture of key American centers, such as Philadelphia in 1777? Each goal appeared possible, and in practice, there was a mutual dependence between them. The British would not be able to defeat the Americans unless they could land and support troops, and for this capability to be maintained, it was necessary to secure port cities. Conversely, these port cities could best be held if American forces were defeated.

The equations of troop numbers made this clear, not least the problems posed for finite British military resources by maintaining large garrison forces. Indeed, the latter point lent further military point to the political strategy of pacification, as such a strategy would reduce the need for garrisons and produce local Loyalist forces, as well as diminishing the number of Patriots.

In an instance of a long-standing issue in both strategy and operational planning, notably, but not only, in counterinsurgency struggles, the British emphasis possibly should have been on destroying the Continental Army, which was definitely a prospect in 1776–77. Instead, the stress was on regaining major centers, not least as this policy was seen as a way of demonstrating the return of royal authority, particularly by ensuring that large numbers of Americans again came under the Crown. Indeed, from the period when the empire struck back, summer 1776, the British gained control of most of the leading cities, either for much of the war (New York from 1776, Savannah from 1778, Charleston from 1780) or, as it turned out, temporarily (Newport from 1776 to 1778, and Philadelphia from 1777 to 1778).

Yet this policy still left important centers, most obviously Boston from March 1776, that were not under British control. This point indicated the fundamental political problem facing the British and more generally true in strategic planning: whatever they won in the field, it would still be necessary to achieve a political settlement, at least in the form of a return to loyalty. The understanding of this issue was an achievement for the British but also posed a major problem. Correspondingly, this understanding was also both achievement and problem for the Patriots.

This point helps explain the attention devoted by Patriot leaders throughout the war to politics, as political outcomes were needed to secure the persistence and coherence of the war effort. The British, in turn, could try, by political approaches and military efforts, to alter these political equations within the Thirteen Colonies. At times, they succeeded in doing so, as in the new political prospectus offered in South Carolina after the successful British siege of Charleston in 1780. Indeed, in tidewater South Carolina, the part of the colony most exposed to British amphibious power and most dependent on trade, British authority was swiftly recognized. This success appeared to be a vindication of the British strategy of combining military force with a conciliatory political policy, one offering a new imperial relationship that granted most of the American demands made at the outbreak of the war. It was scarcely surprising that Northern politicians, such as Ezekiel Cornell of Rhode Island, came to doubt the determination of their Southern counterparts.

To treat this conflict, on either side, therefore simply as a military struggle is to underplay the key role of political goals. Indeed, these goals affected not only the moves of armies (a conventional but overly limited popular understanding of strategy) but even the nature of the forces deployed by both sides. The British use of German "mercenaries" and, far more, of Native Americans and African Americans, provided opportunities for political mobilization on the part of the Patriots hostile to this use, even though, in practice, there was little use of African Americans. The American reliance on France, correspondingly, increased domestic support for war in Britain and greatly hit sympathy there for the Patriots. They could now be presented as hypocrites, willing to ally with a Catholic autocracy (two, when Spain joined in in 1779), and with Britain's national enemy as well.

These alliances brought the war to a new stage, as there was no inherent clarity as to the allocation of British resources between the conflict with the Bourbons and that with the Americans. It was relatively easy for the Patriots to abandon the greater plan of conquering Canada, after failure in 1776 was followed by British military efforts in the Thirteen Colonies that had to be countered. This prefigured the challenge posed by Britain in 1814 and, even more, what would have been Britain's strategy had there been intervention in the American Civil War.

In contrast, during the War of American Independence, there was no such agreement over strategy in Britain among those committed to the war. Partisan politics came into play, not least the politics of justification, with the opposition repeatedly pressing for a focus on the Bourbons (France and Spain), not the Americans, and the ministry unwilling to follow to the same extent. It neither wished nor thought it appropriate to abandon hopes regaining of America. This debate was not settled until Yorktown, not so much, crucially, the surrender of the besieged and defeated British force on October 19, 1781, as rather, the political consequences in Britain, specifically the fall of the Lord North ministry the following March, and the fact that it was succeeded not by a similar one following royal views but rather, that the opposition, under Charles, 2nd Marquess of Rockingham, came to power.

As a consequence, the strategy for fighting on in North America outlined after Yorktown by Lord George Germain, the secretary of state, was redundant. It is instructive, however, to note his plan for mounting amphibious expeditions along the coast, regaining Rhode Island if possible, and exploiting Loyalist support in the lower counties of the Delaware. Germain argued that by retaining New York, Charleston, and Savannah, British trade would be secured and bases maintained from which counteroperations directed against France and Spain could be mounted in the Caribbean.[61]

As a result of the central role of politics in strategy, 1782 was a key year of the war. It was a year, ironically, in which the Patriots had singularly little military success, George Washington, in particular, getting nowhere with his plan to capture New York. Moreover, this failure was more generally significant as it marked the decline in the Franco-American alliance. This decline reflected the problems of pursuing very different military priorities, with the French focused on the West Indies, and far more significantly, a war weariness on the part of the French government that in part arose from the priorities of European power politics, notably French concern about Russian expansionism at the expense of the Turks. This point illustrated the complex and interlinked character of international relations and the resulting context for strategy.[62]

Furthermore, in 1782, the French fleet in the West Indies was heavily defeated by Admiral Rodney at the battle of the Saintes. This was a major instance of the role of battle in determining strategic options. Thus, militarily, the war was going Britain's way by 1782. New warships were being launched, public finances were robust, fears of rebellion in Ireland and of disaffection in Britain were largely assuaged, the Bourbons were increasingly unable to attempt another invasion of Britain, Gibraltar had been held against siege and large-scale attack, and the British position in both India and Canada was more resilient than had been feared. The equations of colonial gains and the likely offsetting in any eventual peace treaty thus altered.

Yet the politics for Britain was now of peace and of a settlement that was not focused on a return of America to its loyalty; and strategy was framed accordingly. Instead, the priority was the disruption, if not destruction, of the coalition of powers fighting Britain and, hopefully, better relations with an independent United States (as it later became). Paradoxically, this strategy was to be successful, and in both the short and the long term, as Britain won the battle of the peace by dividing the opposing coalition and offering peace terms separately. Crucially, the alliance between America and France ceased to be effective. Instead, there was a flexibility that created opportunities for new alignments. In June 1786, William Eden, the British envoy in Paris for negotiating a trade treaty and also a Member of Parliament, reported:

> there are strong appearances here of a disposition to believe that Great Britain and France ought to unite in some solid plan of permanent peace: and many of the most considerable people talk with little reserve of the dangers to be apprehended from the revolted colonies, if they should be encouraged to gain commercial strength and consistency of government.[63]

That was not an option, but in 1787, when Britain and France came close to conflict in the Dutch crisis, there was scant prospect of America wishing to help, or being able to help, the French.[64]

This outcome underlines the conceptual problems of conceiving of strategy in terms of its military operationalization. At the same time, the dynamic character of strategy was amply displayed by the unexpectedness of the challenge posed by the American Revolution. This unexpectedness was not only a matter of the novelty of this revolution but had been seen repeatedly during the previous war. Moreover, the conflicts in which Britain became involved in 1718, 1739, and 1754, were unexpected. So, even more, with the severity of the crisis posed by the 1745 Jacobite rebellion. In reactive terms, challenges were therefore unexpected, at least in their timing, severity, and combination. This was very different to an account of strategy in terms of facilitating imperial expansion. However, the latter was a consequence of conflicts rather than the cause of wars and certainly in so far as military and political planning were concerned.

NOTES

1. J. Black, *Parliament and Foreign Policy in the Eighteenth Century* (Cambridge, 2004).

2. Boutel, French diplomat in London, to Rouillé, French Foreign Minister, September 12, 1754, AE. CP. Ang. 437 fol. 300.

3. Holdernesse to Sir John Goodricke, envoy to Sweden, April 14, 1758, Oxford, Bodleian Library, Ms. Eng. Hist. C. 62 fol. 4.

4. AN. B[7] 359.

5. R. J. B. Muir and C. J. Esdaile, "Strategic Planning in a Time of Small Government: The Wars against Revolutionary and Napoleonic France, 1793–1815," in C. M. Woolgar, ed., *Wellington Studies* (3 vols., Southampton, UK, 1996), I, 1–90; Muir, *Britain and the Defeat of Napoleon 1807–1815* (New Haven, CT, 1996): 12.

6. Richmond to Major-General Charles Grey, April 27, 1782, Durham, UK, University Department of Palaeography, papers of 1st Earl Grey, no. 61.

7. R. Harding, *Amphibious Warfare in the Eighteenth Century: The British Expedition to the West Indies, 1740–1742* (Woodbridge, UK, 1991); N. A. M. Rodger, *The Insatiable Earl: A Life of John Montagu, 4th Earl of Sandwich* (London, 1993).

8. Newcastle to John, 4th Earl of Sandwich, January 19, 1748, BL. Add. 32811 fols. 88–9.

9. See also Sandwich to Cumberland, February 6, 1748, RA. Cumb. P. 31/198.

10. Bernis, French Foreign Minister, to Choiseul, envoy in Vienna, June 6, 1758, Starhemberg, Austrian envoy in Paris, to Chancellor Kaunitz, July 8, 1758, Bernis memorandum to Maria Theresa, delivered on October 19, 1758, in J. C. Batzel, *Austria and the Three Treaties of Versailles, 1755–1758* (PhD diss., Brown, 1974): 454, 469, 498–99.

11. Bristol to Pitt, July 26, 1758, NA. SP. 92/66.

12. Mackenzie to Pitt, December 9, 23, 1758, NA. SP. 92/66.

13. Similar arguments were made in the issue of January 31.

14. R. Knight, *Britain against Napoleon: The Organization of Victory 1793–1815* (London, 2013): 48–49.

15. B. Heuser, "Regina Maris and the Command of the Sea: The Sixteenth Century Origins of Modern Maritime Strategy," *Journal of Strategic Studies*, DOI: 10.1080/01402390.2015.1104670.

16. Richecourt to Austrian envoy in London, February 14, 1748, HHStA. England, Varia, 10.

17. R. Harding, *The Emergence of Britain's Global Naval Supremacy: The War of 1739–1748* (Woodbridge, UK, 2010): 142–46.

18. Holdernesse to Joseph Yorke, envoy in The Hague, April 22, 1755, BL. Egerton Mss. 3446 fol. 105.

19. J. Black, *British Politics and Foreign Policy, 1744–57. Mid-Century Crisis* (Farnham, 2015): 225–28.

20. Memorial by Spanish envoy in London, December 5, and reply, December 13, and Bristol, British envoy in Spain, to Pitt, December 19, 1759, NA. SP. 94/160 fols. 248, 253–54, 299.

21. H. Kleinschmidt, *The Nemesis of Power* (London, 2000), esp. 114–70 and "Systeme und Ordnungen in der Geschicht der internationalen Beziehungen," *Archiv für kulturgeschichte*, 82 (2000): 433–54; A. Osiander, *The States System of Europe, 1640–1990. Peacemaking and the Conditions of International Stability* (Oxford, 1994).

22. Ryder diary, October 6, 1739, Sandon.

23. J. H. Elliott, *Empires of the Atlantic World: Britain and Spain in America, 1492–1830* (New Haven, CT, 2006).

24. Villettes to Horace Mann, envoy in Florence, October 7, 1739, NA. SP. 105/281 fol. 181.

25. Andrew Mitchell, British envoy in Berlin, to Holdernesse, November 11, 1757, NA. SP. 90/70.

26. P. G. Dwyer, "Prussia and the Armed Neutrality: The Invasion of Hanover in 1801," *International History Review* 15 (1993): 661–87, and "Two Definitions of Neutrality: Prussia, the European States-System, and the French Invasion of Hanover in 1803," *International History Review* 19 (1997): 502–40.

27. U. Dann, *Hanover and Great Britain, 1740–1760* (Leicester, UK, 1991).

28. A. C. Thompson, *Britain, Hanover and the Protestant Interest, 1688–1756* (Woodbridge, UK, 2006); B. Simms and T. Riotte, eds., *The Hanoverian Dimension in British History, 1714–1837* (Cambridge, UK, 2007); Simms, *Three Victories and a Defeat: The Rise and Fall of the First British Empire, 1714–1783* (London, 2007).

29. K. Wilson, *The Sense of the People: Politics, Culture and Imperialism in England, 1715–1785* (Cambridge, UK, 1998); D. Armitage and M. J. Braddick, eds., *The British Atlantic World* (London, 2002).

30. T. Claydon, *Europe and the Making of England, 1660–1760* (Cambridge, UK, 2007).

31. Thomas Johnston to Sir Robert Walpole, June 8, 1739, CUL. CH. Corresp. 2875.

32. John Methuen, envoy in Lisbon, to Earl of Nottingham, Secretary of State for the Southern Department, September 19, 1705, BL. Add. 61122 fol. 47.

33. Holdernesse to Mitchell, July 17, 1757, NA. SP. 90/69. See also February 25, 1758, 90/71.

34. See, e.g., R. McJimsey, "England's 'Descent' on France and the Origins of Blue-Water Strategy," in M. Neiberg, ed., *Arms and the Man: Military History Essays in Honor of Dennis Showalter* (Leiden, the Netherlands, 2011): 243–57.

35. N. A. M. Rodger, *The Insatiable Earl: A Life of John Montagu, Fourth Earl of Sandwich, 1718–1792* (London, 1993).

36. Viry, Sardinian envoy in London, to Charles Emmanuel III, June 13, 1758, AST. LM. Ing. 63.

37. C. G. Pestana, *Protestant Empire. Religion and the Making of the British Atlantic World* (Philadelphia, 2009).

38. For the latter, with reference to pressure in 1759 against returning conquests, Bedford, Bedfordshire County Record Office, Lucas papers, L30/9/17/29.

39. Holdernesse to Mitchell, August 2, September 19, 1758, NA. SP. 90/72.

40. Mitchell to Holdernesse, May 23, 1760, NA. SP. 90/76.

41. Joseph to Philip Yorke, September 17, 1754, BL. Add. 35364 fol. 12.

42. M. Schlenke, *England und das friderizianische Preussen, 1740–1763* (Munich, Germany, 1963): 171–225.

43. G. Yagi, *The Struggle for North America, 1754–1758. Britannia's Tarnished Laurels* (London, 2016).

44. George, 2nd Earl of Bristol, envoy in Madrid, to Pitt, March 10, 1760, NA. SP. 90/161.

45. *Monitor*, June 3, 1758.

46. Pitt to Lieutenant-General Sir John Mordaunt, August 5, 1758, NA. SP. 42/100.

47. Newcastle to Sandwich, December 29, 1747, BL. Add. 32810 fol. 425.

48. Newcastle to Cumberland, February 25, Cumberland to Newcastle, February 26, 1748, RA. Cumb. P. 32/116, 119–20.

49. Joseph to Philip Yorke, March 23, f11 1753, BL. Add. 35363 fol. 324.

50. H. W. Richmond, "English Strategy in the War of the Austrian Succession," *RUSI Journal* 63 (1919): 246–54.

51. R. Harding, *"A Golden Adventure": Combined Operations in the Caribbean, 1740–2. A Re-Examination of the Walpole Ministry's Response to War with Spain* (PhD diss., London, 1985): 316–17.

52. Harding, *"A Golden Adventure"*: 313–15.

53. Bristol to Pitt, February 11, 1760, NA. SP. 94/161.

54. *Monitor*, November 19, 1757; M. Robson, *A History of the Royal Navy. The Seven Years' War* (London, 2016).

55. Rodney to George Lyttelton, October 20, November 19, 1759, *Sotheby's Catalogue of the Lyttelton Papers* (London, 1978): 143–46.

56. Yorke to Holdernesse, April 11, 1758, NA. SP. 90/71.

57. Reporting views of Newcastle, Hugh Valence Jones, MP, and Solicitor to the Treasury, to Hardwicke, August 30, 1757, BL. Add. 35417 fol. 38.

58. Yorke to Holdernesse, April 13, 1758, NA. SP. 90/71. For the need for a diversion, see Newcastle to Field Marshal Ligonier, the Commander-in-Chief, June 17, 1758, BL. Add. 35417 fol. 236.

59. Pitt to Mitchell, January 2, 1759, NA. SP. 90/73.

60. M. P. Dziennik, "'Till These Experiments Be Made': Senegambia and British Imperial Policy in the Eighteenth Century," *English Historical Review* 130 (2015): 1161.

61. Piers Mackesy, "British Strategy in the War of American Independence," *Yale Review* 52 (1963): 539–57; W. B. Willcox, "Too Many Cooks: British Planning Before Saratoga," *Journal of British Studies*, 2, (1962): 56–90.

62. J. Dull, *The French Navy and American Independence: A Study of Arms and Diplomacy, 1774–1787* (Princeton, NJ, 1975), and *A Diplomatic History of the American Revolution* (New Haven, CT, 1985); O. T. Murphy, *Charles Gravier, Comte de Vergennes: French Diplomacy in the Age of Revolution, 1719–1787* (Albany, NY, 1982).

63. Eden to Francis, Marquess of Carmarthen, Foreign Secretary, June 6, 1786, NA. FO. 27/19 fol. 116.

64. P. P. Hill, *French Perceptions of the Early American Republic, 1783–1793* (Philadelphia, 1988).

THREE

THE STRATEGY OF THE ANCIEN RÉGIME: FRANCE, 1700–89

COUNTERPOINTING BRITAIN AND FRANCE BY DISCUSSING them in successive chapters can be misleading as it can lead to an emphasis on individual differences between the two countries and on an accentuation of an overall impression of contrast rather than any focus on similarities. At the same time, without making such a contrast the central theme of this chapter, it was readily apparent to contemporaries, and it can still readily be discerned. However, so also can the comparison offered by the extent to which strategic content and context altered in, and for, Britain and in, and for, France. Indeed, that is the most arresting nature of the subject, the way in which change was shaped, and responded to, in both similar and different fashions. The same point can be made of other pairs of states for example of Russia and China, or of the Ottoman (Turkish) and Habsburg (Austrian) Empires. Such an approach leads to an emphasis on the relative nature of strategy and thereby, that aspect of its contextual character.

In the French case, the established political context for strategy in the reign of Louis XIV (r. 1643–1715)[1] is primarily domestic: that of dynastic dynamics, ministerial factions mediated by a powerful and assertive monarch, and a concern with how best to appeal to Catholic interests. This context was subsequently affected by a range of domestic, international, and diplomatic factors. These included a multifaceted reaction against what was seen as Crown autocracy, the rise of transoceanic empire as an issue, at once opportunity and challenge for France, and the new ideals and idioms linked to values that can be defined as Enlightenment, as well as the pervasive pressure of events, notably international events but also those within France. A particular contrast arose from the differences between the response to Louis XIV's policies and the protracted controversy over the alignment with Austria following the Diplomatic Revolution of 1756, an alignment widely seen and presented as both unpopular and unsuccessful.

As with Britain and in the other case studies, the central theme is that of the interplay of strategic culture and strategy. This situation captures the extent to which, alongside long-term interests and structural factors in policymaking and debate, there was no deterministic causation. Supplementing and focusing the unpredictable and fluid character of foreign relations, there were varied and episodic interests and choices over strategy. For example, in 1778, there was a stark choice between intervening in North America or fulfilling treaty commitments to Austria in the War of Bavarian Succession (1778–79). Had the latter choice been taken, France might well not have benefited, as it was to do, from the weakening of British power caused by supporting the American Patriots in order to secure the loss of the Thirteen Colonies, for France would have been involved in war with Prussia, the dominions of which included territories in the lower Rhineland. Prussia would also have been in a position to attack France's other, and more vulnerable, allies in Germany.

Alliance dynamics were more generally crucial to strategic possibilities. The failure of France, during the century, to produce lasting effective relationships with Britain, the Dutch, Spain, Austria, Prussia, and Russia greatly affected France's maritime and colonial position, as well as its hopes and strategies for European power politics. In 1749, Louis, Marquis de Puysieulx, the able French foreign minister, outlined to the British envoy the military basis for partnership between the two powers which had recently been at war from 1743 to 1748 but had been allies from 1716 to 1731:

> the digressions that minister made, on the superiority of Great Britain by sea, and that of France by land; which tended no farther than to explain to my understanding, in what he thought the most advantageous and pleasing light, the propriety of the two nations uniting the superior force of both elements, to keep the rest of Europe in the state of tranquillity.[2]

The failure of such potential alliance dynamics, however, helped ensure that France did not realize the potential it appeared to have in both

Europe and the world. Helped by the lack of German unification, France was the most populous state in Western Europe, its population rising from about 22.4 million in 1705 to about 24.6 million in 1740, and possibly to close to 30 million in 1800. This rise was significant because human labor was the crucial source of power for the economy, and manpower, especially skilled manpower, the vital ingredient of wide-ranging military strength. Moreover, this was the case for naval as well as land power.

Manpower, nevertheless, itself provides an instance of choice, for France did not use conscription to raise regular troops until after the French Revolutionary War started in 1792. Instead of treating this as a demonstration of failure, populous France was able earlier to raise the necessary forces with a minimum of disruption. In addition, while France had a smaller army than either Austria, Prussia, or Russia in the 1760s, 1770s, and 1780s, this size was not a sign of weakness but in part reflected the requirements of its international situation which included investment on the navy. So also with the trajectory of French military reform, which did not match that of Austria or Russia in the crucial interwar period of 1748–56.

In contrast, and as a vital aspect of strategy, one that underlines the problematic character of differentiating it from policy, a need for French military reform was, in the main, perceived only after defeats in the Seven Years' War (175--63). The French did better than is generally allowed in that conflict, particularly in Westphalia in 1757 and in the early 1760s, but their reputation was excessively tarnished by the total success of the Prussian surprise attack at the battle of Rossbach in 1757. Nevertheless, the avoidance of this and other defeats during the war, both in Europe and overseas, as well as a repetition of the repeated triumphs of France's armies in 1745–48, would have offered the French monarchy vital prestige. Such prestige was made more significant by the discussion of French national interest and identity that became more intense from the 1760s, a discussion that owed much to defeats during the Seven Years' War. In turn, success in the war, had it occurred, might have expanded the domestic and international dimensions of France's strategic parameters, possibly indeed leading to additional problems, for example as a result of intervening with force on behalf of its Dutch allies in the Dutch Crisis in 1787, rather than deciding not to do so as was in fact the case.

An emphasis on choice does not imply that free will was unconstrained but draws attention to the contemporary need to adjust strategies to changing circumstances and views, both international and domestic. As part of this process, but also separate to it, the building blocks of strategic culture, strategic debate, and policy, for example glory, honor, and natural interests, or Thucydides's fear, honor, and interests, were not uniform or unchanging in their impact. Instead, they had meanings for specific individuals or groups at particular moments. The nature of the sources, however, can make it difficult to understand and analyze these specific meanings and the resulting differences. For example, it is unclear how best to relate policies from the 1740s to the 1780s to the factional character of French ministerial politics. The differences were reported by foreign envoys and newspapers.[3]

It is also unclear how far to relate these policies and politics to particular social circles. A "party" of high aristocrats keen on military glory and linked to Choiseul, the key figure in foreign policy from 1758 to 1770, has been discerned and contrasted with more cautious ministers, many from a legal background.[4] Moreover, this analysis can be taken forward into the 1780s and back, certainly, into the 1740s, if not earlier. Espionage information in 1758 stressed divisions within the ministry in which military and diplomatic factors were intertwined.[5] However, although social and political differences could, indeed, help drive strategy, and were related to strategic options, there were other key issues in ministerial and wider politics, notably those relating to church policy. Furthermore, individual ministers, particularly Choiseul, had contrasting priorities at particular stages of their career.

Cultural assumptions and notions about the correct nature of policy were related to individual views. The ministers accordingly played major roles, with foreign policy not being determined by military needs. Cardinal Fleury, the leading minister from 1726 to 1743, did not regard war with favor, although during his period in office, France went to war in 1733 and 1741. The Sardinian envoy in Paris in 1738 complained that Fleury would sacrifice France's *gloire* rather than put peace at risk.[6]

It was not only a case of individual views. The regular police reports that the French government received in the 1720s, 1730s, and 1740s provided plentiful information on the views of Parisians on domestic and foreign policies. The Parisians were not selected on any systematic basis, and, essentially, the reports were gathered from the comments made in cafés[7] and constituted individual opinions rather, possibly, than a more shaped public opinion, insofar as the latter can be shaped and reified as a coherent body and force.[8] As a result, they might not appear to have any role in a book about strategy. So also with the comments of foreign diplomats such as Joseph Yorke, a British envoy, in 1749:

> nothing since my coming into this country has surprised me more than to find the French king [Louis XV] spoke of with so little regard, which is so contrary to the notion one generally has conceived, of their outward at least affection for their monarch.[9]

However, as already argued, strategy, as a process involving choices and implementation, cannot be divorced from the assumptions of strategic culture. Rather than treating the latter as a monolith, it was a sphere for, process of, and result of, political contention. This contention had long been a feature of French policy, notably during the lengthy French (civil) Wars of Religion in the late sixteenth century and in the 1620s. It is therefore mistaken to see a rise in French public politics from the 1750s as if that was a new process, even if such a thesis may be attractive if focusing on allegedly transformative change and notably when assessing the background to the French Revolution, which began in 1789. Instead, there was much anticipation of such politics. In particular, the travails of the last years of Louis XIV, travails that owed much to the pressures of the War of the Spanish Succession, led to a rising current of discontent, which fed through into public debate. The most contentious issue was that of religion, an issue that had clear foreign policy implications. Jansenism and relations with the papacy were seen as directly relevant to international alignments and as key aspects of the pursuit of advantage in Catholic Europe.

The death of Louis XIV in 1715, and the subsequent regency government for his infant great-grandson, Louis XV, led to a new range of contention. Foreign policy disputes were intimately related to dynastic issues, notably the claim on the succession of Louis XV's uncle, Philip V of Spain.[10] In this context, it was difficult to think of a stable context for strategy, and especially so when Louis XV, still childless, suffered from smallpox in 1728. French troops had campaigned in Spain during the War of Spanish Succession in order to help Philip V gain the throne: Marshal Berwick commanded the army that helped him capture Barcelona in 1714. Five years later, in contrast, Berwick was invading Spain in command of a French army and in alliance with Britain, while in 1725–29 France (allied to Britain) came close to war again with Spain and Austria, before Spain and France cooperated with Britain in war planning against Austria in 1730 and, without Britain, in fighting Austria in 1733–35.

The extent to which diplomacy continued during most wars, both between allies and with neutrals and opponents, added a further level of complexity to strategy and ensured that a simplistic view of strategy is inappropriate, while at the same time directing attention to the rulers, ministers, and generals who had to handle such relations. In addition, prewar and wartime negotiations and agreements between powers helped set strategy, as with the Franco-Spanish agreements against Britain in 1761 and 1779, and correspondingly left sources.[11]

French strategy in the War of the Spanish Succession (1701–14) is instructive. It was both dependent on events in the field and yet also on diplomacy. For example, Anglo-Austrian victory over a French-Bavarian army at Blenheim in 1704 was followed by the overrunning of Bavaria. This was a campaign verdict that was not to be militarily challenged during the war. Instead, other than in Spain, French strategy became mostly a matter of frontier defense, as was to happen again in 1743, after defeat at Dettingen, and in 1813, after defeat at Leipzig, in each case after major French defeats in Germany. Frontier defense had major and political implications for France as for other powers. It was a course of action that made it difficult to retain and gain allies, that posed a serious logistical strain in the shape of supporting French armies without "contributions" from occupied areas, and which made victory impossible. Moreover, Louis believed his honor involved in supporting Elector Max Emmanuel of Bavaria—a key consideration. Backing allies was also necessary in order to prevent a rallying to Louis's opponents. Indeed, in November 1704, a Franco-Bavarian treaty committed Louis to continue the war until Bavaria was retaken and enlarged. More than honor was involved. French commentators and diplomats were also well aware of the significance of money. Thus, in 1733, considering the possibility of alliance with Bavaria against Austria, Bussy, a diplomat who had recently been to both, commented on the quality of the Bavarian army but argued correctly that Bavaria was very open to attack by Austria and that it required money if it was to arm.[12]

The pattern of warfare was not that of the extirpation of enemies, as in the case of the Chinese treatment of the Zunghars in the 1750s, on which see chapter 5. Instead, diplomacy continued in wartime. Thus, in 1706, a heavy defeat of a French army by John, Duke of Marlborough, at Ramillies and the subsequent expulsion of the French forces from the Spanish Netherlands led Louis XIV to try peace proposals. Again, Marlborough's major victory over the French at Oudenaarde in 1708 and his capture of the major French fortress of Lille later that year made Louis more eager to settle. In turn, Marlborough's pyrrhic victory at Malplaquet in 1709, followed by only slow progress in capturing French fortresses, helped move the political dynamic more toward a position conducive to the French. In part, this was due to the course of the war, but those of politics and diplomacy were also important. The ministry committed to war was overthrown in Britain, and its successor was ready to negotiate a peace with France, the Peace of Utrecht (1713), that involved abandoning some of Britain's allies, notably Austria. In Germany, the Imperial Diet at Regensburg declared in July 1713 that the French proposals would "tarnish the glory of the German nation." However, defeat affected the room available for maneuver. Outnumbered and pushed back by the French, who captured the major fortresses of Freiburg, Kehl, and Landau in 1713, the Emperor Charles VI (r. 1711–40) was forced to negotiate.

In both war and peace, French politics had for long been related to major differences over strategy. A goal of national strength under royal leadership could include many possible strategies, a situation much accentuated by the major divisions in France over policy stemming from the Protestant Reformation of the sixteenth century. The strategic inheritance, and at times, incubus, shaped much of the discussion during the eighteenth century, especially during the first half, as different priorities came to the fore in and after the 1750s. The key differences in France in the seventeenth century had been over religious, dynastic, and geopolitical alignments, notably a tension between *dévot* support for a confessional policy and, in particular, alliance with Spain and, in contrast, a *raison d'état* willingness to seek Protestant (and Muslim) allies against the Habsburgs, a strategy especially associated, from the 1620s to 1661, with the first ministers, successively Cardinals Richelieu and Mazarin. The international strategy of marriage alliances introduced another goal and means, as did the drive for dynastic exultation through territorial expansion. The last can very much be seen in terms of strategic culture.

A fundamental continuity across the century divide was provided by the length of Louis XIV's reign, which lasted, with him active, until 1715, and the extent to which ministers and generals who had served him continued to be active thereafter. Marshal Villars used the example of Louis XIV to press his young successor, Louis XV, to action against Austria in 1733.[13] At the same time, politics and policy debates did not cease during Louis XIV's reign, and the resulting views and tensions provided a background to those seen in the eighteenth century.

For French policymakers, the key elements under the ancien régime were very much affected by changes in the domestic and international context and in the culture of power. For example, with reference to the latter, the War of the Spanish Succession altered French strategy, not least by transforming the nature of Habsburg power.[14] To take the culture of power, Louis XIV was more affected by Counter-Reformation mentality than an emphasis on *raison d'état* politics might suggest. This mentality also provided a way to link domestic and foreign policy. Alongside his orthodoxy and legitimism, this mentality helped lead Louis to support the Catholic James II of England (he was also ruler of Ireland, Scotland, and Wales) (r. 1685–88) after he was overthrown by William III of Orange in 1688.

As an indication of the more general issues of judging practicality, that choice, and the resulting dispatch of French troops to Ireland and mounting of invasion attempts on Britain, can be considered both a foolish distraction from the major military and political tasks in hand on the Continent and, alternatively, as a brilliant way to divert British resources. Both, indeed, were the case, with William III best able to focus on resisting France in the Low Countries only after he had defeated James (and the French) in Ireland and after the destruction of the French invasion fleet at Barfleur in 1692.

Similar issues of past prioritization and present judgment occurred in the eighteenth century. French ministries divided—for example, over war with Britain in 1770 and 1778—deciding not to back Spain in 1770 in the Falkland Islands crisis but to support the Americans in 1778. In addition, foreign policy became far more politicized in France than had been the case in the seventeenth century, and with much of this politics played out in public. The net effect was important to the response to particular military campaigns. Indeed, this process was taken further because of the pronounced overlap of military command with court politics and policy differences, a process also seen in other states. Diplomatic correspondence frequently focused on the intrigues and politics surrounding the choice of generals and their generalship.[15] As a result, French generals, such as Belle-Isle, Noailles, and Saxe in the 1740s and Richelieu in the 1750s, and the moves they made were very much located in a world of appealing to both monarch and a public of sorts, and without any dominant command system to gainsay them. This situation looked toward that during the French Revolution, when some generals, notably Napoleon, pursued political advantage in their campaigning. In contrast, at the time of France's intervention of 1778–83 in the War of American Independence, the theme of politicized command was less prominently to the fore, in part due to the distance of operations and in part due to the focus on the navy.

The politics of command was linked to the struggles for resources and reputation that were so important to the nature of military operations. In place of politics and struggles, the word *strategies* may be inserted, and this possibility highlights the problems involved in both establishing what the latter means and also how the term should be employed. If, indeed, too narrow a definition and application are offered, then the politics of command are misunderstood or neglected. Politics, of course, is a word capable of many definitions.

Turning from Britain, where the focus was on the navy, to France, where the army predominated, offers the possibility of considering the discussion of pre-1800 strategy offered by Martin van Creveld and

Lawrence Freedman.[16] They argued that intelligence-gathering and communication systems were slow and unreliable, such that generals had to be on, or close to, the front line, while they dared not develop plans of any complexity. As a consequence, strategy was perforce primitive. It is not clear, however, that this minimalist view represents a well-founded account of the often complex nature of eighteenth-century strategy. Closeness to the front line may have little place in formulating grand strategy, but that did not necessarily mean that theater strategy was limited. Moreover, closeness to the "front line" in practice described the situation in which rulers directed campaigns in person, as many did including Napoleon. An overall presentation of strategy as primitive or limited is somewhat difficult to reconcile with the published correspondence of Frederick II (the Great) of Prussia (r. 1740–86), or with the efforts of Belle-Isle in the early 1740s to direct French diplomatic and military policy in order to overthrow the Habsburg position and rearrange European politics. The same had been true of the plans of the French foreign minister, Chauvelin, at the time of the War of the Polish Succession (1733–35): Belle-Isle was on campaign, but Chauvelin had been in Paris.

The War of the Polish Succession revealed anew the extent of strategic complexity. France entered the war in response to Russian pressure in Poland to prevent the election as king of the Polish father-in-law of Louis XV, pressure that culminated in a successful invasion. In alliance with Sardinia (Savoy-Piedmont) and Spain, France attacked Russia's ally, Austria. French strategy was very much set by the need to keep its alliance together and to ensure that that of its opponents did not expand. This helped lead to a focus on operations in Italy, although that was also encouraged by the gains that could be made there. Military factors played a role. For example, a war that began late in the year was easier to conduct in a warmer environment. Discussing plans for the 1734 campaign, Fleury told the Sardinian envoy that the French would advance along the Moselle Valley as far as the Rhine in order to cut communications with the major Austrian base at Luxemburg and thus prevent an Austrian attack into France.[17] However, diplomatic factors predominated as so often with strategy. A determination to keep the Dutch and Britain out of the war meant that there was no French invasion of the

Low Countries in 1733–35, unlike in the War of the Spanish Succession (1701–14) and in France's seventeenth-century conflicts. In addition, a wish to lessen German backing for the emperor (Charles VI of Austria) affected the willingness to exploit advantages in the Rhineland by moving eastward, into Hesse-Cassel, possibly to join with Bavaria. Blocking moves were part of the prospectus of response if the French crossed the Rhine. In 1733, the Prussians discussed moving forward into Franconia if that occurred.[18] Conversely, a French advance into Germany was seen as a way to encourage support from states that might back France, notably Bavaria. Such an advance was also regarded as a way to avoid the burdens of defensive campaigning, especially supporting the forces in the field.[19]

Instead of crossing the Rhine, the French concentrated on conquering Lombardy (the Milanese) from the Austrians and, in so doing, acting as a control over Sardinia and Spain. The moves of French units were dependent on political goals, as well as on the economy of gains: the need to make territorial acquisitions in order to compensate for Russian success in Poland. This pattern of conduct was one in which strategy was clearly under political direction. The absence of a relevant word was not of particular consequence.

Alongside the more mundane but pressing concerns about where armies operated, with the consequences for the economies of particular rulers, armies were regarded as the enablers of international transformations. In 1733–35, transformations that were considered included a new order in Eastern Europe in which Russia would not only be thwarted in Poland, but also restrained by a French-supported league of Poland, Sweden, and Turkey. Such a league would see Sweden seek to regain its Baltic losses of 1721 from Russia and maybe both Poland and the Turks do the same. Within Central Europe, negotiations between France and Bavaria were designed to challenge Austria, as was France's unsuccessful attempt to recruit Frederick William I of Prussia. In the event, despite concerns in 1735 among opponents, there was no French movement into Bavaria, as there had been in 1704 and was to be in 1741. Instead, unlike then, Bavaria remained neutral. The contrast between these conflicts indicates the extent to which strategic options were in large part set by the possibilities of alliance support and the extent of political support from within the ministry.[20] In turn, such possibilities rested in large part on a reading of the military situation.

This situation reflected the impact of diplomacy. Thus, Austria and (neutral) Britain supported the westward move of Russian troops into Germany in 1735, a move designed to counteract France's position and prospects there. This demonstrated the way in which the deployment of force (rather than its use in battle) was a key strategic element. It was to be repeated in 1748 when Britain subsidized the westward movement of Russian troops in order to affect the outcome of the War of the Austrian Succession. This policy represented strategy at a very high level: an alignment of the profits of an oceanic commercial system with the manpower and industrial resources of a land power. The British were to support such a movement repeatedly during the French Revolutionary and Napoleonic Wars, notably during the Wars of the Second and Third Coalitions and ultimately it was the guarantee of Allied success in 1815 whatever happened at Waterloo.

In turn, a number of French ministers and commentators urged the need to weaken Britain in its colonies and to build up the French navy and colonial presence. These views were most strongly held in the Ministry of the Marine, notably by Maurepas, minister from 1723 to 1749, but were also seen in mercantile circles.[21] Indeed, a naval strategy can be discerned, although sufficient resources were not always provided to bring it to fruition.[22] In 1739, Maurepas was ready to encourage Spain to act against Britain, whereas the other French ministers were less keen,[23] in part because of a focus on the situation within Europe. In 1755, the need to build up the navy in order to prevent Britain from dominating trade and thus subsidizing its allies was pressed.[24] However, French ministers could be skeptical of such arguments. Abbé Bernis, the foreign minister, responded in 1758 to the suggestion from the French envoy in Spain that peace in Germany would lead Spain to join France in a naval war on Britain by pointing out that it would also free Britain for such a conflict,[25] and Britain's decision, like France, not to take part in the War of Bavarian Succession ensured that this indeed was the case during the War of American Independence. Plans in the early 1760s for concerted Franco-Spanish action against Portugal as a way to hit British trade as well as to make gains for both powers[26] reflected an ability to think in broad strategic terms, albeit one greatly hampered by British naval power.

French plans repeatedly failed not because of an absence of strategic thought but as a result of failures of implementation. In particular, there were serious weaknesses of alliance cohesion in the Wars of the Polish and Austrian Succession and the Seven Years' War, and these weaknesses had a repeated impact on French capability—for example, the repeated lack of Spanish support for French moves in Italy during the first two of these wars. Instead, Spain sought to hold the diplomatic initiative and pursued its own territorial goals. In 1745, France was also challenged by a settlement between its ally Bavaria and Austria, a settlement following a change of ruler in Bavaria. In 1748, Puysieulx, the foreign minister, complained that Spain had always treated France with "la bizarrerie d'une femme remplie d'humeur et de despotisme."[27] This remark, made in private correspondence, is more generally indicative of attitudes with its feminization of Spanish policy even after the death of Philip V (r. 1700–46), who had been dominated by his wife, Elisabeth Farnese, and with its assumption that unpredictability was a female characteristic and could be stigmatized accordingly. The importance of such views as part of the strategic context is indirect, but it is indicative of a personalization of policy.

Clausewitz pointed out in *On War* that allies did not provide a commitment to match that which they expended on their own interests. He wrote: "A moderately-sized force will be sent to its help; but if things go wrong the operation is pretty well written off, and one tries to withdraw at the smallest possible cost."[28] Indeed, the absence of effective coalition integration during the Seven Years' War (1756–63), not least distrust of Russia by its allies, was the fundamental aspect of the war, both strategically and operationally, that provided Frederick II with the opportunities for focusing on his opponents separately and sequentially. France was hit particularly hard by this absence, not least because it was also at war with Britain, whereas Austria and Russia were not, but they also suffered from a lack of coordination.

In 1763, France ended a conflict in which it had made a formidable effort, with humiliating defeats in Europe, especially Rossbach (1757) at the hands of Prussia and Minden (1759) at that of Britain and allied forces, as well as the loss to Britain of most of its transoceanic empire, notably Canada, Guadeloupe, Martinique, and France's bases in India. Failure abroad increased problems within France, not least factional strife. Madame de Pompadour, the royal mistress, and Abbé Bernis, the foreign minister, were associated in particular with the Austrian alliance and faced savage criticism linked to the sense of defeat. Bernis was replaced in 1758. The war conspicuously leached political support from the Crown and ministry, and this process underlined yet again the domestic context and consequences of strategy.

The outcome provided the opportunity and need for rethinking France's position and policies. Doing so would have been much less pressing had France been militarily successful in the war. However, failure threw attention on the Austrian alliance, on the state of the French army, and on its capacity to realize its goals. These factors encouraged the ferment of ideas discussed in the next chapter, and that chapter should be read in the light of this one.

NOTES

1. J. P. Cénat, *Le roi stratège: Louis XIV et la direction de la guerre, 1661–1715* (Rennes, France, 2010).

2. Joseph Yorke to Bedford, March 1, 1749, BL. Add. 32816 fol. 128.

3. *Daily Advertiser,* January 29, 1748.

4. J. Swann, *Politics and the Parlement of Paris under Louis XV, 1754–1774* (Cambridge, UK, 1995).

5. Paris intelligence of April 13, 1758, BL. Add. 32879 fols. 200–1. For more extreme divisions, J. D. Woodbridge, *Revolt in Prerevolutionary France: The Prince de Conti's Conspiracy against Louis XV, 1755–1757* (Baltimore, 1994).

6. Solaro di Breglio to Charles Emmanuel III, May 2, 1738, AST. LM. Francia 136.

7. Paris, Bibliothèque de l'Arsenal, Archives de la Bastille, Gazetins secrets de la Police, vols. 10155–65.

8. T. L. Ewing, *Rumor, Diplomacy and War in Enlightenment Paris* (Oxford, 2014) focuses on 1740–48.

9. Yorke to Cumberland, March 1, 1749, RA. Cumb. P. 43/122.

10. J. M. J. Rogister, "Philippe V, successeur de Louis XV? Les démarches secretes de 1724–1728," in Y. Bottineau, ed., *Philippe V d'Espagne et l'Art de Son Temps* (2 vols., Paris, 1995), II, 141–67.

11. J. R. Dull, *A Diplomatic History of the American Revolution* (New Haven, CT, 1985): 107–8.

12. "Etat de la situation des affaires à la Cour de Vienne au depart du Sieur de Bussy le 19.9.1733," AE. MD. Allemagne 74 fols. 5–6.

13. Marquis de Vogüé (ed.), *Mémoires du maréchal de Villars* (6 vols., Paris, 1884–1904): IV, 309–10.

14. C. Paoletti, "Italy, Piedmont and French Anti-Habsburg Strategy," in F. C. Schneid, ed., *The Projection and Limitations of Imperial Powers, 1618–1850* (Leiden, the Netherlands, 2012): 79.

15. Solaro di Breglio to Charles Emmanuel III, September 11, December 21, 1734, January 4, 1735, AST. LM. Francia 170, 172.

16. M. van Creveld, *Command in War* (Cambridge, MA, 1985): 18; L. Freedman, *Strategy. A History* (Oxford, 2013).

17. Solaro to Charles Emmanuel III, April 5, 1730, AST. LM. Francia 170.

18. Major-General Schmettau to Baron de Zocha, September, 13, 1733, in General Diemar to Landgrave of Hesse-Cassel, September 19, 1733, Marburg, Staatsarchiv, 4f England 202.

19. Reporting discussion with Baron Gedda, Swedish envoy in Paris, Solaro to Charles Emmanuel III, March 10, 1734, AST. LM. Francia 170.

20. Solaro to Charles Emmanuel III, May 3, July 5, 1734, AST. LM. Francia 172. For Fleury's determination not to anger Britain and the Dutch, report of August 2, 1734.

21. R. D. Bourland, *Maurepas and His Administration of the French Navy on the Eve of the War of the Austrian Succession* (PhD diss., Notre Dame, 1978); Memoire by Pelletier, February 14, 1748, AE. CP. Ang. 424 fols. 156–62.

22. D. Pilgrim, "The Colbert-Seignelay Naval Reforms and the Beginnings of the War of the League of Augsburg," *French Historical Studies* 9 (1975–76): 235–62.

23. Reporting Information from Private Secretary of the Foreign Minister, James, 1st Earl Waldegrave, British envoy in Paris, to Newcastle, January 4, 1740, BL. Add. 32801 fol. 353.

24. Champeaux to Rouillé, April 16, 1755, AE. CP. Ang. 438 fol. 413.

25. Bernis to Aubeterre, January 3, 1758, AE. CP. Espagne 523 fol. 6; Choiseul to Ossun, April 17, 1762, AE. CP. Espagne 536 fol. 60.

26. Thomas, 8th Earl of Kinnoull, British envoy to Lisbon, to Pitt, April 16, 1760, NA. SP. 89/52 fols. 65, 69–70.

27. Puysieulx to Marshal Richelieu, February 4, 1748, AN. KK. 1372.

28. Carl von Clausewitz, *On War* (Princeton, NJ, 1976): 603.

FOUR

THE FLOW OF IDEAS

FRENCH DEFEAT IN THE SEVEN YEARS' WAR (1756–63), RATHER than the prior lack of any strategic understanding and practice, helped ensure the developing exposition of a language of strategy in Western Europe from the 1760s. It is always necessary to appreciate the particular context in which ideas and concepts, both established and new, are articulated. Crucially, this particular exposition can be seen as an aspect of the revitalization and attempted revitalization of the French military and more generally of the French state and society as a result of defeat in the war.

In addition, the advancing of the idea and language of strategy was an aspect of the classification, categorization, and exposition of information and ideas that were central to the Enlightenment. Employed to describe key strands in eighteenth-century Western thought and intellectual practice, this term itself is capable of many definitions, and can even be presented as analogous to strategy in this respect. More directly, the Enlightenment is commonly seen as a peaceful process. That, however, downplays the relationship between the Enlightenment and the preparations of states for conflict and indeed the militarized nature of much of enlightened governance and planning.[1] A similar point can be made about the art and culture of the period.

Classification, categorization, and codification were important aspects of Enlightenment activity. A focus on mathematics encouraged a search for precision and in a strongly self-conscious fashion. Rigor was fostered by the development of descriptive geometry, particularly by the French mathematician Gaspard Monge (1746–1818), and was linked to a neoclassical aesthetic in which precision and clarity replaced the exuberant formlessness and insubstantial quality of the Rococo, while the abstract value of mathematics did not solely play an intellectual part. Indeed, mathematical principles and a geometrical science of strategy were to play key roles in *Geist des Neueren Kriegssystems* (*The Spirit of the Modern System of War*; 1799), the theory of a new science of war offered by Adam von Bülow, a former Prussian officer (1757–1807). An English translation of this book was published in 1806, the year, ironically, in which Prussian forces suffered a crushing defeat at French hands at Jena, a defeat that was followed by the French occupation of Berlin and the imposition of crushing and humiliating peace terms.

Changes stemming from the linkage of Newtonian science to fortress engineering, artillery, and military thought were also significant. In particular, ballistics was revolutionized in the mid-eighteenth century West, notably by Benjamin Robins and Leonhard Euler, who were, respectively, British and German. Theoretical and empirical advances greatly increased the predictive power of ballistics and helped turn gunnery from a craft into a science that could, and should, be formally taught. These developments much affected the use of artillery and encouraged the growth of military education, both informal thinking and formal structured thinking. Rulers established military academies. Increased standardization was important for artillery and notably with the French artillery, the background and basis for Napoleon's career. Such standardization increased predictability in the use of artillery and thus enhanced tactical regularity.

This development of ballistics and the artillery was part of a more general search for pattern and rules that would be prescriptive as well as descriptive. The theorization of war, envisaging it as a science and not a craft, was crucial, with a science understood in terms of rules, definitions, and precision. However, this process could, and repeatedly did, lead to an underestimation of the unknown and a trend to seek to control everything, which resulted in an illusion of control over aspects that could not be controlled.

There was also more specific linkage in France between the Enlightenment and the ferment of ideas about the military in the 1760s and 1770s, although the *encyclopédistes*, the contributors to the *Encyclopédie*

(1751–65), themselves were less radical than later writers as far as military operational and organizational factors were concerned.[2] Although measurement of the issue is not possible, the pressure for change in the military and political spheres owed much to the experience of recent failure.[3] This pressure was part of the action-reaction cycle of political and military development, a cycle so often significant in both political and military history. Traveling through France in 1758, en route to his diplomatic post in Turin, James Mackenzie noted widespread disaffection including about the system of military patronage.[4] The following year, his counterpart in Spain reported, "The last letters from France are filled with the murmurs of all ranks of people."[5] There was comparable dissatisfaction within the military.

In the case of France, the experience of failure encouraged both a focus on colonial and naval strengthening,[6] and a notable willingness to challenge the operation, organization, equipment, and ethos of the army. This challenge was an aspect of a more widespread drive for change in policy and structures. This drive was seen both within the government and more generally. The Seven Years' War had left France with a deep sense of humiliation and particularly with serious defeats on land and sea. During the war itself, there was mounting criticism of the government. A sense that French public unrest about foreign policy could be soothed only if France were to produce, on the part of its principal but unpopular ally, Austria, success in the field developed, as on the part of the Austrians did criticism of the French government as overly concerned about the public.[7] In 1760, Frederick II captured the idea of strategically exploiting what he presented as a very divided French ministry when he pressed the British ministry to mount attacks on the French coast, as the reality and fear of such attacks, he argued, "could not fail to raise great murmurings among the people (who were already tired of the war) and might strengthen the hands of those ministers who were disposed to peace."[8]

Memoirs of the period indicate that this sense of systemic flaws was deeply felt in French ruling circles. There was also a response to the more challenging international situation, notably the First Partition of Poland in 1772 and the more general failure of France's anti-Russian policies. This failure was presented as marking a crisis in European civilization as a "barbarian" power reached for leadership. Turkey, a traditional ally, had to cede territory to Russia in 1774. The change in the European system filled some commentators with foreboding.

Pressure for governmental change contributed to the so-called Maupeou Revolution in the early 1770s, which was named after the chancellor who carried through the unpopular remodeling of the *Parlements*. The crisis produced a fierce debate that did not relate to war but nevertheless that owed part of its energy to a determination to improve France so as to be better able to confront the next conflict. Moreover, the arguments encouraged a volatility that influenced other spheres of debate. Writers backing Maupeou argued that the *Parlements* were indifferent to public welfare, while the defenders of the *Parlements* presented them as the protectors of the people against arbitrary government and pressed the need for a society under the rule of law.[9]

The action-reaction cycle encompassed intellectual inquiry and arguments. As an aspect of this, there was already strong interest in France in different fighting methods. Drawing on his experience of the War of the Spanish Succession, Jean-Charles Folard from the 1720s and later François-Jean de Mesnil-Durand between 1755 and 1774, stressed the shock and weight of forces attacking in columns, rather than the customary deployment of firepower and the related linear tactics. The strong influence of the classical past was readily apparent in Folard's work on Polybius and in Mesnil-Durand's *Projet d'un ordre François en tactique, ou la phalange coupée et double soutenue par le mélange des armes* (1755). The interest in the *phalange* (phalanx), a formation of pikemen developed by Macedon, was wide ranging.

More particularly, in his *Mes Rêveries sur l'art de la guerre* (1732), posthumously published in the mid-1750s under a number of titles, Marshal Saxe (1696–1750) criticized reliance on firepower alone. He advocated instead a combination of firepower and shock which he presented as more dynamic. To Saxe, it was necessary to respond to developments and a failure to change accordingly led to failure. In his *Rêveries*, Saxe compared current non-Western societies to past instances in Western history, offering a direct comparison between the Gauls in the first century BCE and the Turks: "the number of years during which the Gauls were perpetually conquered by the Romans, without ever attempting to retrieve their losses by any alteration in their discipline, or manner of fighting. The Turks are now an instance of the same."[10]

The eagerness with which the possibility of improving tactical formations was discussed reflected a sense of flux and a concern that linear formations, while appropriate for maximizing infantry firepower, did not provide the necessary offensive élan or indeed, either élan or a capacity to take the offensive. Concerned about the latter, Folard focused his work on a lengthy commentary on the Roman author Polybius, specifically on the latter's account of the epic clash between Macedonian phalanx and Roman legion. Folard wanted to bring back the wedge (*cuneus*), while the column he advocated was a form of the phalanx. This was intended to restore an offensive capability.[11] Saxe called his ideal formation a legion as a classical affectation and was interested in the reintroduction of armor. Folard and Saxe were also favorable to a revival of the pike, as was the *Encyclopédie* (1751–65), the repository of progressive French opinion. Macedon and in particular, Alexander the Great attracted much attention and not only in France. In 1736, Guy Dickens, the British envoy in Berlin and an army officer, reported, "They make frequent parallels here between the Macedonian troops and theirs."[12] Three years later, the British government was urged to conquer Spanish America in "an expedition equal to Alexander's conquest."[13]

Aside from a conviction of continuities in the practice of warfare,[14] the process of validation put much emphasis on the past as a data set for, and of, analysis. On the pattern of the treatment of Caesar's *Gallic Wars*, the long-standing reverential and referential hold of the fourth- or fifth-century CE *Epitoma rei militaris* (*On Military Matters*) by Flavius Vegetius, was such as to affect historical study and current discussion. Folard, for example, found it normal to debate with Vegetius as if he was a contemporary. Although he offered a different tactical tradecraft, Saxe drew on Vegetius, whose writings went on being published, both in Latin—for example, in Amsterdam in 1744—and in translation— for example, in Vienna in 1759 and in London in 1767. Moreover, Franz Miller, an influential military theorist and the author of *Reine Taktik der Infanteries, Cavallerie und Artillerie* (Stuttgart, 1788), regarded the Roman military as if it were an army of his own time, which he sought to improve.[15] Writing about classical archetypes and exemplars therefore served to validate arguments and try to help separate out present possibilities and policies from political contention.[16]

Saxe liked to present himself as an original thinker offering classical wisdom anew to the modern world. However, in many respects, Saxe, instead, summarized for the French the lessons to be learned from their recent opponents but did so in a fashion made more authoritative by classical references. Most prominently, Eugene of Savoy (1663–1736), one of the foremost generals of the age, successfully served the Austrians against the Turks and the French and thus enjoyed a breadth of experience that most European generals lacked. Although he deployed his troops in the conventional manner, Eugene placed a greater premium on maneuver in campaign and attack in battle than did his unsuccessful French rivals. In northern Italy, in the 1700s, during the War of the Spanish Succession, Eugene did not allow the French emphasis on the defense of river lines and fortified positions to thwart his drive for battle and victory, notably at Carpi in 1701. So also with the British general John Churchill, 1st Duke of Marlborough, another keen attacking commander. He focused on tactical flexibility, notably to retain control and maneuverability prior to delivering a breakthrough strike in the center. Saxe, an illegitimate son of Augustus II of Saxony, served in the Saxon forces in 1709 as part of the allied army under Eugene and Marlborough successfully opposing the French in the Low Countries.

Saxe, the most successful French general of the 1740s, was important because of his prestige, because no French general subsequently matched this prestige until Napoleon (who greatly exceeded it), and because he encouraged fresh thinking. Lieutenant-Colonel Paul-Gédéon Joly de Maïzeroy (1719–80), who coined the French word *stratégique* in 1771, had served as a captain under Saxe, including in his major victories in the Low Countries over Anglo-Austrian-Dutch forces at Roucoux (1746) and Lawfeldt (1747).[17] These battles represented an important advance for France over failures in the region in the 1700s.

It is possible to suggest a developmental project, or at least process, of new ideas and change that in the midst of frequent wars looked toward the elaboration of a formal discourse of strategy. In this perspective, the French Revolution comes as a culmination as well as a stage toward a more distinct use of concepts. That, indeed, is one way to approach the subject, and it is not without value. However, without implying any automatic alternative, it is also pertinent to note the significance in the eighteenth century of a debate with the past. In a way, this debate antici- pated the recent and current fascination with Clausewitz, as well as com- parable interest in his contemporaries and context.

On a long-standing pattern, knowledge in the eighteenth century was in part a matter of the analysis of classical texts in order to establish general principles of war-making or rather, war-making on land. More- over, the classical age could also be cited in current strategic debates. Thus, in 1755, William Pitt the Elder, in the House of Commons' debate on the address, remarked:

> we have been told indeed that Carthage, and that Spain in 88 [1588, the
> Armada] were undone, notwithstanding their navies—true; but not till
> they betook themselves to land operations and Carthage had besides a
> Hannibal who would pass the Alps.[18]

The last was a reference by comparison to the limited success of William, Duke of Cumberland's campaigning on the Continent in the late 1740s, a campaigning that Pitt regarded as foolish. Defeated by Saxe, Cumber- land had failed to match the success of Marlborough.

At least some officers read widely in the history and practice of war. This reading was linked to a more self-conscious professionalism in which continuous training rested on accessing accumulated wisdom through the culture of print. Contemporary writing on war reflected the sense not only that there were lessons to be learned but that they needed learning. In the British army, there was a shift in midcentury from mili- tary history toward a greater emphasis on the practice of war, a shift that may have been linked to Saxe's repeated victories over the British in 1745–47.[19] Drawing on the authority and credentials of the ancients, this analysis sought to match in its rationality the use of mathematics in other branches, including ballistics and cartography.

The engagement with the classics was an aspect of the highly active "ancients and moderns" debate, one that readily encompassed, nota- bly due to the need to discuss the impact of gunpowder.[20] In Britain, there was a strong willingness to engage with modern perspectives. The *Honest True Briton*, a London newspaper, in its issue of April 27, 1724, claimed:

> The old ammunition of bows and arrows, battering-rams and wooden
> engines, which were to be procured and made in all parts of the world, are
> now laid aside; though these were the artillery of the Grecian and Roman
> governments. But now the materials necessary for carrying on a war must
> be by the returns made by the foreign trade that one country drives with
> another ... no nation can resist invasion, or get out of a just and necessary
> war with honor, but from the stores it either has, or must procure by trade
> and navigation.

In France, the "ancients" had more traction. In contrast, the frame
of reference rarely focused on the Middle Ages, whereas the Renaissance
also played a role, notably with frequent references to Machiavelli who
was seen as a reviver of the classical notion of citizen armies.[21] Thus,
discussing the Renaissance was presented as an aspect of considering
the classical legacy, as indeed Renaissance thinkers would have wanted.

A reform-minded intellectual climate gathered pace as a result of
the Seven Years' War (1756–63), at the same time that classical references
remained significant.[22] A public analysis of recent developments was
significant, with histories of the Seven Years' War appearing from John
Wilhelm von Archenholz, Henry Lloyd, Georg Friedrich von Tempelhoff, Johann Gottlieb Tielke, and others. In 1778, Friedrich Wilhelm von
Zanthier produced a work on the art of war that used examples from the
Seven Years' War.[23] In France, the consideration of the country's last
period of victories, largely under Saxe, in 1745–48 was also significant.
The battles in which he was a commander involved large numbers of
men: 200,000 at Roucoux (1746) and 215,000 at Lawfeldt (1747). This,
the fluidity of the fighting, and the extent to which each battle was a
combination of a number of distinct but related struggles all anticipated
aspects of Napoleonic warfare. Saxe's generalship was instructive not
only because of his battlefield ability to control large numbers effectively
in both attack and defense, but also because of his determined espousal
of a war of maneuver with an emphasis on gaining and holding the initiative. His example and writings encouraged fresh thought. Saxe appeared
to disprove the contention that military triumph was impossible, a contention (in part anticipating aspects of recent arguments) advanced by
William Horsley in 1744:

> considering the numbers of people now in Europe, the multitude of
> garrisoned and well-fortified towns, and the excellency to which the art

> of war is arrived, and equally understood by all nations, the making wise
> and extensive conquests now-a-days seems to exist only in the theoretic
> imaginations of Cabinet projectors.[24]

As with all quotations, this is worth considering; but before too much is made of it, it is appropriate to note others that looked in different directions. The following year, after the fall of the possible invasion port of Ostend to French forces, one of a large number of fortified positions they captured, Philip Yorke, MP, wrote of the French, "I think their progress in the Netherlands this campaign has been greater than any of old Lewis's [Louis XIV] except that of 1672,"[25] when the French crossed the Rhine and invaded the Netherlands from the east.

The increase in army numbers offered France enhanced opportunities for military operations but also posed challenges for effectiveness and planning. The French army rose to wartime peaks of 340,000 men in 1695–97, 300,000 in 1710, 303,000 in 1735, 345,000 in 1745, and 347,000 in 1760–1, although all figures for army size have to be handled with much care. In addition, its peacetime strength at 150,000 in 1714, 160,000 in 1735, 201,000 in 1740, and 160,000 in 1770 was considerable and far greater than had been the case in the sixteenth century. This was even more impressive as throughout the century, France had the second largest navy in the world—the largest being that of Britain.

At the same time as peacetime developments from 1763, there was the risk of war, notably with Britain in 1770, a war that eventually broke out in 1778. The French military proved able to respond to challenges. The French occupation of Corsica in 1768, having purchased it from Genoa, was met by initially successful popular opposition, the results of which were compounded by French overconfidence and poor planning. In 1769, in contrast, the French not only increased their troop numbers in Corsica but also responded with established strategic tools of devastation, terror and road construction, as well as by the use of a coordinated three-prong advance based on mobile columns. The opposition was speedily overcome.[26] Napoleon was to study the campaign. The French army and navy emerged very creditably from operations in North America in 1781.

The range of ideas offered after the Seven Years' War was considerable. For example, in his *Essai général de tactique* (1772), Jacques-Antoine-Hippolyte, Comte de Guibert, stressed movement and enveloping maneuvers, advocated living off the land in order to increase the speed of operations, criticized reliance on fortifications, and crucially, urged the value of a patriotic citizen army which was seen as the best means for pursuing a defensive strategy. His writings were reprinted—for example, in Liège in 1775—and were to be praised by Napoleon and to influence Clausewitz. Guibert, who had fought at Rossbach (1757) and Minden (1759) and taken part in the French occupation of Corsica, served as principal rapporteur of the War Council in 1787–89, although in his later works, he favored a professional army rather than a citizen one.[27]

There was also interest in France in new projects for fortification, especially from Marc-René, Marquis de Montalembert (1714–1800). A man of great schemes but not given to costing proposals, to detailed design, or to the practicalities of local topography, he advanced a series of bold projects from 1776 to 1797. In a pattern more generally the case with many of the theorists of the period, Montalembert was concerned primarily with the basic design, which to him, determined whether a fortification was capable of withstanding attack. For him, reason was independent of nature and dominated it: the accidents of terrain and specificities of location could be subordinated to the theoretical plan.[28] With reason, this approach was criticized by contemporaries in France. The debate testified to interest in improvements and commitment to an explicitly rational solution.

Artillery was very much a focus of attention: in France, there was a major effort to achieve enhanced accuracy, standardization, and greater mobility, with Jean Baptiste de Gribeauval a key figure. In his *De l'usage de l'artillerie nouvelle dans la guerre de campagne* (1778), Chevalier Jean du Teil (1738–1820), an artillery officer, argued that the artillery should begin battles, be massed for effect, and be concentrated on the opposing troops and not on counterbattery fire, a process that prefigured later naval ideas on the torpedo. Napoleon's thoughts on the use of massed artillery were drawn from du Teil who taught him.

There was also interest in the development of the division, a unit composed of elements of all arms, and therefore able to operate independently. Such a unit could serve effectively, both as a detached force and as part of a coordinated army operating in accordance with a strategic plan. Indeed, organization in terms of divisions made such a plan more necessary. The divisional system evolved from 1759, initially as temporary units. However, in 1788, French army administration was rearranged along divisional lines: twenty-one combat divisions were created, a development from the concept introduced in 1776 by the Comte de Saint Germain, the minister of war, of the organization of France into military zones, known as divisions, with administrative functions, such as recruitment, as well as permanent garrisons. The system of combat divisions, which became a standard wartime procedure for the French in the 1790s, gave generals the potential to control much larger armies than the sixty thousand to seventy thousand troops that had been considered by some commentators the maximum effective force in midcentury.[29] Operational capability was greatly enhanced as a result of this system. The varied meaning of the term *division* indicated the extent to which words had a range of meanings and applications.

It was in this context, at once varied and dynamic, that the word *strategy* was first deployed. A classical source was crucial, more particularly Byzantium, the Eastern Roman Empire, a state about which relatively little was then known but that had a degree of prestige as the successor of Rome. The *Strategikon* was a manual conventionally attributed to Maurice I, the emperor from 582 to 602. Its title approximated to "On Generals or On the Role of a General," or *strategos*. Written originally in Greek, this was an official manual intended for the management of the army. The issues covered included the use of negotiation to obtain ends. The book also dealt with Byzantium's opponents and the varied ways of fighting them. There was no comparable attention to the Byzantine navy which was essentially treated as a conveyance for the army.

Byzantine views were preserved and developed by Leo VI, emperor from 886 to 912, an armchair general under whose rule there was war with Bulgars and Arabs, and by the commander commissioned to write by the emperor Nikephoros Phokas in the 960s. Leo used the term *strategía* in his military writings, which described the military methods not only of Byzantium but also of its opponents.[30] As a result of being translated into Latin by Sir John Cheke in 1554, Leo's works attracted considerable interest in early-modern Europe, being translated into and cited in a number of languages. Leo's works, for example, were in the library of the Spanish general and military commentator Santa Cruz.[31]

This Byzantine usage remained important in the eighteenth century. The 1770s edition of the *Encyclopédie*, the compendium of French fashionable intellectual opinion, employed the term in reference to classical writing. The article "Extispice" in the 1778 Pellet reprint of the *Encyclopédie*, which was published in Geneva, referred to Onasander's "*Strategique*" and to Bulengerus's *Strategicis*.[32] So also with the 1779 German edition of Folard's work on Polybius's *Geschichte*, which used both *stratège* and *stratégie* in a discussion of Greek warfare. The translator was David Christoph Seybold.[33] These are not the novel usage of the eighteenth century but rather, a translation/transliteration of Greek words, namely *strategos* and *strategikos*. The discussion of the phalanx in the 1778 Pellet reprint cited Polybius and Folard.[34]

In 1771, a translation of Leo's *Tactica* appeared in French, published in Paris, as the *Institutions militaires de l'Empereur Léon le Philosophe*. This translation was the work of Maïzeroy, who used the term *la stratégique* to describe the art of the commander. He defined *la stratégique* as follows:

> La stratégique est donc proprement l'art de commander, d'employer à propos et avec habileté tous les moyens que le general a dans sa main, de faire mouvoir toutes les parties qui lui sont subordonnées, et de les disposer pour le succès. Cette science est si sublime, qu'elle exige non seulement les talens de l'esprit, mais encoure les vertus de l'ame. La philosophie, la morale, la politique et l'histoire sont obliges de lui prêter leurs lumières.[35]

This replaced Maïzeroy's earlier use of the term *dialectic* in his *Traité de tactique* published in his *Essais militaires* in 1762. In this, he had referred to "la dialectique militaire, qui comprend l'art de former les plans d'une campagne, et d'endiriger les operations."[36]

The *Institutions* led to Maïzeroy, a distinguished scholar of ancient Greece, becoming a member of the Academy of Inscriptions and Belles-Lettres in 1775. Maïzeroy had already published, with some overlaps, *Essais militaires* (1762), *Traité des stratagems permis à la guerre* (1765), *Cours de tactique théorique (Traité de tactique pour server de supplement au Cours de tactique)* (1766–67), *La tactique discutée et réduite à ses véritables loix* (1773), *Mémoire sur les opinions qui partagent les militaires, suivi du traité des armes défensives* (1773), and *Traité des armes et le l'ordonnance de l'infanterie* (1776). Affected by poor health and troubled finances, Maïzeroy was nobly born and regarded as an exemplary officer and had become a lieutenant-colonel in 1759. However, Maïzeroy then remained at this rank, although he was on the eve of being named brigadier when he died in 1780. During the Seven Years' War, he served in the forces guarding the coast against British attack, taking part in the battle of Saint Cast in 1758. The reduction in the army in 1762, as the war was coming to an end, had hit Maïzeroy's career, and those of many other officers, but had given him the opportunity to write.

In 1777, Maïzeroy published the *Théorie de la guerre, où l'on expose la constitution et formations de l'infanterie et de la cavaleries, leurs manoeuvres élémentaires, avec l'applicátion des principes à la grande tactique, suivie de demonstrations sur la stratégique.* The influential *Journal de Sçavans*, in its review that November, saw the book as scientific in intention and mathematical in approach. The book dealt in part with "stratégie, c'est-à-dire, de l'art de conduire la guerre et d'en diriger toutes les operations." The review commented that Maïzeroy sought to offer a mathematical approach but noted the dependence in practice on conjunctures, notably the political views of princes, and those that led generals to prefer one operation to another.[37] In his introduction, Maïzeroy referred to the requirement "d'établir une théorie qui serve de guide et d'appui pour s'élever à des parties plus sublimes."[38] He added the need to appreciate rules:

> que la science de la guerre est une partie de celle du gouvernement, qu'elle est même la clef . . . que pour parvenir à connoître cette science, il faut en étudier les régles, ce qui est impossible quand elles ne sont fixées, qu'on flotte dans l'incertitude, ou qu'on n'a que des usages dont on ne peut rendre raison.[39]

Theory was presented as a key means:

> outre la nécessité de posséder à fond la théorie élémentaire, il doit encore étudier les principes de la dialectique qui forme et conduit les projets sur la connoissance qu'on prise du pays, des forces de l'ennemi compares avec les sciences, de la situation des places de part et d'autre: à quoi se joignent souvent des raisons politiques, et des considerations morales sur l'état present des affaires.[40]

To Maïzeroy, this approach represented a revival of the Greek understanding that war was a science with rules.[41]

Maïzeroy continued with the *Traité sur l'art des sieges et des machines des anciens* (1778) and the posthumous *Tableau général de la cavalerie grecque, suivi d'une traduction du traité de Xénophon initulé "Le Commandant de la Cavalerie"* (1781). His influence was further continued by reprints, notably with the 1785 edition of his 1766–67 four-volume *Cours de tactique*.

Translations included into English, the *Traité sur les armes defensives* in 1770 (as *Treatise on the Use of Defensive Arms, translated from the French of Joly de Maizeray, with Remarks*), the *Essais militaires* in 1771 (as *Elementary Principles of Tactics*), and the *Cours de tactique* in 1781, and the last into German in 1771–72. The earliest translations were by Thomas Mante (ca. 1733–ca. 1802), a British officer in the Seven Years' War who in 1769–74 acted as a spy for the French Ministry of War. The key work appeared as *A System of Tactics, Practical, Theoretical and Historical, Translated from the French of M. Joly De Maizeroy by Thomas Mante in Two Volumes* (London, 1781). Written in 1769–71, it was not published until Mante returned to London. He dedicated this book to Lieutenant- General Sir Guy Carleton (1724–1808), a veteran of the capture of Louisbourg (1758), Quebec (1759), and Havana (1762), who had commanded in Quebec against the Americans in 1775–76. Mante used the books in preparing for his *History of the Late War in North America* (1772), an account of the Seven Years' War there. He also paraphrased French works in novels published in 1781–82 and went on to produce a *Naval and Military History of the Wars of England* (1795–1807) that was heavily dependent on the historical works of David Hume and Tobias Smollett.[42] Work that appeared in French was most likely to be translated into English. In contrast to Maïzeroy, Santa Cruz's *Military Reflections*, which was published in Spanish, were not translated into English, whereas it was translated into French, German, and Italian.[43]

The term *strategy* appeared in the third edition of Charles James's *A New and Enlarged Military Dictionary, or, Alphabetical Explanation of Technical Terms*, which was published in London in 1810. James (d. 1821), an active writer, had traveled in France in the 1780s and published *Hints Founded on Facts, or a View of Our Several Military Establishments* (1791) before serving as a militia officer in the 1790s and as a major in the corps of artillery drivers in 1806–12. His military dictionary included a glossary of French terms, and the other editions appeared in 1800, 1805, and 1817. James also exemplified the process by which there was interaction between European and Asian military techniques, one focused by the British presence in Asia. Thus, in 1813, he published *Military Costumes of India, Being an Exemplification of the Manual and Platoon Exercise for the Use of the Native Troops and British Army.*

Maïzeroy's emphasis was on a reasoning and reasoned response to circumstances in order to make command appropriate and successful. Like many writers of the period, Maïzeroy presented the present age as an opportunity to regain the perspectives of antiquity. In the preface to his new 1781 edition of his *Cours de tactique applique les exemples aux precepts, développe les maxims des plus habiles généraux, et rapporte les faits les plus intéressans et les plus utiles, avec les descriptions de plusieurs batailles anciennes*, a work that first appeared in 1776 (the same year as the first volume of Edward Gibbon's *Decline and Fall*), the period since the fall of the Roman Empire was presented as "les siècles d'ignorance," one, however, ended by "une revolution dans les esprits," namely the Renaissance. Maïzeroy added an insight based on his view of the international system, namely that smaller states would have to have better militaries than "grandes monarchies" reliant on an idea of their power. As a result, he proposed a domestic character linked to strength, one that called for a strategy of reform.[44] Maïzeroy, who emphasized the complexity of command, also pressed for an understanding of "la science de la guerre," a science, he claimed, in the fashion of the age, that was linked to "des regles certaines."[45] He continued:

> Quoique l'invention de la poudre et les nouvelles armes aient occasionné divers changemens dans le méchanisme de la guerre, il est certain qu'elle n'a dû influer que très-peu sur les principes de la Tactique; et point du tout sur ceux de la Stratégie. C'est l'opinion contraire qui, depuis environ un siècle, a fait prévaloir de mauvaises maxims, et nous a écarté de la bonne route.[46]

Maïzeroy felt it necessary to provide a footnote to explain the term *stratégie*:

> La Stratégie comprend les plans d'opérations, les mouvemens d'armées, l'art des campemens, des marches, la distribution des troupes relativement aux projets formés, et généralement la science du raisonnement comme

celle du coup d'oeil: c'est pourquoi on la nomme plus communément
Dialectique militaire, qui est la partie sublime de la guerre, et la science
proper du Général. Cette science est toujours imparfaite, si elle n'est fondée
sur la connoissance des principes avoués par ce qu'il y a de plus habite.[47]

He had used the term in his *Mémoire sur les opinions qui partagent les militaires* (1773) and with more weight, in his *Théorie de guerre* (1777).

After Maïzeroy, the term *stratégique* was used by the Marquis de Silva in his *Pensées sur la tactique, et la stratégique ou vrais principes de la science militaire: Considérations sur la guerre de 1769 entre les Russes et les Turcs* (1778). Marquis Emanuele de Silva Taroicca (1727–96), was a Portuguese who served as an officer in the Spanish army, then as a staff officer in the army of Sardinia (Piedmont), subsequently in that of Russia under Catherine the Great (as a Sardinian observer in 1769), and finally in that of Sardinia (Piedmont) again. *Pensées* was published in Turin by the royal printers and dedicated to Victor Amadeus III of Sardinia (Piedmont). This was a development of Silva's *Pensées sur la tactique et sur quelques autres parties de la guerre* (Paris, 1768), and also reflected his *Remarques sur quelques articles de l'Essai general de tactique* (Turin, 1773), a comment on Guibert's work of the previous year.[48] In the "Avertissement" to *Pensées*, Silva referred to his emphasis since his 1768 study: "j'ai fait mon étude principale et continuelle de cette partie, qui est la base de la Stratégique et de toute la science militaire," with a footnote explaining: "La Stratégique est proprement la science du Général. Elle enseigne à former les projets des opérations, et à bien employer et combiner tous les moyens que lui fournissent les différentes branches de la Tactique."[49]

Silva very much struck an Enlightenment tone, opening the first chapter of *Pensées* by claiming that better war-making would make battles more decisive and wars, accordingly, shorter and less ruinous. This was presented as a public good based on understanding the true laws, which, he stated, could be demonstrated in a geometric fashion.[50] Thus, mathematical reasoning was part of the equation.

Silva was interested in modern warfare, as reflected in his *Considérations sur la guerre présente entre les Russes et les Turcs*, written in late 1769 and published in Turin in 1773. His *Pensées* devoted much attention to recent military history, although there were also references to classical warfare, and the citing of texts, including Polybius and Caesar. Silva emphasized the value of situational awareness, notably an understanding of the country in which operations were to be conducted. The Seven Years' War was the presence most apparent in the text. Frederick the Great was presented as the imitator of the Romans and history as the way to instruct present-day officers.[51] Reflecting the impact of more recent generalship, Silva devoted far less attention to Saxe than to Frederick.

Silva pressed on to argue that all considerations on which a plan of war was devised related to three points: the country in dispute, the force, and that of the enemy.[52] The political dimension cited by Silva did not attract his particular attention. Nevertheless, he did make political points—for example, that grand alliances did not make war with the same ardor and unanimity that they declared them.[53] Silva also emphasized the value of the systematic peacetime preparation of war plans and of national military education, the latter a theme he took back to the classical world.[54] In his proposal for a military academy, he argued the importance of a mathematical understanding:

> La géometrie est comme le tronc d'où partent presque toutes les branches de la théorie militaire, et le nombre de ces branches est immense. Il est vrai qu'il ne s'agit point d'une géométrie transcendante, plus admirable qu'utile, et qu'on ne doit enseigner des mathématiques que ce qui a un rapport direct et immédiat à l'art de la guerre. Mais que de parties à apprendre! La géométrie élémentaire, l'algèbre, la trigonometrie, la méchanique, l'hydraulique, la fortification, l'attaque et la défense des places, la tactique, la stratégique.[55]

Silva was keen on the last word. Thus, the "Avertissement" for the second edition of his *Considérations sur la guerre présente entre les Russes et les Turcs*, a work appearing as *Considérations sur la guerre de 1769 entre les Russes et les Turcs*, that was published as part of his 1778 *Pensées sur la tactique, et la stratégique*, declared the value of strategy, not least in clarifying lessons:

> Je le crois au contraire assez propres à constater plusieurs principes que j'ai établis sur la Stratégique, et ceux surtout qui concernent la manière de former le plan et de régler l'état de la guerre. En raisonnant sur les premieres operations j'ai entrevu, et en quelque façon deviné, les événemens qu'elles devaient produire, et qu'elles ont réellement produits: ce qui prouve bien que la science de conduire les armées a des principes sûrs, des quells on peut tirer les consequences les plus justes.

In practical terms, Silva's use of strategy was in order to emphasize able operational command, due preparation for war, and in particular, military education. Most of his work related to tactical and operational matters, and part of it revolved around the established question of the best formation and fighting method for infantry, a question that, in part, he answered with reference to the classics. The other key issue was how to respond to Prussian proficiency.[56]

Silva was important in Sardinian circles, playing a role in the reorganization of the army in 1773–77, a reorganization pushed by Victor Amadeus III. In particular, in 1775, the army was restructured into four departments, essentially divisions, one composed of cavalry and three of infantry. Each was divided into two "wings," each of which was composed of two brigades. Silva was influenced by the French "Réglement pour l'infanterie."[57] As part of the interest in military affairs in Sardinia, the Marchese di Brezé (1727–96), a senior officer, also wrote on military affairs, including *Observations historiques et critiques sur les commentaires de Folard, sur la chevalerie* (Turin, 1772) and *Réflexions sur les préjurgés militaires* (Turin, 1779).[58]

The impact of Prussia reflected the prestige of its methods after the Seven Years' War. Those interested in military matters attended Prussian maneuvers and studied Frederick the Great's campaigns. Prussian military regulations were translated and Prussian drill adopted, while those who had served under Frederick were able to gain posts elsewhere, Catherine II of Russia recruiting her relative Count Frederick of Anhalt in 1783. Charles III of Spain used Prussia as a model for both infantry and cavalry tactics, while in December 1777, Nathanael Greene cited Frederick the Great, "the greatest general of the age," when attempting to dissuade George Washington from launching an attack on British forces.[59] From 1764 to 1785, the British kept yearly summaries of the annual Prussian maneuvers and the British drill regulations of 1786 were based on a manual by the Prussian inspector general. Three years earlier, Louis-Alexandre Berthier, later Napoleon's chief of staff, was much impressed by the Silesian maneuvers of the Prussians.

This situation, however, did not encourage the development of strategic argument. In part, this was because the Prussians during the Seven Years' War had focused in large part on reacting to a more powerful alliance and on the operational, rather than the strategic, level of war, which in the latter case, prefigured the failings of German war-making in the twentieth century. So also with the War of the Bavarian Succession (1778–79) in which Frederick had responded to Austrian territorial schemes. Frederick's response to the Seven Years' War had included the consideration of more flexible tactical ideas but not any fundamental reassessment of Prussian war-making.

Jean-Claude-Eleónore Michaud d'Arçon also used the word *stratégique* in his *Défense d'un système de guerre national* (1779) but without really defining it. Thus, the word was known, although many authors, for example Guibert, did not pay great attention to it, which suggests that the word was not considered significant. Guibert was both jealous of others who wrote on military matters and critical of what he described as attempts to intellectualize military affairs. Guibert's major contribution, the idea of *l'ordre mixte*, exemplified his notion that a flexible response to circumstances was crucial. This notion led Guibert to criticize Frederick II's tactics and to reject what he regarded as formulaic and intellectual solutions in part because he saw them as inflexible.

Appearing in 1787, volume three of the *Encyclopédie Méthodique* dedicated to the military art had a massive section on tactics and a short entry on *strategême* (pp. 572–73) but none on *stratégique*. Underlining the extent to which the establishment of the word *strategy* was an aspect of a more general state of volatility and flexibility in language, as well as a search for precision and exactness, the entry on "*tactique*" began by defining it as the art of "disposer et de mouvoir les troupes en ordre" and then added a classification reflecting a sense of flux:

> On divide la tactique en grande ou générale, et en petite ou particulière . . . la grande tactique comprend les positions et mouvements des armées, relatifs aux pays qu'elles doivent attaquer ou defender, et aux armées enemies et de toutes leurs dépendances, telles que les munitions de guerre et de bouche, les machines de guerre et les bagages. Il est d'autant plus necessaire de distinguer ces deux parties principals de l'art de la guerre, qu'on les a confondues de notre temps.[60]

The subsequent account of "grande tactique" was of what would now be termed operational warfare.[61] Also in 1787, Jacques, Vicomte de Grenier, in his *L'Art de guerre sur mer, ou Tactique navale*, complained that earlier writers had covered little beside orders of battle. He himself did not dwell on strategy and was to be criticized in 1802 for his narrow technical approach.[62]

In François Louis Hérold de Wimpffen's *Mémoires*, published in 1788, he wrote of the "conceptions aux connaissances purement intellectuelles de la stratégie et de la logistique" and of "ce genre de stratégie."[63] This usage suggests an established meaning by this point. Wimpffen was an infantry colonel at this point. Born in the German territory of Zweibrücken, from which many served in the French army, he made the transition in that army from the Bourbons to that of Revolutionary France, holding divisional command in 1792–93. Other works by Wimpffen were published in French and German in 1797–99, with a translation of one into English in 1804 as *The Experienced Officer; or Instructions by the General of Division to his sons and to all young men intended for the military profession: being a series of rules laid down by General Wimpffen, to enable officers of every rank, to carry on war, in all its branches and descriptions, from the least important enterprises and expeditions, to the decisive battles, which involve the fate of empires. With an introduction by Lieutenant Colonel Macdonald*. Having served in the army of the East India Company from 1780 to 1796 and in the Scottish Volunteers during the French Revolutionary War, John Macdonald (1759–1831) visited France during the peace of 1802–3 following the Treaty of Amiens, and later published translations of several French military works. Wimpffen's younger brother, Georges Felix de Wimpffen (1744–1814), served as a general.

The value of the term *stratégique* was to be pushed to the fore in part because war became a more pressing and continual feature in European civilization from 1792. Indeed, it may be asked whether the use of the term *strategy* would have spread had there not been this period of war. The fourth volume of the *Encyclopédie Méthodique* on the *Art Militaire*, a supplementary volume issued in 1797, contained a *Table Analytique*, and its seventeenth section was dedicated to strategy. This began:

> Dans cette dix-septième section, sous le titre de *Stratégie*, on réunira tous les mots qui ont des rapports avec l'art de former des projets de guerre, de les faire cadrer avec les moyens de l'état, de les mettre en usage avec intelligence et économie, d'exécuter les desseins projetés de disposer

les marches, les plans de campagne, les campemens, les fourrages, les
convois, les approvisionnemens des places, les passages des rivières, les
subsistances, etc.[64]

Turning back to the pre-Revolutionary ancien régime, the existence
of strategy prior to the word attracts reconsideration. Guibert, in his
Essai général de tactique (1772), had distinguished grand from elementary
tactics, and by 1779, the year of his *Défense du système de guerre modern*,
was referring to "la stratégique," which was a version of the former. The
quest for a scientific account of war was linked to the categorization that
led to the use of a separate term. Moreover, the hierarchy of knowledge
that commentators sought as an aspect of classification encouraged the
view that strategy was superior as a task to tactics. What this meant, or
might mean in practice, was less clear. As a linked issue, France's failure
to enter the War of the Bavarian Succession (1778–79) ensures that there
is no conflict with which policymaking and practice in the earlier wars
can be readily compared prior to the French Revolutionary War, because
France's intervention in the War of American Independence from 1778
to 1783 was very different in character.

The major contrast between French war-making from 1792 and the
earlier situation was not the development of a language of strategy nor
a new military context within which such an idea appeared relevant but
instead, the move from the wartime coalition politics France had earlier
displayed to a much simpler situation. Indeed, if anything, France, as
a result, needed strategy less from 1792 because the establishment and
implementation of goals was far less affected by the exigencies of alliance
politics than on occasions earlier in the century.

Indeed, the term *strategy* did not gain a meaning or usage that led to
what it described being seen as a solution to the pressing needs of war.
There is scant sign that the word altered policy in this period any more
than the launching of the word *geopolitics* at the end of the nineteenth
century.[65] The limited impact of the term is suggested by the relatively
slow adoption of the word as far as dictionaries were concerned or of
usage, at least insofar as generals left records, on which see also chapter
8. The French Academy Dictionary of 1798 did not have *stratégie* but
had *stratège* for an officer who commanded the army in Ancient Greece
and *stratagème* as a ruse de guerre. In contrast, the Robert dictionary

gives a first usage date of 1803 for *stratégie*: "Art de faire évoluer une armée sur un theatre d'opérations jusqu'au moment où elle entre en contact avec l'ennemi: parti de la science militaire qui concerne la conduit générale des operations de grande envergure, élaboration des plans." In short, *stratégie* is defined as the planning that preceded contact with the enemy—in other words, all the work that goes into planning a military operation. Both were already present before the term was devised. *Stratégique* followed for the first time in the Robert dictionary in 1823, defined as "qui concerne la *stratégie*." On the *Dictionnaires d'autrefois* website, most usage is from 1835.

That the terms took a while to get attested in dictionaries is of considerable interest. The early history of the term is largely obscure precisely because the reference back to the classics was not one that continued to command interest. Instead, the role of Maïzeroy was ignored. The focus was placed instead on Guibert because those he had influenced were significant, while it was easy to relate his writings to the subsequent developments in the Revolutionary and Napoleonic Wars. These developments did not, however, lead to any immediate flowering of French writing about strategy.

NOTES

1. J. Black, *Eighteenth-Century Europe*, 2nd ed. (Basingstoke, UK, 1999).

2. K. H. Doig, "War in the Reform Programme of the *Encyclopédie*," *War and Society* 6 (1988): 1–9.

3. E. Dziembowski, *Un nouveau patriotism français, 1750–1770. La France face à la puissance anglaise à l'époque de la guerre de Sept Ans* (Oxford, 1998) and *La guerre de Sept Ans 1756–1763* (Paris, 2015): 568–81.

4. Mackenzie to Pitt, November 22, 1758, NA. SP. 92/66.

5. Bristol to Pitt, November 19, 1759, NA. SP. 94/160.

6. H. M. Scott, "The Importance of Bourbon Naval Reconstruction to the Strategy of Choiseul after the Seven Years' War," *International History Review* 1 (1979): 17–35.

7. Kaunitz to Starhemberg, June 12, 1758, Batzel: 458.

8. Mitchell to Holdernesse, April 20, 1760, NA. SP. 90/75.

9. D. Echeverria, *The Maupeou Revolution: A Study in the History of Libertarianism: France, 1770–1774* (Baton Rouge, LA, 1985): 138.

10. E.g., *Les rêveries ou memoires sur l'art de la guerre* (The Hague: Pierre Gosse, 1756); *Mes rêveries* (Amsterdam

and Leipzig: Arkstée und Merkus, 1757); R. S. Quimby, *The Background of Napoleonic Warfare: The Theory of Military Tactics in Eighteenth-Century France* (New York, 1957).

11. J. Chagniot, *Le Chevalier de Folard, la strategie de l'incertitude* (Paris, 1973).

12. Dickens to Horatio Walpole, September 18, 1736, NA. SP. 90/41.

13. Thomas Johnston to Sir Robert Walpole, June 8, 1739, CUL. CH. Corresp. 2875.

14. For an emphasis on continuity, see A. Ferrill, *The Origins of War from the Stone Age to Alexander the Great* (London, 1985): 7, 217–22.

15. D. A. Neill, "Ancestral Voices: The Influence of the Ancients on the Military Thought of the Seventeenth and Eighteenth Centuries," *Journal of Military History* 62 (1998): 487–520.

16. Saxe, *Rêveries* (London, 1757): 47.

17. A. David, "'L'interprète des plus grands maîtres.' Paul-Gédéon Joly de Maïzeroy, l'inventeur de la stratégie," *Stratégique* 99 (2010): 63–85.

18. Horace Walpole, *Memoirs of King George II*, edited by J. Brooke (3 vols., New Haven, CT, 1985): II, 70.

19. S. Powers, "Studying the Art of War: Military Books Known to American Officers and Their French Counterparts during the Second Half of the Eighteenth Century," *Journal of Military History* 70 (2006): 781–814; I. D. Gruber, *Books and the British Army in the Age of the American Revolution* (Chapel Hill, NC, 2010).

20. B. Heuser, "Denial of Change: The Military Revolution as Seen by Contemporaries," in M. Mantovani,

ed., *International Bibliography for Military History* 32 (Leiden, the Netherlands, 2012): 3–27.

21. Anon., memorandum, May 1745, AE. Mémoires et Documents, Ang. 40 fol. 129.

22. A. Gat, *The Origins of Military Thought from the Enlightenment to Clausewitz* (Oxford, 1989).

23. G. F. von Tempelhoff, *Geschichte des Siebenjährigen Kriegs in Deutschland in Deutschland zwischen dem könige von Preussen und der kaiserin königin mit ihren allirten* (Berlin, 1787); Johann Wilhelm von Archenholz, *Geschichte des Siebenjährigen kriegs in Deutschland* (Berlin, 1793); D. Hohrath, *Ferdinand Friedrich Nicolai und die militärische Aufklärung in 18. Jahrhundert* (Stuttgart, 1989); Speelman, ed., *Lloyd*.

24. W. Horsley, *A Treatise on Naval Affairs: Or, A Comparison between the Commerce and Naval Power of England and France* (London, 1744): 76.

25. Philip to Joseph Yorke, August 25, 1745, BL. Add. 35363 fol. 94.

26. T. E. Hall, *France and the Eighteenth-Century Corsican Question* (New York, 1971): 187–204.

27. *Guibert: Stratégiques*, edited by J.-P. Charnay and M. Burgos (Paris, 1977); Charnay, ed., *Guibert ou le soldat philosophe* (Paris, 1981); B. Heuser, "Guibert. Prophet of Total War?," in S. Förster and R. Chickering, eds., *War in an Age of Revolution: The Wars of American Independence and the French Revolution, 1775–1815* (Cambridge, UK, 2010): 49–67.

28. J. Langins, *Conserving the Enlightenment: French Military Engineering from Vauban to the Enlightenment* (Cambridge, MA, 2004).

29. S. T. Ross, "The Development of the Combat Division in Eighteenth-Century French Armies," *French Historical Studies* 1 (1965): 85–86.

30. J. Haldon, *A Critical Commentary on the "Taktika" of Leo VI* (Washington, DC, 2014); G. T. Dennis, *The Taktika of Leo VI* (Washington, 2010); G. Dragon and H. Mihaescu, eds., *Le traité sur la guerrilla de l'empereur Nicéphore Phocas* (Paris, 1986).

31. B. Heuser, *The Strategy Makers: Thoughts on War and Society from Machiavelli to Clausewitz* (Santa Barbara, CA, 2010): 125.

32. *Encyclopédie* (Geneva, 1778), VI, 328.

33. Polybius, D. C. Seybold, J.-C. de Folard, K. T. Guichard, *Geschichte: Aus dem griechisch en aufs neue übersetzt und mit anmerkungen wie auch auszügen aus den werken des Herren von Folard und Guischard über die kriegkunst der alten beleitet von D. C. Seybold* (8 vols., Lemgo, 1779).

34. *Encyclopédie* (Geneva, 1778), XII, 483.

35. *Institutions Militaires*: I, 6.

36. *Essais Militaires* (Paris, 1762): 130.

37. *Journal de Sçavans* (November 1777): 718–19.

38. *Théorie*: 1.

39. *Théorie*: ii.

40. *Théorie*: iii–iv.

41. *Théorie*: vii.

42. R. C. Cole, *Thomas Mante: Writer, Soldier, Adventurer* (New York, 1993).

43. Heuser, *Strategy Makers*: 126.

44. *Cours de Tactique*: xx.

45. *Cours de Tactique*: xxi.

46. *Cours de Tactique*: xxii–xxiii.

47. *Cours de Tactique*: xxii.

48. F. A. Pinelli, *Storia militare del Piemonte: dalla pace di Aquisgrana al 1850* (2 vols., Turin, 1854): I, 38; F. Venturi, *Settecento riformatore: III. La prima crisi dell'antico regime, 1768–1776* (Turin, 1979): 132–33.

49. Silva, "Avertissement": 1.

50. Silva *Pensées* (Turin, 1778): 1–3.

51. Silva, *Pensées* (Turin, 1778): 147, 188.

52. Silva, *Pensées* (Turin, 1778): 305.

53. Silva, *Pensées* (Turin, 1778): 310.

54. Silva, *Pensées* (Turin, 1778): 342–44.

55. Silva, *Pensées* (Turin, 1778): 348.

56. Silva, *Pensées* (Turin, 1778): 4.

57. P. Bianchi, *Onore e mestiere. Le riforme militari nel Piemonte dei Settecento* (Turin, 2002): 233–46, 296.

58. *Dizionario biografico degli Italiani* 14 (1972).

59. R. Snowman, ed., *The Papers of General Nathanael Greene*, II (Chapel Hill, NC, 1980): 235.

60. *Encyclopédie méthodique: Art militaire*, vol. 3, part 2 (Paris, 1787): 658.

61. *Encyclopédie méthodique: Art militaire*, vol. 3, part 2 (Paris, 1787): 658–59.

62. A. Ramatuelle, *Cours élémentaire de Tactique Navale* (Paris, 1802): xii. For a British equivalent, see John Clerk of Eldin, *An Essay on Naval Tactics, Systematical and Historical* (London, 1790).

63. François Louis, Baron de Wimpffen, *La vie privée et militaire du Général Baron de Wimpffen. Memoires écrits par lui-même* (Paris, 1788): I, 154, 212.

64. *Encyclopédie Méthodique: Art militaire*, IV, *Supplément* (Paris, 1797): 984.

65. J. Black, *Geopolitics and the Quest for Dominance* (Bloomington, IN, 2016).

FIVE

THE STRATEGY OF
CONTINENTAL EMPIRES

THE STRENGTH AND INTENTIONS OF CONTINENTAL EMPIRES
were a matter of great concern not only to one another but also to the
maritime powers. Indeed, despite triumphalism at particular moments,
there was scant sense at the time that geopolitical destiny necessarily lay
with the latter as was subsequently frequently to appear the case to later
commentators. In the British House of Commons in 1778, Charles Jenkinson, a key official who became secretary at war that year, declared that

> the great military powers in the interior parts of Europe [Austria, Russia,
> Prussia], who have amassed together their great treasures, and have
> modelled their subjects into great armies, will in the next and succeeding
> periods of time, become the predominant powers. France and Great
> Britain, which have been the first and second-rate powers of the European
> world, will perhaps for the future be but of the third and fourth rate.[1]

Jenkinson's sense of flux appeared particularly pertinent to contemporaries who were witnessing the crisis of British imperial rule in North
America and from 1776, reading Edward Gibbon on the fall of the Roman
Empire, having, in the Seven Years' War, earlier seen repeated triumphs
for Britain. Gibbon, moreover, addressed the question of whether European Christian civilization as a whole would fall anew to "barbarian"
assault, thus repeating the overthrow of the Roman Empire.

Jenkinson was referring to Europe, but his comments were more
generally relevant. This chapter offers a way to consider a number of the
leading land powers in the world: China (the Manchu Empire), Japan,
Turkey (the Ottoman Empire), Russia (the Romanov Empire), Austria
(the Habsburg Empire), and Spain, as well as of certain smaller land

142

powers. Had the chapter focused solely on the early years of the century, then it would have been appropriate as well to consider the Mughal and Safavid empires of India and Persia (Iran), respectively. However, the former was greatly weakened by midcentury, and the latter was overthrown in 1722. The consideration of the major land powers offers a way to examine the balance of opportunities and pressures that helped mold continental expansionism. There will be a short introduction looking for common themes, then a brief discussion of each in turn, and then a conclusion considering how the situation changed.

Although most historical work adopts the specificities of distinctive traditions in the form of area studies, and notably for China, the comparative theme for major Eurasian land empires is not a new one, and it continues to yield many valuable insights. Most comparisons focus on socioeconomic similarities or contrasts, notably between China and Russia, but there is also a consideration of political counterparts.[2] In functional terms, it is readily possible to differentiate between the relations of empires with one another and their relations with weaker polities and/or ones they were determined to treat in a tributary fashion.

In the eighteenth century, as opposed to the seventeenth, there was less hostility at the level of relations between empires. Such hostility remained important to Persian-Turkish relations in the 1720s–40s, and became more so for Russo-Turkish relations, with large-scale conflict between the two in 1768–74 and 1787–92 playing a major role in the escalating problems of the Turkish Empire and in the sense elsewhere that it was in crisis. In contrast, whereas, following a short and episodic conflict, the Chinese had driven the Russians from the Amur Valley in the 1680s, a verdict the Russians accepted with the Treaty of Nerchinsk in 1689, the two empires did not clash at all in the eighteenth century. The significance of this point has been underplayed due to the general tendency not to focus on what did not happen. Understandable in terms of the space available, this counterfactual tendency, nevertheless, underplays both the possibility that it might have happened and, separately, that this possibility can throw some light on what actually occurred and thus the how and why and notably the question of accident or policy?

In the case of Russia and China, there is no reliable form of historical patterning to provide guidance, either in terms of the history of the two states or of potentially analogous cases. To take the latter, the total Spanish overthrow of the Aztec and Inca empires in 1519–36 indicated how major empires could be overthrown by far smaller forces (albeit with significant local allies at the expense of the Aztecs in 1519–21), and this point was also germane in the case of Persia in 1722. However, these comparisons offer scant guidance to the likely resilience of China. Spanish ideas of conquering China in the sixteenth century were fantasies. In terms of Spanish force projection, operating with forces on the littoral of the Far East, either from Mexico across the Pacific, which was the basis of the establishment of a Spanish colony in the Philippines in the 1560s, or via the Indian Ocean, as the Portuguese did from the 1490s, was not practicable. With the Pacific and the Indian oceans, there was no comparison to the more confined geopolitical sphere of the Atlantic.

Russia itself had made formidable gains in Siberia during the late sixteenth and seventeenth centuries, and it might appear plausible to ask whether the same could not have been repeated. There were to be major Russian gains in the mid- and late nineteenth century, at the expense of China and, even more, in Central Asia. In addition, the ability of Russia, despite its lack of a good Pacific port, to project power across the north Pacific to Alaska in the eighteenth century throws further light on Russian capability.[3] Looked at differently, this capability appears irrelevant given Chinese strength in the period. In Russian operations in the Aleutian Islands, their relative numerical strength and the benefit of warships was aided by the contribution of firearms and the savage impact of smallpox on the local population, factors that had already been the case with Russian expansion in Siberia from the 1580s. The Russians met their first organized resistance in the Aleutians in the early 1760s when they reached the Fox Islands. However, in 1766, a Russian fleet successfully attacked the islands. These operations provided no indication of what would have happened against more populous and powerful China. Nevertheless, the situation might have been different had Russia intervened in the islands to the north of Honshu, the main island of Japan, as the Japanese government indeed feared with regard to the island of Hokkaido where Japanese colonialism was at the expense of the indigenous Ainu population.

The fall of the Ming Empire at Manchu hands in the 1640s[4] does not provide guidance as to what might have occurred at the hands of Russia had it sought to resume its earlier expansionism at the expense of China. In particular, that approach underplays the extent to which this fall owed much to large-scale rebellion within China. Such rebellion did not recur until the Rebellion of the Three Feudatories in the 1670s, and that was not as serious as the situation in the 1640s. At that stage, Russia was in no state to project its power against China, if indeed it really ever was prior to the late nineteenth century and then only against northern China. In the eighteenth century, there were major rebellions in China but not on the scale of those in the 1640s, 1670s, or 1850s, the last the Taiping Rebellion.

Alongside strong feeling of hostility to Turkey and Islam, the Russian elite lacked any sense of Russia as an Asian power involved in a struggle for dominance with China. The spatial preponderance of dominions east of the Urals did not match Russian assumptions. This is one of the many instances in which maps offer only a poor guide to strategy. More generally, there was a focus on Russia's part on Europe. No effort was made to repeat the intervention in Persia in 1722–23 by Peter the Great (r. 1689–1725). In 1761, a British diplomat noted that "the Russian sovereigns, instead of taking the fairest opportunity, during the troubles of Persia, to erect a mighty, Asiatic empire, have turned their views wholly upon Europe."[5]

The means of strategy was deliberative and accretional, rather than the bold advances seen with Peter the Great. New lines of Russian forts were added as ambitions and settlements advanced southward from Russia's existing possessions. Control over the Bashkirs was anchored by a new line of forts from the River Volga to the new fort at Orenburg built from 1733, a fort that was to be important in resisting the Pugachev rebellion four decades later. In addition, the Usinskaya Line based at Troitsk (1743) was constructed along the River Uy to protect the agricultural zone to the east of the Urals. Farther east, the Ishim line of forts was replaced in the 1750s by Petropavlovsk and its Presnogor'kovskaya Line in modern northern Kazakhstan. By the second half of the century, a chain of forts, more than four thousand kilometers in length, extended eastward from the Caspian Sea to Kuznetsk in the foothills of the Altay Mountains.

It was more plausible to think that Russia, and indeed China, could have played differently their relationship with the other key player in the region, the Zunghar confederation of Xinjiang, which is also mentioned in the following chapter. Until the mid-1750s, the Zunghars were a significant challenge to the Chinese position in Mongolia and Tibet as well as to the Chinese and more particularly, ruling Manchu sense of success and destiny. There was also an important religious dimension in the shape of competing authority over Buddhism between China and the Zunghars, a dimension that echoed that of rivalries between Shi'a and Sunni and between Protestant and Catholic powers. To Chinese commentators, China's eventual success made it the proven recipient of heavenly grace.[6]

The Chinese appear to have been most concerned to avoid Russian support for the Zunghars, which would have been destabilizing for China's position in the steppes. Indeed, both Russia and China sought stability, rather than the more unpredictable strategy of using the Zunghars to pursue gains at the expense of the other. This stance, whether regarded as strategy or policy, or both, can be linked, on the part of each empire, to a politics of prudence and on that of China, to a strong desire for a stable and protective world order. With the centers of power of the two empires, St. Petersburg and Beijing, far removed, and neither challenging the ideological role of the other, as rival Muslim and Christian empires did, it was possible, as well as desirable, for China and Russia both to coexist and to pursue other goals, including those on other frontiers.

The last point is crucial, whether a functional and instrumental approach to strategy is taken, or one that concentrates on the dominance of drives and means derived from ideological roles and values. The major work on Russian strategy, that by J. P. LeDonne,[7] focuses heavily and valuably on the location of troops in terms of opportunities and threats. Both opportunities and threats can be seen in terms of functional and ideological factors. As the former were perceived in terms of assumptions, different ideological factors can also be seen in play. These considerations serve as a useful basis before briefly separately assessing the strategies of the major Eurasian land empires. After that, the concluding section will reexamine the question of overall similarities and differences.

CHINA

The leading land power in the world was both a "satisfied" state, in that it had a clear world vision that it appeared able to sustain, and also pursued an expansionist policy designed to leave no doubt about the applicability of this vision. Each approach has been taken to Chinese military history, as a whole and in specifics, and both is valid if in concert with the other. The particular need is for a nuanced account that allows for significant variations between individual dynasties and indeed rulers, while also accepting the impact of other contingent aspects.[8] The play of contingency and conjuncture is generally underrated due to the tendency to focus on a structural account of Chinese policy or at least on a structural exposition and explanation. Such an account certainly matched Chinese ideology, but it was a less-than-complete presentation of the situation.

The rise of the Manchu (or Qing) dynasty and its replacement of the Ming in 1644, encouraged interest in further expansionism, made conquest more possible, and thus both countered possible threats and made it easier to sustain the Manchu presence in China. The awareness of challenge and threat was a key element in Manchu strategy. Indeed, the balance between positive and defensive reasons for expansionism is one that repeatedly has to be struck with care. Moreover, as an additional complication, the two could be readily compatible and indeed were frequently part of the same equation. The Manchu created a dynamic system willing and capable of subjugating at least some of China's neighbors, and this expansionism contrasted with a very different situation for the Safavids and Mughals in the eighteenth century. Looked at differently, Manchu success at the expense of Ming China in the mid-seventeenth century, a success that was obtained only due to serious divisions within China and with the support of important military elements there, anticipated the efforts of the Marathas in India against the Mughals and of the Afghans in Persia and India against the Safavids and Mughals. However, neither the Marathas nor the Afghans were as able to ground temporary achievements as the Manchu were.

The comparison offered with the Marathas and Afghans might, instead, be the Zunghars, although they were far less successful than either. However, had the Zunghars continued powerful, maybe, for example, prefiguring in that the Durranis of Afghanistan from the late 1740s in maintaining the independence of their homeland and in pressing on their neighbors, then they might have been in a position to apply greater pressure in China. Indeed, far from assuming a certain success, the Manchu feared the creation of a hostile Mongol confederation and notably from the 1690s. As so often, the porosity of the frontier operated both ways, and the Zunghars, in effect the western Mongols, would probably have contested Manchu influence among the Khalkas in eastern Mongolia as well, possibly as control of the Chinese provinces of Gansu and even Shaanxi. This contest, which had a strong religious dimension,[9] might well have weakened China prior to the onset of European pressure in the mid-nineteenth century, possibly leading to fissiparous tendencies in the state. For example, it might have proved far harder for China to suppress rebellions such as the large-scale White Lotus Rebellion in the late 1790s.

Equally, it could be argued, using the challenge and response model, that continued Zunghar pressure would have kept the military center stage and maintained the viability of Chinese armed forces, although if this had been the case with Manchu pressure on the Ming, it was not successfully so then for the Ming. Such what-if counterfactuals may appear questionable, but they were very much part of the context within which strategy was formulated and evaluated. To leave out counterfactualism is to fail to understand contemporary approaches, not least the "scientific" stance advocated by Joly de Maïzeroy, an approach that included a dialectic focused on the assessment of respective strength and thus possible moves.[10]

In the event, in 1680–1760, China conquered more territory than any other power in the world. The Manchu repeatedly fought to expand. Their expansionism was imperialistic and for glory and possessions, rather than for resources and trade. Traditionally, the chief characteristic of the Chinese military was a certain remorseless persistence, but the Manchu brought a new dynamic and a greater ability to campaign successfully in the steppe. Thus, they took forward the traditional Chinese strategy of playing off steppe forces in order to win allies and weaken opponents, a strategy that was a way to cope with the scale of the steppe and the seeming intractability it posed. The Manchu, indeed, created a military system that was in effect a Manchu-Chinese hybrid as well as having distinctive goals. Impressive in its operational extent, the army was able to act in very different terrains. The ability to deliver power at a great range matched the situation within the European world: organizational developments, range, and capability were more important than military technology itself. These are points that to a degree challenge the standard interpretation of military development, especially that of technology-based revolutions.[11]

This ability was at the service of a set of cultural and geographical assumptions and of the need to revise constantly the empire-building strategy. In a mechanistic interpretation, this was a case of adjusting the strategy to changed realities,[12] although there is always the risk that such an interpretation ignores the role of cultural assumptions in both the perception of realities and the adjustment and thus of what is referred to as strategic culture. The Chinese were more ambitious and more successful in Central Asia than on their southern frontiers where in their most significant conflict to the south during the century, they were defeated in Myanmar (Burma) in the late 1760s. This was in part because the southern frontiers were not of central strategic interest to China, and plans by the Qianlong emperor, who felt the humiliation of failure, to try to reverse the defeat were abandoned. War with Myanmar began in 1765 over what had hitherto been the buffer zone of the Shan states, but this was less important to China's rulers than eastern Mongolia, which had been contested with the Zunghars in the 1690s, a struggle followed by one over western Mongolia. The Manchu, indeed, were much more comfortable with the people and cultures of Central Asia than with the south. The more loyal and reliable Banner Armies of the Manchu garrisoned north China but had little presence in the south. Instead, the Manchu relied there on the Green Standard troops, those of the Han Chinese. In addition, the generals sent to the southern frontiers were less competent.

In the case of Vietnam in 1788–89, China failed anew. In 1786, a successful peasant revolt against the Le dynasty, the Hanoi-based rulers of northern Vietnam, had been followed by the flight of the new Le ruler to China where he sought Chinese backing. This cause was backed by Sun, governor of the frontier provinces of Guangxi and Guangdong, and he persuaded the Qianlong emperor to support a new Chinese-dominated

order in Vietnam. The governors to the south tended to be more autono-
mous than their counterparts closer to Beijing. The Chinese attempt to
capture Hanoi was defeated by Nguyen Hue, as the result of a surprise
attack on Chinese forces in January 1789. Rejecting advice for a renewed
invasion, the emperor dismissed Sun and accepted Nguyen Hue's effort
to negotiate peace, which included the recognition of vassal status.

The campaign had not been helped by the lack of domestic (Vietnamese) support for the incompetent Le ruler, while the Vietnamese
were well familiar with the use of firearms. At the same time, there was
no Chinese tradition of sustained attempts at conquest in Southeast
Asia, where a Vietnamese revolt had overthrown only recently established Chinese control in 1429, the area was not of crucial strategic interest, and the heavily forested environment was unsuitable for Manchu
cavalry.[13] China was to fail anew when it attacked Vietnam in 1979.

Strategic prioritization, therefore, itself a product of a number of
attitudes and factors, was not the sole issue in respective Chinese failure
or success in different areas. In addition, there were important environmental and political factors. They presumably were fed back into
assumptions and prioritization, but it is unclear how and how far. For reasons of terrain and climate, cavalry, the key Manchu element, could not
function adequately on the southern borders, while the heavily forested
environment there was very difficult for large-scale military operations
and certainly caused delays that exacerbated logistical issues. Disease
also proved a crippling problem in operations in Myanmar. In addition,
the military organization and achievement of Myanmar was greatly
improved in the 1750s and 1760s by its dynamic new ruler, Alaung-hpaya,
although he focused on campaigning against Siam (Thailand), a pattern
that was to be repeated in the 1780s. Environmental factors were more
generally significant. In the case of India, the strategy of the Marathas
faced the problem that their key element, their cavalry, became nonop-
erational during the monsoon.

The extent to which the problems of campaigning were fed back
into strategic prioritization for both China and its opponents is unclear.
Indeed, the very process of framing tasks is a matter of uncertainty.
For China, strategic prioritization was also apparently involved in the
relationship between focusing on outer borders as opposed to inner

borderlands. Indeed, this focus has been regarded as the cause of growing social disorder and opposition in the latter, opposition that led to large-scale uprisings, particularly the White Lotus Rising in the 1790s.[14]

The alternative opportunities that were not pursued are striking. The Mongols, after, as a result of major and sustained efforts, they had conquered China in the thirteenth century, had (unsuccessfully) pursued maritime expansion against Japan and Java. In contrast, Manchu goals by sea were restricted to nearby Taiwan, gained in 1683. There was no attempt to invade Japan as a counter to earlier Japanese expansionism into Korea in the 1590s, nor, on land, any wish to repeat the brief frontier war with Russia in 1683–89 and to drive the Russians back beyond Lake Baikal repeating the success and range shown against the Zunghars. As a result, the Manchu heartland was not to be protected and expanded to north and northwest as it had been to the south, although expansion to the north and northwest would have been across barren terrain.

Like the Ming and the Mughals in India, the Manchu maintained coastal navies and were not interested in strategic power projection outside China and India. Their strategies were continental in nature, and to a considerable degree, Manchu expansion in Central Asia in the eighteenth century and Mughal operations in Afghanistan in the seventeenth century both arose from attempts to stabilize key frontiers including integrating their enemies within the imperial framework. Similarly, in India, the Marathas in the mid-eighteenth century sought to secure the Indus frontier.

In the process of framing tasks, the role of determined and successful leadership appears readily apparent. The personal determination of the Kangxi (r. 1662–1722) and Qianlong (r. 1736–95) emperors was crucial to the defeat of the Zunghars. Both made it a personal crusade and pushed hard those generals who were more hesitant about campaigning on the steppe. The latter, indeed, was a risky proposition in part for military reasons, including logistics, but also for political ones focused on the unreliability of local support. The Kangxi emperor wanted victory, and he appreciated the transient nature of the possession of territory, as opposed to the destruction of the opposing army. In turn, the Qianlong emperor, who was well versed in dynastic history, wished to surpass the achievements of his grandfather, the Kangxi emperor, by putting an end to the frontier problem. He essentially did so and notably so on the steppe. The destruction of the Zunghars brought control over the Mongols while, farther to the west, the Kazakhs accepted tributary status. In France, Louis XIV (r. 1643–1715) was similarly affected by the reputation of his grandfather, Henry IV (r. 1589–1610), and not interested in the example set by his father, Louis XIII, who was regarded as less successful and, in a psychologically significant fashion, less manly.

The importance of personality is illustrated by the Qianlong emperor's predecessor and successor, as neither was so successful. The Yongzheng emperor (r. 1723–35) launched only one expedition against the Zunghars and did not persist after its defeat at Hoton Nor in 1731, which suggests that had he ruled for long, the Zunghars might have revived and expanded. Neither was this reign characterized by major military initiatives. This point, however, raises the questions of assessment and of how best to characterize strategy. The Yongzheng emperor's financial reforms laid the basis of the Qianlong emperor's military successes; each was a strategy toward a policy of triumph. The Yongzheng emperor established a grand council to facilitate the conduct of the conflict with the Zunghars, and its remit was expanded under his successor in order to receive and analyze monthly reports of grain prices across China and thus guide the use of stockpiled grain.[15]

By the end of the eighteenth century, China was at peace with all its neighbors and on acceptable terms. Russia had tried in the 1720s to gain from Persian weakness and more consistently, was not willing to respect the territorial integrity of Poland or Turkey and successfully pursued expansionism at their expense. In contrast, the boundaries with China negotiated in 1689 and 1728 were accepted by Russia. Within China, nomadic peoples increasingly found their movement and pastures under direction. More generally, bureaucratic control by government appointees was repeatedly pushed in place of an earlier reliance of control of non-Han peoples via tribal chiefs. The strategies against risings were more brutal. As in response to the Miao revolts in Hunan and Guizhou in 1795–97, they included the creation of garrison positions, building walls, introducing military agricultural colonists, and employing brutal repression.

Yet, for China, as elsewhere, the extent to which there was strategic consistency is unclear, and this situation undermines any attempts to suggest a single strategic culture or, a very different point, to point to geopolitical determinism. Instead, the situation repeatedly returns us to the realm of history, in the shape of considering the role of choice in developments, the impact of the past, and its remaking under the stress of circumstances, ideas, personalities, and their repeated and inconstant interplay.

RUSSIA

As with China, Russian strategy was characterized by "the application of overwhelming force" to specific objectives, creating a perception of strength and invincibility[16] and aiding the success both of military operations and of their fulfilment in a new political order. Adam Smith observed:

> Whoever examines, with attention, the improvements which Peter the Great [r. 1689–1725] introduced into the Russian empire, will find that they almost all resolve themselves into the establishment of a well-regulated standing army. It is the instrument which executes and maintains all his other regulations. That degree of order and internal peace, which that empire has ever since enjoyed, is altogether owing to the influence of that army.[17]

As in the case of China, Turkey (the Ottomans), and Britain, Russia faced a range of different challenges and operated in markedly contrasting military and political environments. In this, each of these powers differed from Prussia and albeit less markedly, France under Napoleon, and this point compromises the military reputations of the latter. However, China, Turkey, Britain, and Russia were far from identical in their political cultures and spheres of operation. Indeed, China and Turkey did not engage in transoceanic operations in this century, while those of Russia were not on the scale of Britain. Only France and Spain came close to matching Britain in this respect.

Taking Britain out of the equation for this reason and because of its political structure and culture, there were major similarities between Russia, China, and Turkey, notably the need to deal with large-scale domestic risings (which was also seen with Britain) and also the marked contrast between operating on the frontiers against major polities with large forces and against far more diffuse polities with smaller forces. Thus, Prussia, Myanmar, and Persia, for Russia, China, and Turkey, respectively, were very different to native peoples in northeast Siberia and the southwestern borderlands of China or the Bedouin, respectively. In every case, however, there was felt to be the need to maintain control as well as concern about the possible consequences of failure.

This need and concern, indeed, helped ensure the need to command the narrative in the shape of reporting success. This was the situation even if this supposed success was in practice problematic in its extent or consequences. The contrast between achievement and presentation could create a major tension over the perception of strategy. Failure could be perceived as reflecting a lack of divine support and thus as an existential challenge. In that respect, success and failure were about far more in the domestic sense than the pursuit of *gloire* in order to strengthen control.

Separately, there was also the issue of the relationships between addressing insurrections and confronting foreign rivals. In the 1770s, China did not resume its unsuccessful campaigns against Myanmar, and Russia did not sustain its successful war with Turkey in part because both had to confront large-scale insurrections: the Second Jinchuan War and the Pugachev rising, respectively. Each insurrection in large part arose from the difficulties of control over a region that traditionally enjoyed considerable autonomy. That these choices, respectively, entailed not resuming an unsuccessful war and cutting short a successful war indicated the far from fixed interrelationship of strategic tasks, challenges and opportunities, and therefore, the danger of reading from individual cases. This is the case not only for particular chronological conjunctures but also for individual states as a whole.

For Russia, as for other societies, the legacy of the past was crucial. The Romanovs, like the Manchu, and later, like the Communists in both Russia and China, had gained power as a result of a fundamental crisis, one that had linked insurrections to attacks from abroad. That this process occurred in the seventeenth century, albeit in the 1610s, and not further back in time, helped ensure the prominence of the memory. The same was true for the Bourbons, albeit for the 1590s for France and the 1700s–10s for Spain, and for the Hanoverians in Britain, albeit for the 1710s. In Russia, the Romanovs had been the key beneficiaries of overcoming this threat, whereas in China, it was the Manchu who rose to power through this process. In each case, however, there was an awareness of the past. Indeed, such a "deep history" was more generally true for dynastic systems and for ones that grounded their legitimacy upon the reality and presentation of continuity. In part, such a grounding could lead to a refusal to give due attention to earlier dynasties.[18]

The challenge of the 1600s–10s might have appeared very distant after the consolidation of Romanov power under Michael (r. 1613–45) and the large-scale military activity, especially against Poland and Sweden, under Alexis (r. 1645–76), but in practice, this challenge recurred in the 1700s. Sweden and Poland were the international players in the earlier "time of troubles," and Russia's heavy defeat in 1700 at Narva at the hands of Charles XII of Sweden was followed by his overthrow of Peter the Great's alliance system with Charles's conquest of Poland and his replacement as king there in 1704 of Peter's ally, Elector Augustus II of Saxony, by his own protégé, Stanislaus Lesczczynski. Repeated victories by Russian forces over Polish-Saxon armies, however, demonstrated the difficulties of translating victory into political outcomes and the consequent need to win in order to maintain control of the situation. The intervention in Polish politics underlined the role of choice in strategy. Then, in 1708, Charles invaded Russia in combination with Ivan Mazepa, the rebellious hetman of the Cossacks, thus reopening an issue of major concern in the 1640s–60s and the 1680s. Even after being heavily defeated at Poltava in Ukraine in 1709, Charles continued to pose a threat to Russia for he fled to Turkey and played a role in court politics there. He helped direct Turkey against Peter, who was defeated in the subsequent Russo-Turkish war at the river Prut in 1711.

Again, this might appear an irrelevant memory as a result of Peter's overrunning of much of the Swedish Empire, such that when the Great Northern War came to an end in 1721 with the Treaty of Nystad, Russia very much appeared the rising power: under the treaty, Russia annexed Estonia and Livonia and returned Finland. The development of a navy made Peter's gains and reputed schemes appear more threatening. Nevertheless, Russian anxieties about the present and future continued from the 1730s to draw on concerns about the past. In 1733, Russian military intervention in Poland was primarily in order to prevent the election as king of Stanislaus Lesczczynski, who had been earlier chosen at the behest of Charles XII, only to be driven out by Peter the Great after Poltava.

The strategic threat was clear at the international level, where it was alliance politics that provided the crucial equations of strength and sphere of competition. This was true in details and at the larger scale. In the late 1730s, bold Russian schemes at the expense of the Turks collapsed, not so much due to military difficulties, for Russia was increasingly successful, but because of the breakdown of the supporting diplomatic coalition as, encouraged by France, Austria made peace with the Turks in 1739. Conversely, Russian policymakers were concerned that a hostile Poland might seek to revise territorial losses to Russia in the seventeenth century, and might cooperate with Sweden and Turkey in opposing Russia. These concerns remained, with France trying to operate such an alliance in the late 1730s and early 1740s and again were seen in play with the French *secret du roi* policy of the 1750s–70s and subsequently with French and then British opposition to Russian expansionism in the 1780s, the early 1790s, and in the nineteenth century.

Russian concerns thus rested on a basis of real plans and hopes on the part of others, although the concerns were extrapolated into a more fixed pattern of threat. Moreover, this was one that was located not only in terms of Russian anxieties but also with reference to a strong and growing feeling of entitlement to dominate Eastern Europe. In opposition to defeated Sweden, weak Poland, Muslim Turkey, and distant France, Russia, at least in the person of Alexis and even more clearly under his son, Peter the Great, felt that it had a destiny and right to be the dominant power, an attitude that continues to the present, as in strategy toward Ukraine.

In this context, in the eighteenth century for Russia strategy, or what would later be termed *strategiia*, was largely a matter of keeping potential opponents separate and of exploiting the ability to focus on individual ones. For example, the invasion of the Turkish Empire in 1711 followed the crushing defeat of Charles XII at Poltava in 1709, while the successful end of the Great Northern War with Sweden in 1721 was to be succeeded in 1722–23 by successful Russian campaigning in the eastern Caucasus and northern Persia. In turn, Persian revival under Nadir Shah led Russia to return gains in 1735 in order to try to ensure that Nadir did not settle with the Turks. He did so in 1736, which put Russia in a far more difficult strategic situation than would otherwise have been the case. So also with Frederick II of Prussia's need in the 1740s for Austria to focus on Bavaria and France rather than Prussia and his wish during the Seven Years' War to force opponents to separate peace agreements, which encouraged him to focus on the most vulnerable—Austria.[19]

Strategic success did not always require formal hostilities. Instead, intimidation and influence worked with both Poland and Sweden, although different methods were used. Against Sweden, Russian strategic capability was very different to that in the conflicts between the two powers in the sixteenth and seventeenth centuries. The deployment of galley-borne Russian troops in the eighteenth century was a challenge to Swedish security that became an important aspect of Baltic power politics. Aside from wars between the two powers, there were also frequent threats of Russian attack—for example, in 1749 and 1772—as Russia sought to affect or direct Swedish policy. The ability to affect or seek to affect policy by means of intimidation linked strategy and the flow of international relations, giving a point to military preparedness and ensuring that war was not the only measure of strategy.

Russian policy was rather like Chinese in that the pace of expansionism varied by individual rulers. In the case of Russia, it is easier than with China to note the role of court factionalism, in large part because there were foreign envoys able and eager to report on the matter. These envoys were linked to prominent Russian figures, each seeking to influence the other. A somewhat overly factionalized account of Russian policy was presented as a result, but this account presented the extent to which rivalries between ministers and other figures indeed largely played out in terms of diplomatic alignments. Military events proved a major part of this politics. Foreign commentators also speculated on which frontier was more sensitive and thus on Russia's likely strategy.[20]

The ability of Russia to deploy troops westward into Europe was a key strategic tool, both militarily and diplomatically. The consequences were unclear. Thus, in January 1748, Frederick II of Prussia observed the need to establish if such a deployment would impose on French policy.[21] The deployment led to planning and speculation both pro and anti, as with the unfounded suggestion by the French envoy in Dresden that France would invade Germany in order to block Russia's march.[22]

Russian strategic capability was repeatedly enhanced as a consequence of organizational improvements. For example, during the Seven Years' War, the Russian army made operational and tactical progress, including in the use of field fortifications and light troops and the handling of battle formations. The adoption of more flexible means of supply helped to cut the baggage train of the field army, making it less like that of an oriental host. The slow rate of march had affected the assumptions of other powers,[23] but the daily rate increased during the Seven Years' War, although logistics remained makeshift. This had a serious impact on operations—for example, forcing the Russian army to retreat to the Vistula in late 1760.[24] General Korsakov's army crossed the Russian frontier on May 15, 1799, and reached Prague two months later, an average daily speed of less than fifteen miles,[25] but one that still delivered capability.

A different form of enhancement was seen in the war with Turkey in 1768–74 in which under the leadership of Count Peter Rumyantsev, traditional linear tactics were replaced by independent columns able to reform into hollow squares and to provide mobility and firepower. These tactics prefigured those of Revolutionary France, although the Russians tended to compartmentalize their military experience and to argue that conflict on their southern steppe required distinctive practices to those necessary for victory against Western forces.[26] This offers an important reminder of the significance of command decisions for relationships between organizational effectiveness and strategic capability.

JAPAN

Unlike in the sixteenth, nineteenth, and twentieth centuries, Japan did not fight China, nor unlike in the twentieth century, did it fight Russia. In 1792, a Russian request to open diplomatic and commercial relations led a hostile Japan to order the establishment of coastal defenses, but nothing happened because the Russians did not pursue the matter.[27] Conflict, trade, and disease all played a role in the extension of Japanese rule over the Ainu of Hokkaido, but this was a peripheral engagement.[28]

Despite a lack of large-scale conflict, there was an earlier sense of strategic understanding that is instructive because it indicates that conflict was not necessary to the existence of such a sense. The word *Hei-ho* was the equivalent of *strategy* or, more specifically, *war strategy*. "*Hei*" means soldiers and "*ho*," in this case, "rule" or "the way to follow." "*Hei-ho*" is sometimes translated as the "art of war." In addition, the words *Hei-gaku* and *Gun-gaku* could mean *study of strategy*: "*Gun*" means *army* and "*Gaku*" means *study*.

In Japan, the study of military strategy had emerged in the early seventeenth century. It was founded on several Chinese classics, and later, on the basis of these key texts, several schools developed. Together with other disciplines, such as the study of Confucianism and that of medicine, this study of military strategy became one of the important disciplines in Japan during the Edo period, that is from the beginning of the seventeenth century to the mid-nineteenth century. During this period, almost no war occurred in Japan and even actual military mobilization was extremely rare. Peasant revolts were the major military issue. As a result, as the Edo period (1600–1869) progressed, the study of military strategy became less practical. Moreover, being influenced by Confucianism, the theories of some schools came to assume a moralistic tone on the pattern of Western developments over the last half century. In Japan, more modern and practical concepts of military strategy did not emerge until the arrival of Western military science in the early nineteenth century via the Dutch.

TURKEY

The strategic legacy of the Ottoman Empire was a long one, with, again, functional and ideological factors playing a role, as did the need to reconcile priorities on different frontiers and the interests of specific groups within the empire. Linked to an active process of information gathering that was readily apparent from the sixteenth century,[29] Ottoman forces could be deployed in accordance with a strategy based on a considered analysis of intelligence and policy options.[30] Geography was certainly an element in prioritization and in the response to it. In particular, there were major problems in campaigning against Persia. As far as bases were concerned, Baghdad was 1,334 miles from Constantinople, compared with Belgrade's 597. Moreover, there was no sea and river route to Iraq comparable to the Black Sea and the Danube and Dniester rivers to ease campaigning and logistics. Conversely, it was easier for Persian rulers to campaign against the Turks in modern-day Iraq than into Central Asia, Afghanistan, or even India. This strategic asymmetry served as a key element in helping frame the conflict between Turks and Persians but did not dictate its course. Such strategic asymmetries are more generally important.

The situation in Turkey became more dynamic due to the experience of serious failure from the 1680s, failure linked to the overthrow of sultans in 1703 and 1730. The eighteenth century was to be seen as one of Ottoman decline, with strategy "done to" the empire, rather than being done by it—an aspect of strategy as relative. However, to a degree, that is an overly simplistic approach as well as a misleading assessment that only emerges as plausible in hindsight. It was certainly the case at the outset that the empire appeared to be in great difficulties. Important territories were conquered by Austria, Poland, Russia, and Venice in 1684–97, and the peace treaties of 1699–1700, notably the Peace of Carlowitz of 1699, saw the Turks make major territorial cessions, particularly most of Hungary to Austria and the Morea (Peloponnese) to Venice. Defeat helped lead to political crisis. Sultan Mustafa II was regarded as compromising Muslim honor by accepting Carlowitz, which was a peace entailing recognition of Christian Europe, rather than merely a truce. These terms contributed to a crisis of authority in 1703 that led to Mustafa's overthrow.[31] In turn, major defeat at the hands of Austria in 1716–17 was followed by significant territorial cessions (in modern Hungary, Romania, and Serbia) in the Peace of Passarowitz in 1718. Subsequently, the mismanagement of war with Persia, led to the overthrow of Mustafa's successor, Ahmed III, in 1730. In 1737–39, Russia achieved major successes against Turkey, including capturing Iasi, the capital of Moldavia in 1739.

These events contributed to the strain of war on the empire. Whereas that strain was scarcely a novel feature, it had been accompanied for most of the period up to the 1580s by a high level of success, a level that had brought glory and profit. Each had acted as the lubricant of success. The situation had become more problematic from the 1590s, contributing to a mid-seventeenth century political crisis for the empire. Revival from the 1650s had indicated the resilience of a political culture in which bellicose values helped ease the experience of war or at least maintained the determination of the leadership and elite.

However, this element of elite strategic culture was accompanied by changes in the socioeconomic and political contexts that altered the parameters for Turkish war-making. An absence of new conquests and success in battle acted as a powerful constraint, causing a loss of prestige as well as a lack of pillage and fresh land to distribute. Alongside political tensions, the inability to pay the army reduced the sultan's control and led to rebellions, notably in 1717–19 and more seriously in 1730. Moreover, desertion affected the number of Turkish troops, and in an important shift in the capacity for implementation, there was an increased need to turn to provincial militias as well as to forces raised by local strongmen. These were important to a more general crisis in recruitment and command practices.[32] As a related point but at a different level and tempo, one that created a dynamic that contrasted with that in the past, the Turks were a settled society and developed state and no longer the apparently inexorable people that had terrified Westerners in the fifteenth and sixteenth centuries.

Linked to this, moving onto the defensive created serious problems for the Turkish Empire, both structurally and in terms of ethos. There was a marked deficiency in preparations for defenses. Nevertheless, key fortresses, such as Ochakov, were improved. This defensive emphasis and improvement to fortifications affected strategy. The greater strength of fortresses, the determination to secure territorial gains, and the need to dominate supply routes ensured that sieges were very significant in campaigning north of the Black Sea, as in the Danube Valley where they had for long been to the fore. The Turkish fortresses on the rivers athwart Russia's advance into the Balkans, such as Izmail and Silistria on the Danube, played a key role in campaigns, affecting Russian mobility.

Changes in goals were significant. In particular, there was no attempt to intervene against Austria and Russia in the War of the Austrian Succession (1740–48) and Seven Years' War (1756–63), as Frederick II would have liked, because such intervention would have lessened the pressure on Prussia. As a result, Holdernesse wrote of Mustafa III (r. 1757–74) that if he had "a military turn . . . the least surmise of that kind cannot fail, in the present conjuncture, to have the greatest influence upon the affairs of Europe."[33] There was no such intervention. As a consequence, the pacific Koca Mehmed Ragib Pasha, *reis* (foreign minister) and grand vizier for much of 1741–63, was a significant figure in the military history of the period. In 1764–65, moreover, Turkey refused to respond forcibly to Russian intervention in Poland as France would have liked.

In contrast, despite heavy costs and repeated defeats at the hands of Russia in 1768–74, in part due to the absence then of an effective plan, it was the Turks who took local disputes in the 1780s to the state of full-scale war. Turkey declared war in 1787 having decided to fight until Russia was driven from the Caucasus and Crimea, the latter a loss in 1783 that compromised the force structure of the Turkish army.

Whether on the offensive or on the defensive, it was necessary for the Turks to consider their range of possible commitments. For example, in 1715, the Turks were encouraged to turn against Venice by the absence of problems elsewhere: Russia had been beaten and there was peace with Persia which was under pressure from Afghan rebellions. Looking forward to the opportunity to regain the Morea, the Turks were also angered by the refuge granted by Venice to Montenegrins who had unsuccessfully rebelled in 1711 against Turkish control. In turn, the Austrian ruler, Charles VI, allied with Venice in 1716 because he was no longer anxious about a weakened France, Austria's recent opponent, but one affected not only by defeat but also by the political instability following the accession of the infant Louis XV in 1715. Turkish ministers and foreign envoys seeking a Turkish focus on one opponent tried to ensure peace for Turkey elsewhere.[34]

Alongside disadvantages, the Turks defeated the Russians in 1711, the Venetians in 1715, and the Austrians in 1739. Western commentators were concerned. In 1715, Sir Robert Sutton, the British envoy in Constantinople, warned about the possible consequences of Turkish success: "If they are suffered to possess themselves of the Morea, now they are grown so powerful at sea and growing daily stronger, the kingdoms of Naples and Sicily, as well as all Italy will lie greatly exposed to their insults." In 1732, the French envoy in Rome thought the major issue was whether the

Turks would attack the Christian powers, and in 1740 his counterpart in Constantinople commented on the size and logistical capability of the Turkish army.[35] In 1739, the Austrians obtained peace but at the cost of ceding Belgrade, northern Serbia, and western Wallachia, thus reversing many of the Austrian gains under the Peace of Passarowitz. These successes emphasized the difficulties, then and now, of assessing effectiveness and of advancing the concept of strategic redundancy.

The conceptualization of strategy took time. In the 1850s, the Turks began to use the term *sevkülceys*, the dictionary meaning of which is *strategy* in the sense of managing the troops. The Turks employed more general terms, such as *art of war* or *business of war*, for *strategy* earlier.

AUSTRIA

The quality of the scholarly work on Austrian foreign policy and the wealth of archival material permits an understanding of the role of political contention within the governing elite and its significance for whatever may be dubiously segregated as foreign policy, policy, and strategy. In particular, individual lobbies and ministers were associated with an emphasis on specific geographical areas and as a result, with particular approaches toward their interdependence.

The peace treaties of 1713–14 reflected the significant downplaying of past Austrian and Spanish dynastic policies and the emergence of a geopolitical approach to war and diplomacy that focused on the hereditary provinces, the *Erblande*, and an approach that centered on regional challenges.[36] In 1718, the Austrians abandoned their successful war with the Turks in order to cope with the crisis created in Italy by Spanish expansionism.

The military was integral to the process of focusing on specific areas, and not separate from it or charged only with implementation. Thus, Prince Eugene, the president of the Council of War, was identified in the 1720s and 1730s with attempts to protect recent gains from the Turks by strengthening fortress cities and building up local militias[37] and with a diplomatic strategy. The latter contered on developing good relations with Britain, Prussia, and Russia. Moreover, Eugene sought to further this goal by means of having protégés, several from a military background, appointed as diplomats, and also by pursuing a personal correspondence with diplomats. This process extended to military figures who served other rulers and were judged appropriate as means to influence policies and thus give effect to strategy. General Diemar of Hesse-Cassel and General Grumbkow of Prussia were leading examples.[38]

In turn, in the 1720s and 1730s, there were alternative prescriptions. A strategy of cooperation with France was pushed particularly hard by the chancellor, Count Sinzendorf, one of cooperation with Spain, by the Marquis of Rialp, and a Catholic, authoritarian stance hostile to German Protestant princes by Count Schönborn, each also major officeholders.[39] These were strategies designed to serve the policy of dynastic interests, notably aggrandizement but at least security. These strategies had implications that were defined or at least affected by the probabilities of particular enemies and allies. Geographical priorities were in part a matter of responses to an assessment of the threat environment. Strategy had to adapt to the dynamic character of this assessment, with offensive and defensive priorities changing accordingly but also being adopted in an attempt to shape this very dynamism and to reflect political exigencies. Generals were participants in the continued struggle of military politics and pursued approaches to campaigning based on whose interest their ambition allied them with.[40]

Austria was in a very different position to China, not least because of issues of scale but also due to the real or potential interconnectedness of these threats. For China, there was a relationship in the first half of the century between stability in both Mongolia and Tibet and the threat from the Zunghar Confederation, but there was no equivalent for nonneighboring threats. In contrast, Austria had to face attempts at cooperation by its opponents as well as the consequences for such cooperation arising from its size and location. Thus, in the Thirty Years' War (1618–48), as in 1703–4 during the War of the Spanish Succession, there was attempted cooperation with hostile advancing Hungarians, in the first case by Bohemian rebels and in the second by Bavaria,[41] and similar efforts were made on other occasions. Linked to this, France's concept of an Eastern alliance system proved highly adaptable. Developed against the Habsburgs in the early sixteenth century, with the Turks and the

German Protestants playing the key alliance roles, this concept subsequently also encompassed, or sought to include, Denmark, Sweden,
Poland, Russia, and Hungarian rebels.

In the eighteenth century, this strategy changed as France's international position altered, but the strategy also explained military moves.
The dispatch of a French squadron to the Baltic in 1739 was designed to
encourage a Swedish attack on Russia, which was then allied to Austria, and that of French forces to attack the Habsburg heartland in 1741
was seen as a way to keep Prussia and Saxony in the French alliance
system. As a consequence, a key element for Austria was that of thwarting these moves and possible moves. In this strategy, at once reactive
and proactive, there was no separation between military and political
dimensions.[42]

Diversionary attacks were a prime strategic resource. Thus, in
November 1746, during the War of the Austrian Succession, Austrian
forces invaded Provence in southern France from northern Italy. Encouraged by the British and supported by their navy, the invasion was in part
mounted to divert French efforts from the Low Countries.

The prime change in Austrian strategy was one that arose from
alterations in rulers. Whereas the Kangxi and Qianlong emperors of
China had both been focused on the Zunghars, there was a major change
between Charles VI (r. 1711–40) and his eldest grandson, Joseph II (r.
1780–90). As a legacy of his struggle, as a second son, to take over the
Spanish Habsburg inheritance, Charles focused on the Mediterranean
and in particular, proved willing to go on listening to advisers, such
as Rialp, who had served him before he succeeded his elder brother,
Joseph I (r. 1705–11). This concern with Spain and Italy and with their
significance when Austria was involved in alliances[43] was not to characterize Charles's daughter and successor, Maria Theresa (r. 1740–80),
and even more, Joseph II. Instead, Joseph in particular responded to the
opportunities created by Polish and Turkish weakness as well as to the
need to respond to the strength and ambitions of Prussia and Russia.
This assessment was aided by the willingness of the Italian powers and
Spain to accept a territorial settlement with Austria, notably with the
Treaty of Aranjuez, in 1752, one that ensured that there was no conflict
in Italy between 1748 and 1792. Thus, strategic parameters were again

set by international needs and opportunities, each of which had a highly contingent character.

Powers that were potential allies could also be seen as threats. Russia, a key support against Prussia from 1726, was increasingly regarded as a threat to Austrian prospects in the Balkans. The Austrians feared both a Russian conquest of Crimea, which would create the possibility of an amphibious attack on Constantinople, and a Russian conquest of Moldavia and Wallachia, which would open the Balkans to Russian penetration.[44]

Defeat at the hands of Prussia in the early 1740s led to a major attempt to revive and strengthen the Austrian state and military and thus to be prepared for whatever challenge occurred. This was an aspect of strategy that was not too different to the more specifically military policy of preparing and maintaining fortifications. The strengthening of the military involved a structural process of reform designed to raise and support greater numbers. These made it possible to envisage more wide-ranging commitments—for example, the planning for war with both the Turks and Prussia in 1790—as well as to deploy larger field forces, such as those that thwarted the Prussian invasions of Bohemia in 1778 and 1779.

There had been an earlier attempt at strengthening the state after the War of the Spanish Succession, one in particular using protectionism to develop trade and industry. This strategy clashed with the British attempt to develop trade with the *Erblande* in order to make it part of an informal empire of British trade, an attempt pursued without success by Britain in the late 1730s, that was designed to have direct consequences for power politics.

The case of Austria offers a means to consider other empires including some of those already discussed. The need to reconcile a range of commitments was more pressing than for states of a smaller scale. That raises the issue of the relationship between state size and strategy, which is one way to approach the issue of geopolitics. The problems of strategy appear much greater as the scale of an empire increased. Possibly, that also encouraged the exercise of what we can term strategy. This would provide another instance of the process by which the issues and problems of imperial governance, more generally, encouraged a search for new governmental solutions and political languages. Strategy can in part be located in this context.

SPAIN

With Spain, strategy was very much linked both to rulers and to dynastic issues. The crucial consideration was that the new dynasty that replaced the Spanish Habsburgs in 1700, a cadet branch of the French Bourbons under Philip V (r. 1700–46), the younger grandson of Louis XIV, only acquired part of the inheritance as a result of the consequent War of the Spanish Succession. The quest for the remainder, most of which was in Italy, was enhanced by the independent Italian dynastic interests of Philip's second wife, Elisabeth Farnese, a member of the ruling House of Parma. Ambitious policies in Italy led Spain into three wars in 1717–20, 1733–35, and 1741–48. To that end, the army and navy were greatly strengthened and made more fit for purpose.[45]

Capability followed ambition, and Spanish strategy is best understood in terms of this equation. Thus, Spanish naval power was rapidly revived in the late 1710s. This revival indicated a key point about strategy. Despite the limitations of the Spanish navy militarily,[46] it had by 1717 achieved its strategic purpose of enabling Philip to take an aggressive stance in the Mediterranean. This capability fell foul in 1718 of British opposition and also suffered then from a lack of French support. Indeed, the Anglo-French alliance was a precondition of the effective British response to Spanish naval power in 1718, and this remained a factor until the alliance collapsed in 1731.

As the uncle of Louis XV, who did not have a son until 1729, Philip maneuvered to retain his interest in the French royal succession, which underlined the difficulty of seeing states as distinct units. Indeed, within France, Philip had the benefit of figures of influence who looked to his interests. These diplomatic goals were central to his international and military strategies, which are best considered as means to further these goals, means that were adapted, combined, and discarded in accordance with the nuances of court politics. The latter were unstable and divisive.[47] In turn, Philip found that bilateral relations were affected by broader-ranging international concern. For example, Britain, in its relations with Spain, was very concerned by the issue of Portuguese security.

Under Ferdinand VI (r. 1746–59), Philip's surviving son by his first marriage, the emphasis shifted to what can be seen as more national goals, although it is necessary to be cautious in counterpointing dynastic and national interests because the sovereign and the state were often perceived as one. From the end of the war in 1748, expenditure on the navy increased greatly and its size rose rapidly. This made the navy a more important element in discussions about the Anglo-French naval balance, a situation accentuated by the growing importance of colonial considerations in the strategies of the three governments.

This process was continued by Ferdinand's half-brother, Carlos III (r. 1759–88), who added a particular focus on the pursuit of the strengthening of the Spanish Empire. Thus, strategy was overwhelmingly a matter of responding to royal priorities.[48] At the same time, foreign diplomats discerned public opinion as existing there. Benjamin Keene, a British envoy long experienced in Spain, reported in 1749:

> The putting an end to so destructive a war has been so agreeable to
> all ranks of people, that here is not a person of any distinction of one
> sex but what has been to visit me, nor of the other that has not sent me
> compliments, and even the lower sort have shown their satisfaction at
> seeing me again in this country.[49]

BURMA AND SIAM

Imperial sway was on a continuum with the attempts of powers to gain control over weaker polities. For example, Burma (Myanmar), Siam (Thailand), and Vietnam all saw a mixture of external warfare and state-building by force. There was a process of competitive state-building, a process in which outside powers, notably China, played an episodic role. Operations revealed what would generally be considered strategic planning. In 1785, conscripting about two hundred thousand men, Bo-daw-hpaya of Myanmar (r. 1781–1819) launched an advance on Siam from the north, as well as a pincer offensive on southern Siam focused on Junk Ceylon/Phuket Island. In the latter, one force moved overland from Tenasserim through the Kra Isthmus, while a second force proceeded by sea from Tavoy. However, the campaign failed because of Siamese attacks on Myanmar's communications.

Instability in individual states encouraged intervention by others, as by China in Vietnam in the 1780s. In addition, there was an attempt to assert suzerainty over weaker neighbors, as Siam did over the northern Malay sultanates in the 1780s. For individual rulers, it is appropriate to consider their strategic choices and military effectiveness by looking at the totality of their commitments. Thus, commitments on Burma's western frontier help explain its failures against Siam in the 1780s. At the same time, Burmese failure against Siam also reflected leadership factors on both sides, as well as the development of effective defensive strategies by the Siamese.

The Siamese strategic approach against the Burmese invasions in the eighteenth century was primarily the defense in depth that relied on the highly centralized mobilization of military subjects in the capitals and the nearby fortified cities. In addition, Taksin (r. 1767–82) successfully reasserted Siamese hegemony over Laos and Cambodia, which allowed Siam to obtain more manpower. Under Rama I (r. 1782–1809) Siamese strategy switched to a preemptive defense focused on defeating the Burmese at the borders: operating guerrilla warfare to harass and exhaust Burmese supplies before using the main army to defeat the Burmese. In 1785–86, this strategic shift occurred. Such a strategic trajectory had also occurred in the sixteenth and seventeenth century, which reflected the need to choose between different modes of defensive warfare. Manpower was a key element and one necessary in order to wage aggressive wars. At the same time, the decline of the corvée system obliged Siam to conduct more military ventures in order to forcefully gather more manpower. These and other instances underline the need for a complex reading of effectiveness and strategy and for a wariness toward glib dismissals. Moreover, consideration of this region encourages disquiet about explanations of Europe's rise in terms of a distinctive bellicosity and political fragmentation.[50]

CONCLUSIONS

Public politics were far less clearly to the fore in the empires discussed in this chapter than in the case of Britain and France. However, work on later authoritarian and even totalitarian political systems has indicated that they also had a public politics. This was also the case in the eighteenth century. In part, the symbolism of success staged by the empires of the period represented an attempt to get to grips with its public politics. Linked to this, the achievement of success was a key point. Indeed, this underlined a central aspect of strategy. It was frequently not a matter of achieving specific goals but rather of obtaining success. Means and ends thereby were closely linked, with the goal of war being victory itself or at least of a conflict that enabled victory to be claimed.

Alongside common tones, there were differences in strategic assumptions. In particular, the extent to which elites saw themselves as "facing an assortment of discrete, localized challenges, or a single, integrated crisis involving the empire as a whole"[51] varied. There was a contrast between a wide-ranging struggle for alliances on the part of many empires and the extent to which no such challenge was seen in the case of China and Japan, and notably for the former after the Zunghars were crushed in 1757. There were, therefore, no foreign threats leading to pressure for military modernization.

Relationships between strategic assumptions, in turn, created a wider strategic context. This was seen in the dynamics at particular geopolitical levels. Thus, in Europe, the course of conflict served to prevent the emergence of a hegemonic power. For example, by 1735, Don Carlos, Philp V's elder son by his second marriage (later Charles III of Spain), was established in Naples and Sicily after a decisive victory over the Austrians the previous year at Bitonto, one of the most underrated battles of the century. Thus, the Austrian hegemony in Italy, which had been created by military victories in the 1700s and affirmed in the peace settlement of 1713–14, had been overthrown in southern Italy. This was important in the challenging of the Austrian reach for more general predominance, and prefigured the Prussian success in doing the same against the Austrians in Germany and East Central Europe in the 1740s and 1750s.

As a result, the absence of a European hegemony was related to the failure of hegemonic ambitions in particular regions of Europe. The interaction of the latter involved rival coalitions, military prioritization, and diplomatic strategy, each a key element of European power politics.

The overthrow of the Austrian position in southern Italy was an aspect of the failure of such regional ambition. The interaction of developments in particular spheres was also seen in 1740 when Frederick II of Prussia's decision to invade Silesia owed much to Russia's inability to help Austria at that point.[52]

The course of Frederick's campaigning also indicated a key element of strategic opportunity on land—namely, the opening and closure both of capability advantages and of equivalents in the international system. This was the case with the anti-Austrian coalition of 1741 and with the tactic of the oblique attack, just as was subsequently to be the case for French war-making in 1792–1815 and for its Prussian/German counterpart in 1866–1945. Frederick was to find that the offensive-defensive dichotomy he had used during the Seven Years' War did not work in the War of the Bavarian Succession (1778–79) when the Austrian reliance on the defensive, at the tactical, operational, and strategic levels, denied Frederick the opportunity to catch advancing forces at a vulnerable moment. In addition, Frederick did not benefit then from the inherent problems of coalition warfare, the lack of cooperation that his opponents had demonstrated during the Seven Years' War. In February 1760, reporting that Frederick thought that in the campaign he would be outnumbered by 250,000 troops to 90,000, Andrew Mitchell, the British envoy, noted, "The King of Prussia is reduced to the fatal necessity of depending upon the faults and blunders of his enemies."[53]

The Austrian success in the War of the Bavarian Succession ensured that ancien régime warfare appeared indecisive, thus, subsequently putting a focus on the success of the French Revolutionaries and later, Napoleon. That approach, however, underrates Austrian success in 1778–79. It later served Frederick's purpose to represent what had happened as a "cabinet war," and this is the misleading version that has gone down to posterity, rather than the decisive victory he in fact pursued. This war was followed by a postwar Austrian fortification strategy designed to block possible Prussian invasion routes into Bohemia, particularly at Theresienstadt (later a concentration camp) and Josefstadt, which were built to complement the prewar construction of Königgrätz. Similarly, Prussian success against the Dutch in 1787, Russian against the Turks in 1787–91, Austrian against the Turks in 1789, and Russian against the French in 1799 scarcely suggested that the ancien régime system was ineffective.

Relative strength helped ensure that strategies successful in some areas were not necessarily so elsewhere. For example, Spain in the southwest of what is now the United States was less successful in winning allies than China on the steppe. In part, this was because Spain lacked the resources and the traditions of intervention on the steppe that might serve to help win allies, but also because it did not have the powerful army that the Chinese were repeatedly able to deploy in advance of their fortifications.

Returning to the wider comparative perspective, it is readily apparent that the variety of circumstances makes it very difficult to offer a typology of military history or to see any common strand in strategic development. This is the case not solely if the basis for comparison is at the national or dynastic level, but also if it is thematic—for example, in terms of environmental, technological, international, or domestic political factors. Nor is there any marked sense of convergence on a common theme, and certainly not to the extent that was to be seen in the second half of the nineteenth century. Nevertheless, one valid strand is that of the contrast between Western transoceanic maritime power capacity and the lack of similar capability for non-Western powers, a contrast that reflected capability, opportunity, and strategic vision. The long-range plans of Western naval forces were not always successful, but no non-Western state could pursue a strategy at this range. Tipu Sultan of Mysore dispatched four warships to Basra in Iraq in 1786 in an attempt to seek Turkish support, but the failure of the mission was matched by the disastrous fate of most of the squadron. Indian rulers tended to focus on continental goals and on their armies.[54] Whereas the Turks had sent significant naval forces into the Indian Ocean in the sixteenth century, they no longer did so. This was a significant change in strategic capability and therefore in the context for Western activity, one that matched the end, in the fifteenth century, of Chinese operations into the Indian Ocean. Such changes were important to the "deep history" that established the context for strategic choices.

NOTES

1. W. Cobbett, ed., *The Parliamentary History of England from the Earliest Period to the Year 1803* (36 vols., London, 1806–20), vol. 19, col. 948.

2. P. C. Perdue, "Boundaries, Maps, and Movement: Chinese, Russian, and Mongolian Empires in Early Modern Central Eurasia," *International History Review* 20 (1998): 263–86; P. C. Perdue, *China Marches West: The Qing Conquest of Central Eurasia* (Cambridge, MA, 2005); A. Stanziani, *Bâtisseurs d'empires. Russie, Chine et Inde à la croisée des mondes, XVe–XIXe siècle* (Paris, 2012); L. Hostetler, "Imperial Competition in Eurasia: Russia and China," in J. Bentley, S. Subrahmanyam, and M. E. Wiesner-Hanks, eds., *The Cambridge World History: VI. The Construction of a Global World, 1400–1800 CE. Part 1. Foundations* (Cambridge, UK, 2015): 297–322.

3. G. Barratt, *Russia in Pacific Waters, 1715–1825* (Vancouver, BC, 1981).

4. K. M. Swope, *The Military Collapse of China's Ming Dynasty, 1618–1644* (London, 2014).

5. Walter Titley to Edward Weston, May 23, 1761, Farmington, CT, Lewis Walpole Library, Weston papers, vol. 21.

6. P. C. Perdue, "Fate and Fortune in Central Eurasian Warfare: Three Qing Emperors and Their Mongol Rivals," in N. Di Cosmo, ed., *Warfare in Inner Asian History, 500–1800* (Leiden, the Netherlands, 2002): 390, 394.

7. J. P. LeDonne, *The Grand Strategy of the Russian Empire, 1650–1831* (New York, 2004). See also W. C. Fuller, *Strategy and Power in Russia, 1600–1914* (New York, 1992).

8. H. van de Ven, ed., *Warfare in Chinese History* (Leiden, the Netherlands, 2000).

9. J. Waley-Cohen, "Religion, War and Empire-Building in Eighteenth-Century China," *International History Review* 20 (1998): 336–52.

10. J. Black, *Other Pasts, Different Presents, Alternative Futures* (Bloomington, IN, 2015).

11. J. Black, *War and Technology* (Bloomington, IN, 2013).

12. Y. Dai, *The Sichuan Frontier and Tibet: Imperial Strategy in the Early Qing* (Seattle, WA, 2009): 3.

13. T. B. Lam, "Intervention versus Tribute in Sino-Vietnamese Relations: 1788–1790," in J. K. Fairbank, ed., *The Chinese World Order: Traditional China's Foreign Relations* (Cambridge, MA, 1968): 165–79.

14. Dai, *Sichuan Frontier*: 241–42.

15. B. S. Bartlett, *Monarchs and Ministers: The Grand Council in Mid-Ch'ing China, 1723–1820* (Berkeley, CA, 1991).

16. LeDonne, *The Grand Strategy of the Russian Empire*: 221.

17. Adam Smith, *An Inquiry into the Nature and Causes of the Wealth of Nations* (Oxford, 1976): 706.

18. W. Franke, "Historical Writing during the Ming," in *The Cambridge History of China, vol. 7, pt. 1, The Ming Dynasty, 1368–1644*, edited by F. Mote and D. Twitchett (Cambridge, UK, 1988): 781–82; P. K. Crossley, *A Translucent Mirror: History and Identity in the*

Transformation of Qing Imperial Ideology (Berkeley, CA, 1999).

19. Yorke to Holdernesse, April 12, Mitchell to Holdernesse, July 8, 1758, NA. SP. 90/71, 72.

20. Amelot, French Foreign Minister, to Villeneuve, French envoy in Constantinople, November 4, 1739, W. Holst, *Carl Gustaf Tessin* (Lund, Sweden, 1931): 356.

21. Frederick II to Count Podewils, envoy in Vienna, January 1, 1748, *Polit. Corresp.* VI, 1.

22. Sir Charles Hanbury-Williams, British envoy in Dresden, to Newcastle, March 3, 1748, NA. SP. 88/69.

23. Reporting view of British government, Viry to Charles Emmanuel III, July 4, 1758, AST. LM. Ing. 63.

24. J. Keep, "Feeding the Troops: Russian Army Supply Policies during the Seven Years War," *Canadian Slavonic Papers* 29 (1987): 270, 272.

25. Lieutenant-Colonel John Ramsay, British Commissary with Korsakov, to Lord Grenville, July 14, 1799, BL. Add. 63819 fol. 2.

26. B. W. Menning, "Russian Military Innovation in the Second Half of the Eighteenth Century," *War and Society* 2 (1984): 37.

27. J. W. Hall, ed., *The Cambridge History of Japan, IV: Early Modern Japan* (Cambridge, UK, 1991): 475.

28. B. L. Walker, *The Conquest of Ainu Lands: Ecology and Culture in Japanese Expansion, 1590–1800* (Berkeley, CA, 2001).

29. G. Ágoston, "Information, Ideology, and Limits of Imperial Policy: Ottoman Grand Strategy in the Context of Ottoman-Habsburg Rivalry," in V. H. Aksan and D. Goffman, eds., *The*

Early Modern Ottomans: Remapping the Empire (Cambridge, UK, 2007): 80–81 and "Where Environmental and Frontier Studies Meet: Rivers, Forests, Marshes and Forts along the Ottoman-Hapsburg Frontier in Hungary," in A. C. S. Peacock, ed., *The Frontiers of the Ottoman World* (Oxford, 2009): 57–79; A. T. Karamustafa, "Military, Administrative, and Scholarly Maps and Plans," in J. B. Harley and D. Woodward, eds., *The History of Cartography, Vol. II/I, Cartography in the Traditional Islamic and South Asian Societies* (Chicago, 1992): 209–27; R. A. Abou-El-Haj, *Formation of the Modern State: The Ottoman Empire, Sixteenth to Eighteenth Centuries* (Albany, NY, 1992).

30. Ágoston, "Information, Ideology, and Limits of Imperial Policy": 77.

31. R. A. Abou-El-Haj, *The 1703 Rebellion and the Structure of Ottoman Politics* (Istanbul, 1984).

32. D. N. Crecelius, *The Roots of Modern Egypt: A Study of the Regimes of Ali Bey Kabir and Muhammad Bey Abu al-Dhabab, 1760–1775* (Minneapolis, MN, 1981); V. H. Aksan, "Manning a Black Sea Garrison in the 18th Century: Ochakov and Concepts of Mutiny and Rebellion in the Ottoman Context," *International Journal of Turkish Studies* 8, nos. 1 and 2 (2002): 63–72.

33. Holdernesse to Mitchell, September 12, see also September 19, 1758, NA. SP. 90/72.

34. Robert Olson, *The Siege of Mosul* (Bloomington, IN, 1975).

35. Sutton to Sir Luke Schaub, June 15, 1715, New York, Public Library, Hardwicke papers, vol. 42; Cardinal Polignac to François de Bussy, February 16, 1732, AE. CP. Autriche, supplement

vol. 11; Villeneuve to Amelot, French Secretary of State, January 16, 1740, Paris, Bibliothèque Nationale, Manuscrits Français, 7191 fol. 5.

36. C. Ingrao, "Habsburg Strategy and Geopolitics in the Eighteenth Century," in B. Király, G. E. Rothenberg, and P. Sugar, eds., *War and Society in East Central Europe* XI (1982): 53–54.

37. Jean Nouzille, *Le Prince Eugène de Savoie et le Sud-Est Européen, 1683–1736* (Paris, 2012).

38. M. Braubach, *Die Geheimdiplomatie des Prinzen Eugen von Savoyen* (Cologne, Germany, 1962).

39. G. Mecenseffy, *Karls VI spanische Bündnispolitik 1725–29* (Innsbruck, Austria, 1934); H. Hantsch, *Reichsvizekanzler Friedrich Graf von Schönborn* (Augsburg, 1929).

40. E. Lund, *War for the Every Day: Generals, Knowledge, and Warfare in Early Modern Europe, 1680–1740* (Westport, CT, 1999).

41. K. Benda, *Le projet d'alliance hungaro-suédo-prussienne de 1704* (Budapest, 1960).

42. Ingrao, "Strategy and Geopolitics": 49–66; C. Ingrao and Y. Yilmaz, "Habsburg vs. Ottoman: Motives and Priorities," in P. Mitev, I. Parvev, and M. Baramova, eds., *Empires and Peninsulas: Southeastern Europe between Carlowitz and the Peace of Adrianople, 1699–1829* (Sofia, 2010): 5–18.

43. L. Frey and M. Frey, *A Question of Empire: Leopold I and the War of the Spanish Succession* (Boulder, CO, 1983).

44. K. A. Roider, *Austria's Eastern Question, 1700–1790* (Princeton, NJ, 1982).

45. C. Storrs, "The Spanish Risorgimento in the Western Mediterranean and Italy 1707–1748," *European History Quarterly* 42 (2012): 555–77 and "Philip V and the Revival of Spain, 1713–48," in T. J. Dadson and J. H. Elliott, eds., *Britain, Spain and the Treaty of Utrecht, 1713–2013* (London, 2014): 84 and *The Spanish Resurgence, 1713–1748* (New Haven, CT, 2016).

46. For the lasting problem of a mismatch between warships and sailors in this navy, see Bristol to Pitt, February 25, June 2, 1760, NA. SP. 90/161.

47. See, e.g., Keene to Newcastle, June 9, 1739, BL. Add. 32801 fol. 24.

48. Strategy is not given much space in the otherwise excellent and lengthy C. Iglesias, ed., *Historia militar de Espana. Edad moderna. III. Los Borbones* (Madrid, 2014).

49. Keene to Bedford, February 25, 1749, NA. SP. 94/135 fol. 57.

50. See, e.g., P. T. Hoffman, *Why Did Europe Conquer the World?* (Princeton, NJ, 2015): esp. 120–34. For the addition of experimental science to geopolitical friction within Europe, see T. Andrade, *The Gunpowder Age: China, Military Innovation, and the Rise of the West in World History* (Princeton, NJ, 2016): 244–56.

51. M. W. Mosca, *From Frontier Policy to Foreign Policy: The Question of India and the Transformation of Geopolitics in Qing China* (Stanford, CA, 2013): 11.

52. T. Blanning, *Frederick the Great. King of Prussia* (London, 2015).

53. Mitchell to Holdernesse, February 12, 1760, NA. SP. 90/75. In this report, he warned of the difficulties of reporting conversation and numbers

with precision, a point that is more generally applicable.

54. P. Macdougall, "British Seapower and the Mysore Wars of the Eighteenth Century," *Mariner's Mirror* 97 (2011): 306 and *Naval Resistance to Britain's Growing Power in India 1660–1800: The Saffron Banner and the Tiger of Mysore* (Woodbridge, UK, 2014).

SIX

THE STRATEGY OF THE
"BARBARIANS"

THE WESTERN STADIAL THOUGHT OF THE PERIOD ASSUMED
that there were very distinct and clearly progressive stages in development, stages that set the background for Western consideration and
expansion. "Barbarians" were presented as lacking the more formal state
structures and settled economies of those presented as more opulent and
civilized. These views, for example, were expressed by Edward Gibbon,
William Robertson, and Adam Smith as they sought to provide account
of human history that was not dependent on a religious approach and
that extended to non-Christian societies. In his *Wealth of Nations* (1776),
Smith began book five, "On the Revenue of the Sovereign or Common-
wealth," by arguing that

> the first duty of the sovereign, that of protecting the society from the
> violence and invasion of other independent societies, can be performed
> only by means of a military force. But the expense both of preparing
> this military force in time of peace, and of employing it in time of war, is
> very different in the different states of society, in the different periods of
> improvement.
>
> Among nations of hunters, the lowest and rudest state of society, such as
> we find it among the native tribes of North America . . . an army of hunters
> can seldom exceed two or three hundred men. . . . An army of shepherds on
> the contrary, may sometimes amount to two or three hundred thousand.[1]

Smith linked complexity to the socioeconomic developments that permitted the establishment of professionalized regular armies able to
sustain themselves and presented this establishment as an inevitable
consequence of these developments. He referred to the "opulent and
civilized" in contrast to the "poor and barbarous."[2]

Far from simply being abstract, an account from the cutting-edge was offered by Dean Mahomet, a quartermaster with the powerful Bengal army of the British East India Company. He recorded the advance of a brigade from Bihar to Calcutta in 1772–73 and the response to resistance by the hill people of the passes through which Bengal was entered. Mahomet clearly thought weaponry and discipline were important and also commented on the savagery of the conflict. After the "licentious savages" had attacked those cutting grass and gathering fuel for the camp, two companies of sepoys (Indian infantry trained to fight like their European counterparts) advanced:

> Our men, arranged in military order, fired . . . the greater part of them
> [savages], after a feeble resistance with their bows, arrows, and swords,
> giving way to our superior courage and discipline, fled . . . two hundred . . .
> prisoners . . . severely punished for their crimes; some having their ears and
> noses cut off, and others hung in gibbets.[3]

Smith's approach offered a way to discuss "barbarians," a way that remains influential today. This method was (and is) one that primitivized them and thus made them apparently easy to dissect and explain and thus to justify control and brutality. This approach was misleading in a number of respects and notably because the strategies of these peoples were well developed and fit for purpose, although lacking the form of public political discussion and published theory seen in the West.

There is related tendency that minimizes the "barbarians," one in which they are seen as unsuccessful because anachronistic and as irrelevant as a consequence. In short, they were motivated by primitive drives and strategy was "done" to them. This tendency is linked to and in part stems from the argument that the power of major states increased in the eighteenth century, in part as a consequence of growing population and improving climate. It is argued that this increase ensured that the "barbarian" peoples or nomads or seminomads or pastoralists were driven back by the expanding territorial sway of the major settled peoples and their states, one linked to a general territorial consolidation of these states that was seen in the spread of agriculture, settlement, and military service.[4]

There is a parallel in the contemporary and later treatment of "pirates," as with the British response to the predatory coastal powers on the west coast of India.[5] Contemporary accounts brought out ethnographical assumptions. In turn, these assumptions and categories were applied to new groups that were encountered as when the British extended their scope northward along that coast, although there was also an ability to respond to local circumstances and to alter treatment and response accordingly.[6]

The focus on growing state power in the eighteenth century strikes a chord with the leading historical traditions, those of the European imperial powers, of the United States, and of China. Each of these was to achieve such expanding sway, while China, Russia, and the United States still enjoy its consequences. Moreover, in the eighteenth century, each saw major expansion. Thus, parallels can be found between the Chinese conquest of the Zunghars, Russian victory over the Kalmyks in Central Asia and the Itelmen and Koraks in Kamchatka, eventual American success in the Ohio River Basin, and many other episodes.

The strategy followed by the Russians was brutal while the resistance to them was characterized by the strategy of desperation. Relying on bone or stone-tipped arrows and on slings, the poorly armed Itelmen were brutalized in the Russian search for furs. They rose in 1706 but were suppressed. When they resisted in 1731, the Itelmen had some firearms obtained from the Russians and were able to inflict many casualties as a result, but they were eventually crushed. Disease was part of the equation. Largely isolated communities such as those of the Itelmen proved especially vulnerable to disease as their immunity was low. Another rising in 1741 was defeated. As with British colonists in North America, in response to opposition there the Russians responded brutally to resistance by the Koraks and were willing to kill as many as possible, not least in the war of 1745–56. The Koraks then submitted.

A clear pattern of outcome and consequence apparently emerges. Such an account, however, is flawed for two reasons. First, the strategic practices of those who are defeated are still of consequence, and not least given the light they throw on the victors, a point underlined by the extent to which strategy is relative and contextual. Second, and more to the point, the impression of continual defeat is deeply flawed. There were successes as well as failures in the cases mentioned above.

In addition, there were major successes for the "barbarians," and notably for the Afghans, especially in the conquest of Persia in 1722 and in invasions of northern India in midcentury and toward its close. With Afghan forces capturing the Safavid capital, Isfahan, in 1722, Delhi in 1757 and 1761, and Lahore on a number of occasions including 1749, 1752, 1756, 1762, and 1797, it is a little difficult to understand why they are regarded as redundant. Their continued role provides a clear demonstration of the significance of cavalry and calls into question accounts of military progress centered on the rise of infantry. Although eventually totally defeated in the 1750s by China, the Zunghars conquered Tibet from Chinese protégés in 1717, advanced into central Kazakhstan in 1723 and overran Turkestan in 1724–25.

So also with the expansion of Saudi power in Arabia under Abdul-Aziz bin Muhammad (r. 1765–1803). The Shʻia of al-Hasa were hard hit by this Saudi expansion, while there were also advances into the Ottoman Empire. In particular, there were advances into Iraq, where the Shʻia holy city of Karbela was sacked in 1802, and into the Hejaz, where Mecca and Medina were occupied in 1805. Religious fundamentalism was an important aspect of this expansionism. In response, the Turks and their local agents organized defensive measures, notably building new forts on the route of the hajj from Damascus to Mecca, and launched an unsuccessful expedition in 1790 against the Al-Saud heartland of Najd. This then was not an account of the failure of the "barbarians."

The tension between settled societies and attacking pastoralists was also seen in Africa, notably with Berber incursions on the plains of Morocco and Tuareg raids out of the Sahara Desert against the city of Timbuktu on the River Niger. The latter was part of a pattern of pressure still seen with Tuareg attacks in Mali and Niger in 2012–16. Timbuktu was raided in 1729, its trade routes were attacked in 1736 and 1737, and in 1737, the Tuareg were victorious in battle. The *pashalic* (provincial government) of Timbuktu was destroyed by the Tuareg in 1787.

These general points demonstrate why it is necessary to reexamine the question, a question, moreover, that can be phrased in terms of the "barbarians," or in a more restricted sense, of Inner Asia, or Central Asia, or of the Turkic peoples, although other areas and peoples were also involved—for example, the nomadic Oromo who repeatedly raided Ethiopia and the Iroquois and other tribes in North America. The Araucanians of Chile not only stopped Spanish penetration southward but also advanced across the Andes to challenge the Spanish position in Argentina. Throughout his reign, Iyasu I of Ethiopia (r. 1682–1706) fought the Oromo. Although he developed support from Oromo tribes who had converted to Christianity, Iyasu found it very difficult to gain lasting success in his protracted warfare with the other Oromo.

An economic interpretation sees conflict as one way to gain trade and the benefits that came with it or alternatively, to obtain payments as bribes in order to cease attacks.[7] A cultural approach emphasizes differences between the two sides, as well as the anthropological, psychological, and sociological predisposition of raiding societies to use violence in order to establish and affirm status, a long-standing process, with strategy in part seen as a cultural phenomenon. Indeed, the term *strategy* has, as a result, been employed to discuss Stone Age activity.[8]

Returning to the eighteenth century, it has been argued, for example, that in northeastern North America the Iroquois were concerned with glory, honor, and revenge, rather than economic issues such as access to wild animals. This argument has been deployed to argue that the Iroquois interest in control over the fur trade did not provide a set of motives for policy similar to those of the Europeans.[9] More generally, conflict was in some respects not unlike hunting, both because opponents could be regarded as akin to animals and because the emphasis was both on the masculinity of the individual, who was pitted against other individuals and against the environment, and on the group, which was also important in hunting.[10]

Any emphasis on anthropological, psychological, and sociological factors can be linked to a political focus on the divisions within the ruling families and groups of these raiding societies, and the use of conflict in order to establish, affirm, and maintain status. Each of these elements was pertinent and even more so in the combination that led to an inherently dynamic character in the political and military culture and practice of "Barbarian" societies and in the resulting international system.

A discussion of strategy needs not only to take note of these points but to also appreciate the degree to which sources that fix their relative importance are absent. Similarly, although control over hunting grounds was a form of territorialism, it is difficult to appreciate differences in interest in control over territory. Instead, the sources available are those from the societies the "barbarians" attacked. These sources are apt to simplify and primitivize the latter. In particular, tribal peoples were presented as attacking from outside or as rejecting the imperial sway of rulers, notably the "Son of Heaven," the Chinese emperor. Linked to the problems posed by a lack of written sources, the remembrance of the past in the oral culture of "barbarian" societies can be highly misleading.[11]

Looked at differently, this imperial sway was a matter of pretension in which imperial rulers were apt to devote insufficient attention to the views of those whom they regarded and treated as subject peoples. Instead, in attempts to introduce or enforce uniformity, to secure resources, or to demonstrate control in the face of rival imperial powers, there was frequently a drive to give force to an alleged or apparent subjection that did not, in practice, capture a reality of divided authority and limited strength. Added tension could be derived in the case of religious division.

The Afghans fully demonstrated the role of religious division, a role that was linked to policy, including in the destruction of religious sites. This was a sphere in which strategy and policy were closely aligned. Just as it had played a key role in its establishment, so religion helped provoke the overthrow of Safavid rule. The Safavid attempt to impose Shʿite orthodoxy on Sunni Muslims led to widespread opposition—for example, from Kurds and from the Lezghis of the Caucasus but more particularly, from 1709 among the Afghans. The Afghan seizure of the major Safavid position in the region, the city of Kandahar, represented an obvious demonstration of strength and also provided resources, including money from controlling the trade to India. The classic "anti-Barbarian" strategy, that of "divide and rule," a strategy much used by China and one for which Afghan divisions left many opportunities, failed to work for the Safavids in part because of the poor leadership of the indolent Shah Husain (r. 1694–1722).

Moreover, as so often, the inherent dynamic nature of the strategic context for Afghan operations operated to encourage a process of swelling challenge to the Safavids, just as, in other contexts, the context could lead to failure. In the case of swelling challenge, the nature of war-making, with the problem of keeping forces together and operating, was especially apparent for polities that lacked an institutional basis to support regular armies. This was seen with the successive Afghan advances against the Safavids. Thus, in 1716, the Abdalis of western Afghanistan, a powerful confederation of tribes, captured Herat, the major city in western Afghanistan. In 1719, Mahmud, the leader of the Ghalzai tribe, advanced west to Kirman in eastern Persia, capturing the city and looting it savagely before returning to Afghanistan. In 1722, the Ghalzais advanced farther, indeed to the center of Persia, defeated a far larger Persian army at Gulnabad, and captured the Persian capital, Isfahan, the shah abdicating in favor of Mahmud.[12] Given the much smaller size of the Afghan force and the Afghan drive for loot and legitimacy, a drive matching that of the Visigoths under Alaric, who sacked Rome in 410, the decision to advance on Isfahan was fully understandable.

An aggressive strategy was made necessary by the ethos and economics of this "Barbarian" society, and it is not helpful to present ethos and economics in an either-or scenario. This point can be seen with the most successful Afghan ruler of the century, Ahmad Khan Abdali (Ahmad Shah), the able and energetic founder of the Durrani Empire based in Afghanistan (r. 1747–73). The force structure, operational means, and tactical methods of the Durranis all contributed strongly to an aggressive strategy. The Durranis obtained effective cavalry horses from Central Asia and armed their cavalry with flintlocks. Aggressive warfare ensured support and stability, providing plunder and finding occupation. Moreover, these benefits helped the tribal chiefs who provided Ahmad Shah with troops. Victory against others overawed opposition, as when the defeat of the Marathas in winter 1759–60 led the emir of Sind to end his rebellion. Northwest India, the most prosperous neighboring region to Afghanistan and one that was vulnerable as a result of Mughal weakness, was repeatedly attacked by the Afghans from 1748. Financial contributions were extorted from defeated regions, with the Mughal emperor Ahmad (r. 1748–54) in 1750 promising the Afghan leader fourteen lakhs of rupees.

The Marathas, however, posed a major challenge to the Afghans in the late 1750s and early 1760s, and the situation became even more difficult for the Afghans with the rise, from 1762, of Sikh power. This rise was an aspect of the repositioning and reconceptualization of power and strategy in India as the Mughals declined.[13] The Sikhs were a military confederacy.

The assessment of the Afghans as having a predisposition for conflict does not lessen the more general rehabilitation of "barbarians," so that they are no longer seen as a product and part of an inchoate "other" against which civilization must defend itself but, as instead, part of the world of civilization. In this reevaluation, "barbarians" enter into specific wars, rather than being in a permanent state of war, but that does not make them inherently pacific. Moreover, they also are able to play off opponents and to exploit "divide and rule" strategies to their own benefit. This was seen in the very different environments of North America, where the Native Americans played off the competing European powers, and in India, where the local princes did the same.

To refer to the Afghans and, even more, the Persians under Nadir Shah as "Barbarians" is deeply problematic in a number of respects, as well as an aspect of the "Orientalism" that is decried. For example, the contrasts between these polities and those of India or the Ottoman Empire are limited. Moreover, the Persians continued to think of themselves as a great nation and power throughout the period. This possibly affected military means, making it harder to adopt guerrilla tactics for resistance to Russian expansionism in the early nineteenth century. Guerrilla warfare was seen as beneath them.[14]

Linked to this were the particular characteristics of cavalry-based armies. They were excellent for mobility and for offensive operations but less so for such operations against Western-style infantry and also in defense. If "barbarians" are to be defined in terms of those who brought down empires, then the Marathas, a Hindu warrior caste especially strong in light cavalry, can be seen in that light because they played a key role in bringing down Mughal India. Threatening Mughal control was the prime Maratha means. The mobile and decentralized style of Maratha campaigning undermined the logistical basis of their slower-moving opponents' operations. At the same time, alongside logistical considerations, Maratha strategy reflected political and cultural assumptions about place, more particularly the belief that forts were necessary for the symbol and reality of power, a Maratha belief that provided the Mughals with clear targets. Position warfare was different from its maneuverist counterpart which favored the Marathas.

Nevertheless, the Mughal strategy in the early 1700s of attacking Maratha forts did not end resistance. Moreover, this strategy was expensive, and the impression of failure it created was damaging and helped sustain opposition there and elsewhere. The impression of success was a key strategic goal as it was a significant attribute both of generalship and of rule.

Having successfully resisted Mughal attacks in the 1700s, the Marathas made important gains from the 1730s onward. Although they could defeat the Mughals in battle, as at Talkatora in 1738, the more mobile Marathas generally refused to engage in a major battle. Instead, they concentrated on cutting off their opponent's grain supplies Nagpur and reinforcements, forcing the Mughal general to buy them off with a cash tribute in 1735. The major Mughal defeat at the hands of Nadir Shah of Persia at Karnal in 1739 enabled the Marathas to raid as far as distant Bengal in 1741. From 1745 to 1751, Orissa was raided every year by a Maratha leader who had established himself in Nagpur. Farther south, the Carnatic was invaded in 1740. In 1752 and again in 1760, the Nizam of Hyderabad, the major ruler in south-central India, ceded large territories to the Marathas.

Maratha armies grew larger and more professional, which, however, increased the cost of their operations. The change in the armies was related to that of Maratha ambitions, finance, and governance. It was related to an operational shift from a deep battle long-range penetration by cavalry into the rear of their enemy, to a slower battle-centric strategy in which infantry and artillery played key roles. A consideration of the Marathas underlines the problems of defining "barbarians" or more generally, of categorization. Any stress on progress invites such categorization, however misleading.

Much of the resistance to the Afghans came from similar groups, notably the Marathas. The latter pressed north at the same time as the Afghans were moving southeast into India. The search for wealth to plunder was linked not only to an opportunistic politics but also to an attempt at legitimation. Indeed, the struggle in northern India in the late 1750s and early 1760s was contemporaneous with the Seven Years' War in Europe and the Atlantic world, and this simultaneity invites questions about the nature of strategy and of respective significance, questions that have not been adequately addressed. Indeed, it is striking that recent scholarship on the Seven Years' War, while sometimes willing to treat it as a world war, does not consider the issue of comparisons.

That of Ahmad Shah of Afghanistan and Frederick II is instructive. Each had commitments on a number of fronts, although Amad Shah's were more far-flung, while he also had to suppress rebellions, as Frederick did not have to do. Frederick's opportunistic conquest of Silesia in 1740–41 was the key military event of his reign and one that, despite treaties, he could not really legitimate by winning Austrian acceptance. Ahmad Shah faced similar problems. He left the governor of Punjab in position when he conquered it in 1752 and had it ceded to him by the Mughal emperor, the ineffective Ahmad Shah (r. 1748–54). However, the death in 1753 of the governor was followed by chaos there and by a Mughal attempt to regain control. In turn, Ahmad Shah crossed the River Indus in December 1756, going on, next month, to defeat at Narela the Marathas who had come to Mughal assistance. This was victory over a larger force, on the pattern seen with Frederick's victories. The sequel was somewhat different. After Narela, the Afghans occupied defenseless Delhi, deposed the emperor, Ālamgir II, and stormed the cities of Brindaban, Mathura, and Agra.

This campaign can be treated in highly contrasting fashions. One is to emphasize destruction and to use that to imply "barbarism" and anachronistic behavior. Thus, Delhi was extensively pillaged. Moreover, the mass slaughter of the inhabitants of the stormed cities contributed to an outbreak of cholera that led the Afghans to return home. Conversely, pillaging can be seen as economically rational. It provides short-term advantage, especially under the assumption that the pillagers know that they cannot hold for long the city they have conquered. In addition, when the conquering army has no logistical train and has to live off the conquered land, pillaging is rational.

In the case of Ahmad Shah, political purpose can also be pointed out. He had his son, Timur Mirza, marry Ālamgir II's daughter, with the major provinces of Punjab and Sind granted as her dowry. When Ahmad Shah returned to Afghanistan, he left his son to govern his lands east of the Indus. Similarly, after extensive campaigning in 1758, Ahmad Shah ended a rebellion by Nasir Khan, the ruler of Baluchistan, by means of an agreement that included an acknowledgment of overlordship, the provision of troops for his army, and a matrimonial alliance. Far from being an unskilled "barbarian," Ahmad Shah was a skillful negotiator able to play his role in power politics with great skill.

In 1759–61, renewed Afghan-Maratha conflict saw both the Rohillas and the Nawab of Oudh join the Afghans. The Rohillas were to play a key role in Ahmad Shah's victory at Panipat in 1761, although, after the victory, disagreements between the allies helped undermine Ahmad Shah's position. Moreover, Sikh opposition became a key factor, and Ahmad Shah was unable to end it despite operations in 1762, 1764, and 1767. His eventual settlement reflected the strategy of place: he left the Sikhs the central Punjab, while he retained the city of Peshawar, the gateway to Afghanistan.

Like the Marathas, Ahmad Shah benefited from the weakness of the Mughals, rather as Frederick II did from that of the Habsburgs. Ahmad Shah had to respond to the Marathas, as Frederick also did to those of others seeking to maneuver in terms of the opportunities of the period, notably France and Russia. Frederick might seem to be more successful, although that conclusion appears less well founded from the perspective of Prussia's total defeat by France in 1806. Unlike the Habsburgs, the Prussians certainly did not face the problems posed by the succession problems that led to a short civil war when Ahmad Shah died in 1773 and to more serious rivalry and conflict from 1793. It is also unclear how far Ahmad Shah should be seen as the ruler of a viable unit and how far as the leader of a tribal confederation.[15]

More generally, the collapse of Mughal power was followed by the creation of a new political and social order in which the rulers of successor states across India were matched by other important individuals, including large landholders, service gentry, and prominent members of mercantile groups. In combination, these groups provided the patronage and protection that kept both society and the economy functioning.[16] In turn, these rulers and other individuals sought protection in the midst of the instability of the period. Thus, the decline of the Mughal Empire was not solely at the hands of "barbarians." Instead, there was a complex process of state-building.

State-building, indeed, is a problematic concept. If the emphasis is to be on generals seizing power and creating empires, then it is difficult to see how Napoleon can be regarded as different to Nadir Shah who made himself shah of Persia in 1736 after being the key military figure there from 1729. Nadir's strategy is more generally instructive. It was in part designed to gain spoils in order to reward his army and also to transfer the burden of the army's support from Persia to other countries, a situation that prefigured Napoleon's strategy. Moreover, just as Napoleon's imperial model was more that of Charlemagne than that of Revolutionary France, so Nadir's imperial model was not the earlier Safavid one but a more far-flung ambition similar to that of Timur (1336–1405), later called Tamerlaine, a Turkic figure who, based in Samarkand in Central Asia, had campaigned widely, capturing Delhi, Baghdad, Damascus, and Ankara, and creating a far-flung empire. As such, there was a parallel between Nadir Shah and the situation in China where Manchu interests, ambitions, and commitments were more far-flung than those of the previous Ming dynasty. However, China offered the Manchu a bureaucratic strength and institutional continuity that neither Timur nor Nadir enjoyed, and partly as a result, their achievements proved ephemeral.[17]

In terms of creating a dynasty that survived its creator, both Napoleon and Nadir Shah were less effective than Ahmad Shah or Haidar Ali of Mysore. In each case, the logic of military success in terms of opportunities and needs helped determine commitments and interests, as much as any strategic parameters set by the nature of the military or by the inherited strategic culture of the particular polity they had taken over. None compared to George Washington in helping secure a new polity within what became a distinct and different strategic environment. Napoleon went down to total defeat in 1814 and 1815, whereas Nadir Shah was assassinated in 1747 when at the height of his power and his empire swiftly disintegrated. Its rapid rise and fall served commentators as an instance of the unpredictability of international relations and their dependence on military leadership. Thus, in 1787, John Shore, a senior British official in Bengal and later governor-general of British India, wrote to the then governor-general: "the House of Timur I believe is fallen never to rise again; unless a Nadir Shah should arise from the degenerate stock."[18]

It is tempting, in this context, to treat these and other questions of difference and asymmetries in terms familiar to the discussion of

Orientalism. For example, in his next letter, Shore wrote, "the motions of an Asiatic despot are not to be tied by the strictest rules of reason."[19] The same theme of the irrational nature of non-Western power was struck that year by William Kirkpatrick, British resident with Scindhia, one of the Maratha leaders, who wrote of a struggle involving Scindhia:

> In the present case, when the conduct of either party is so little regulated by any fixed or steady principles of policy, and when so much depends upon a variety of contingencies which either do not occur or have not so much influence, in states further advanced in political or military knowledge, such conjectures are to be received with particular caution.[20]

At the same time, it is worth noting that republics and limited monarchies attracted the criticism of commentators who regarded their own states as more stable and who thereby thought others less capable of formulating or pursuing strategies. Horatio Walpole, an experienced British diplomat, reported from the United Provinces (Dutch Republic) in 1739: "this government is at present weak, divided and distracted that the prospect of coming to a resolution is as uncertain as in a Polish Diet."[21]

In practice, however, more than perception, whether Orientalism or not was involved, and in particular, there were, and are, broader issues about the range of societies and polities in the world and concerning treating them all as similar. On the one hand, monarchies were a common form across the world. Some monarchies elsewhere, indeed, showed parallels with those of Eurasia, albeit in very different contexts. Thus, in the Hawaiian archipelago, Kamehameha I expanded his power from his base on the west coast of the island of Hawai'i, the big island. He won dominance of that island in 1791 and of those of Manui and Oahu in 1795. This was a warfare of clan conflict in which weaponry and determination both played a role.[22] Dominant rulers able to deploy large forces were also seen in some other parts of Oceania, notably Tonga. They provided a different strategic environment to those where the many warring tribes were not brought into such subordination to a dominant ruler— for example, the Marquesas, Tahiti, and New Zealand—or indeed most of both North America and Amazonia. Moreover, as North America showed, it was difficult, despite the fears of Anglo-American opponents, to create a pan-Native alliance.[23]

The nature of politics was significant but so also, to take a functional view, akin to those of the European "stadial" writers of the period, were those of sociological context. Thus, in certain island groups, such as Hawai'i and New Zealand, higher population densities and more developed social and political systems enhanced the possibilities of large-scale military action. In contrast, in the vastness of Australia, small migratory hunting groups formed the population. A similar contrast can be seen in Africa. Population levels and governmental development were again significant for military attainment and activity. Areas of low population density and limited economic development, such as the Kalahari Desert of southwest Africa, had a different level of military preparedness and warfare from that of monarchical states able to deploy armies of considerable size, such as Asante and Dahomey, both in West Africa, and Ethiopia in Northeast Africa.

The nature of the sources makes it difficult to analyze the character and causes of military transformation in Africa. It is all too easy to write in terms of optimizing processes of change without allowing enough weight for issues of choice and thereby strategy. There were clearly interactions between environment, trade, and politics. In the forest zone of West Africa, for example, power was related to the replacement of bow and javelin by muskets, and this replacement was linked to the slave trade. The significance of the latter and more generally, the extent to which power rested on control over people, ensured that the latter was a key goal of strategy, rather than simply over territory. This factor was also seen elsewhere, for example in North America, and in South Asia where Alaungpaya returned from his invasion of Manipur with prisoners marched back to provide labor and invaded Siam in part in a search for subjects. Hsinbyushi of Myanmar (r. 1763–76) also saw a need to secure more servicemen.

Environmental borders, notably those between savannah and forest, were important to the character of warfare in Africa (and elsewhere).[24] At the same time, the role of individual rulers was significant. Thus, in modern Sudan, two states, the Funj kingdom of Sinnar in northern Sudan, and the rising state of Darfur in western Sudan, competed over the area of Kordofan, where warrior rulers gained tribute by using their cavalry both to intimidate subjects and to defend them from foreign rulers. In 1745 and 1755, Sinnar campaigned against Kordofan. Abu Likaylik, who served in the 1745 campaign, was the commander in 1755. Having built up a power base, he invaded Kordofan from Sinnar and deposed the Sultan.[25] Haidar Ali was to follow a similar trajectory in Mysore in southern India in 1761. One of his generals, Mir Zainul Abedeen Shushtari, produced a work discussing the subsequent military reforms in Mysore.[26]

The quest for personal power was also significant in Ethiopia, where Mika'el Suhul (d. 1780), ras of the province of Tigrai (Tigré) and later of Gondar, played a key role, building up a powerful army and opposing Iyasu II, the negus (emperor; r. 1730–55) and his successor Iyoas I (r. 1755–69). This was linked to a strategy of mobilizing support. Mika'el was opposed to Muslim and Galla influences at the imperial court and posed as a Christian and national champion. He tried, without success, to persuade Iyoas I to attack the Funj kingdom. The negus was hanged after being defeated at Azezo in 1769. However, in 1771, Mika'el was defeated by rival provincial warlords. Division and conflict between the effective rulers of the provinces continued into the twentieth century.

It is mistaken to adopt too contrasting an account of ideologies, one in which those of major states are supposedly rational, while "primitive" societies have irrational, fundamentalist beliefs, notably those of revivalism and millenarianism. Prophets play a role in the latter. Such a contrast is latent in developmental accounts focused on modernity, but it is wrong to assume that revivalism and millenarianism were somehow separate to the political culture of major states and large developed economies. Both communism and National Socialism (Nazism) displayed these characteristics, whereas liberal cultures, with their stress on the views and rights of individuals, are inherently different in their values. These societies represent different types of modernity.

Allowing for that general point, it is still necessary to consider how best to approach value systems and indeed to assess societies where literacy was limited and written texts very few. Those characteristics are true for most of history, but by the eighteenth century, there were significant contrasts between literary societies and those where reliance was on oral communication. The ability to record information was more widespread in societies not dependent on oral records.

As a different point but one related to the problems of comparing dissimilar societies, it is misleading to regard firearms technology as the key indicator of modernity and the means of ensuring a military transformation that led to centralization and greater stability.[27] The process of conflict was far more complex, as were the consequences. For example, none of the Western powers had the military impact in Africa of the jihad launched by Usman dan Fodio and the Fulani against the Hausa states in modern northern Nigeria in 1804. Militarily, this jihad was not dependent on firearms. Instead, its tactics were based on mobility, maneuver, and shock attack. Ideology, in the shape of marshaling some spiritual drives in order to ensure group coherence, also played an important role in the success of the Merina ruler, Adrianampoinimerina (r. ca. 1783–ca. 1810), who spread his power in Madagascar.[28] Aung Zega, the rebel who established a new dynasty in Myanmar in 1752, called himself Alaung-paya (r. 1752–60), meaning the great lord who will be a Buddha one day.

It was possible to be highly effective without making much use of firearms. Thus, in the Philippines, swords and other handheld cutting and stabbing weapons were used in the islands of Jolo and Mindinao against the Spaniards, while the headhunting mountain people of northern Luzon employed machetes, spears, head-hunting axes, and three-pronged shields. In North America, the bow offered much, although musket shot was less likely to be deflected by vegetation. The spread of horses was very important in bringing greater mobility and range. The absence of large armies did not entail any lack of organized and deadly conflict.[29]

More particularly, there is a danger that the perspective of the settled societies ensures that the "barbarians" are perceived as valiant but limited. The situation was more complex. For example, as in North America, the settled societies and the goods and opportunities they provided were fed into local antagonisms helped to fuel them at the same time that the powers were affected, if not manipulated.[30] Strategic interaction was highly complex, and this was seen in North America as well as in India.

Nor were the "barbarians" unchanging. For example, rather than presenting Eurasian nomadic warfare in terms of innate environmental characteristics, stemming largely from the possibilities for horsemanship and thus as a somewhat passive or unchanging counterpart to the development of firearms technology by settled society, it is appropriate to consider the extent to which nomad skills and success varied and changed, alongside the limitations of nomads and the extent of internomadic warfare.[31] There was a capacity for reflection and informed argument. For example, in 1547, Sahib Giray, the khan of the Crimean Tatars, advised his ally and overlord Süleyman the Magnificent, the Turkish sultan, that the large armies used by the latter against the Safavids were less useful than a reliance on smaller, more mobile forces, such as those offered by the Tatars. Such forces were easier to support logistically and thus less of a pressure on local resources as well as less expensive, and they were also better able to fix and fight the Safavids who used similar forces.[32]

At the same time, the tactical and operational aspects of cavalry warfare on the steppe had profound effects on the strategic understanding of what constituted victory. Conditions were extremely fluid, the enemy could always ride away, there were few strongholds to capture, and therefore, it was difficult to achieve and impose a sense of victory and hard for those opposing steppe forces to control the situation. In this context, gaining some kind of hold over a population without the regular application of force was far from easy.

Alongside a past process of hierarchical organization dominated by the West, a situation still seen in much current discussion of military history, there was also the development in the eighteenth century of comparative linguistics, comparative religion, and cultural relativism—the last, for example, seen in Johann Gottfried von Herder's *Auch eine Philosophie der Geschichte* (*An Alternative Philosophy of History*; 1774). Many modern writers on strategy scarcely rise to that significant challenge of range and relativism. The points made in this and the previous paragraph indeed lead toward a critique of many of the assumptions associated with the idea of an early-modern military revolution. The flaws of this thesis have already been assessed,[33] but at this juncture, it is more appropriate to draw attention to the deficiencies as far as those societies not included in this movement or development are concerned. They, instead, are generally presented as societies that are acted upon. They therefore appear redundant and uncivilized, with civilization understood in terms of this particular project. However, that perspective creates a somewhat circular and self-validating approach to the topic that is unhelpful and misleading. This problem is underlined by the process of reading back from the nineteenth century, which again is unhelpful. Far from being a constant, technological factors may well have been more significant then, rather than in earlier centuries.

The resonances of this argument for the treatment of strategy are readily apparent. There is an equivalent, indeed linked, tendency to offer a hierarchy of development and significance. This tendency is based on the stadial thinkers of the eighteenth-century West, but it alike suffers from a tendency to assume a teleology that is problematic. A typology, instead, can be offered by reference to the nature of rule and its clear significance for military capability and practice. Military systems with political continuity and stability and administrative strength, especially China, Britain, and Russia, proved more able to survive setbacks and to sustain a projection of their power than monarchies on horseback, such as those of the Zunghars, Nadir Shah in Persia, Ahmad Shah in Afghanistan, and Napoleon, or with the exception of their not using horses, Alaungpaya in Myanmar and Tamsin in Thailand. However, governmental systems of continuity, stability, and strength were not invariably successful in war, as the Chinese discovered in Myanmar and Vietnam, the Russians in Persia, the Afghans in Persia and the Punjab, and the British, eventually, in North America—the last an effort that was more central to their military effort than the Chinese and Russian examples given. Systems of continuity, stability, and strength could fracture, with these divisions providing opportunities for assailants. Nevertheless, such divisions were more common in the horseback monarchies. Thus, Chinese success over the Zunghar ruler Galdan Boshughtu in 1696–97 owed much to support from his rebellious nephew, Tsewang Rabtan. This was an aspect of China's long-standing strategy of trying to play off steppe forces and to use steppe allies.[34] The problems of a typology emerge repeatedly, but so also do the existence and extent of comparisons.

NOTES

1. A. Smith, *An Inquiry into the Nature and Causes of the Wealth of Nations* (Oxford, 1976 ed.): 689–91. See also W. Robertson, *The History of the Reign of the Emperor Charles V. With a View of the Progress of Society in Europe*

(London, 1769; 3 vols., 1782 ed.), I, 5–6; E. Gibbon, *The History of the Decline and Fall of the Roman Empire* (1776–88), edited by J. B. Bury (7 vols., 1897–1901 ed.), I, 93, V, 358–59, VII, 2.

2. Smith, *Inquiry*: 708.

3. M. H. Fisher, ed., *The Travels of Dean Mahomet: An Eighteenth-Century Journey through India* (Berkeley, CA, 1997): 55.

4. T. Barrett, *At the Edge of Empire: The Terek Cossacks and the North Caucasus Frontier, 1700–1860* (Boulder, CO, 1999); W. Sunderland, *Taming the Wild Frontier: Colonisation and Empire on the Russian Steppe* (Ithaca, NY, 2004); B. J. Boeck, *Imperial Boundaries: Cossack Communities and Empire-Building in the Age of Peter the Great* (Cambridge, UK, 2009).

5. P. Risso, "Cultural Perceptions of Piracy: Maritime Violence in the Western Indian Ocean and Persian Gulf Region during the Long Eighteenth Century," *Journal of World History* 12 (2001): 293–319; D. Elliott, "Pirates, Polities and Companies: Global Politics on the Konkan Littoral c. 1690–1756" (Economic History Working Papers, London School of Economics, 136, 2010).

6. L. Subramanian, "Whose Pirate? Reflections on State Power and Predation on India's Western Littoral," in S. Davies, D. S. Roberts, and G. S. Espinosa, eds., *India and Europe in the Global Eighteenth Century* (Oxford, 2014): 241–65.

7. T. J. Barfield, *Profits from Power: Nomadic Empires and China, 221 BC to AD 1757* (Oxford, 1989).

8. M. Sahlins, *Stone Age Economics* (Chicago, 1972).

9. J. A. Brandão, *"Your Fryre Shall Burn No More": Iroquois Policy toward New France and Its Native Allies to 1701* (Lincoln, NE, 1997).

10. For a later period, see K. Hoganson, *Fighting for American Manhood: How Gender Politics Provoked the Spanish-American and Philippine-American Wars* (New Haven, CT, 1998).

11. Regarding the 1850–53 Cape-Xhosa war, see T. Stapleton, "The Memory of Maqoma: An Assessment of Jingqi Oral Tradition in the Ciskei and Transkei," *History in Africa* 20 (1993): 321–35.

12. R. Matthee, *Persia in Crisis: Safavid Decline and the Fall of Isfahan* (London, 2011).

13. J. J. Gommans, *The Rise of the Indo-Afghan Empire. c. 1710–1780* (Leiden, the Netherlands, 1995) and "Indian Warfare and Afghan Innovation during the Eighteenth Century," *Studies in History* 11 (1995): 261–80.

14. M. Axworthy, *Iran: Empire of the Mind* (London, 2008): 183–84.

15. A. Tarzi, *"Tarikh-I Ahmad Shahi*: The First History of 'Afghanistan,'" in N. Green, ed., *Afghan History through Afghan Eyes* (London, 2015): 95–96.

16. C. A. Bayly, *Rulers, Townsmen, and Bazaars: North Indian Society in the Age of British Expansion, 1770–1870* (Cambridge, UK, 1983).

17. M. Axworthy, *Sword of Persia: Nadir Shah, from Tribal Warrior to Conquering Tyrant* (London, 2006) and "The Army of Nader Shah," *Iranian Studies* 40 (2007): 635–46.

18. Shore to Cornwallis, September 3, 1787, NA. PRO. 30/11/122 fol. 17.

19. Shore to Cornwallis, September 9, 1787, NA. PRO. 30/11/122 fol. 20.

20. Kirkpatrick to Cornwallis, June 13, 1787, NA. PRO. 30/11/121 fol. 60.

21. Horatio Walpole to Harrington, August 11, 1739, NA. SP. 84/381 fol. 50.

22. R. Tregaskis, *The Warrior King: Hawaii's Kamehameha the Great* (New York, 1973).

23. R. M. Owens, *Red Dreams, White Nightmares: Pan-Indian Alliances in the Anglo-American Mind, 1763–1815* (Norman, OK, 2015).

24. J. Thornton, *Warfare in Atlantic Africa, 1500–1800* (London, 1999).

25. J. J. Ewald, *Soldiers, Traders, and Slaves: State Formation and Economic Transformation in the Greater Nile Valley, 1700–1885* (Madison, WI, 1990): 45–46.

26. M. Husain, ed., *Fath-ul-Mujahideen: A Treatise on the Rules and Regulations of Tipu Sultan's Army and His Principles of Strategy* (Karachi, 1950).

27. For this claim, see, e.g., B. Hacker, "Gunpowder and the Changing Military Order: The Islamic Gunpowder Empires, ca. 1450–ca. 1650," in B. Steele and T. Dorland, eds., *The Heirs of Archimedes: Science and the Art of War through the Age of Enlightenment* (Cambridge, MA, 2005): 95.

28. G. M. Berg, "The Sacred Musket: Tactics, Technology and Power in Eighteenth-Century Madagascar," *Comparative Studies in Society and History* 27 (1985): 263, 278–79.

29. D. H. Dye, "The Transformation of Mississippian Warfare: Four Case Studies from the Mid-South," in E. N. Arkush and M. W. Allen, eds., *The Archaeology of Warfare: Prehistories of Raiding and Conquest* (Gainesville, FL, 2006): 101–47; C. S. Keener, "An Ethnohistorical Analysis of Iroquois Assault Tactics Used against Fortified Settlements of the Northeast in the Seventeenth Century," *Ethnohistory* 46 (1999): 777–807.

30. A. Gallay, *The Indian Slave Trade: The Rise of the English Empire in the American South, 1670–1717* (New Haven, CT, 2002): 337; W. L. Ramsey, *The Yamasee War: A Study of Culture, Economy, and Conflict in the Colonial South* (Lincoln, NE, 2008).

31. N. Di Cosmo, ed., *Warfare in Inner Asian History, 500–1800* (Leiden, the Netherlands, 2002).

32. R. Murphey, "The Garrison and Its Hinterland in the Ottoman East, 1578–1605," in A. C. S. Peacock, ed., *The Frontiers of the Ottoman World* (Oxford, 2009): 369.

33. J. Black, *Beyond the Military Revolution* (Basingstoke, UK, 2011).

34. F. W. Bengholz, *The Partition of the Steppe: The Struggle of the Russians, Manchus, and the Zunghar Mongols for Empire in Central Asia, 1619–1758: A Study in Power Politics* (New York, 1995).

SEVEN

THE RISE OF REPUBLICAN
STRATEGIES, 1775–1800

THE FACES OF THE MARATHA TROOPS WHO CAME OUT OF THEIR position at Panipat, north of Delhi, on January 14, 1761, to attack the Afghans were anointed with saffron, a sign that they had come out to conquer or die. In what was the largest battle in the century, one that the Afghans won, allegedly at least thirty thousand Maratha soldiers were killed. A focus on determination and conflict outside the West, however, does not suit Western-based narratives of significant development. Nor, more pertinently for this book, is it germane to the dissemination of a new language of strategy. As a result, the focus in this chapter is Western-centric. Nevertheless, it is necessary, at every point, to recall the significance of warfare outside the West.

There were a number of long-established republics in 1775, notably the United Provinces (Dutch Republic, Netherlands), the Swiss Confederation, Venice, and Genoa. The most significant as a major state was the first. The United Provinces was one of the world's leading naval powers, as well as having colonies from the New World via southern Africa to the East Indies and deploying a large army in Europe. The Dutch had had to devise a strategy as part of a struggle for independence from Philip II of Spain during the late sixteenth century and in the context of a divided domestic politics. Thereafter, the Dutch had faced attacks from Spain and France. As such, the Dutch prefigured the situation that was to face the United States and France in the late eighteenth century. Lacking a court context or dynastic goal for policy, each had to produce a new strategic logic, not least for public consumption but also to help define goals and means in a competitive environment. Each also probed optimistic, even utopian, conceptions of policy and strategy, for ends as well as means, before finding that the situation they faced was more difficult as well as divisive.

At the same time, the situation for the long-standing republics by the late eighteenth century suggested that distinctive republican features could become less significant with time and certainly in so far as comparison with limited monarchies, notably Britain, Poland, and Sweden, were concerned. In part, this was because both categories of states were affected by the interaction of inherited political practices with an assertive public politics.[1] The latter has very much been a theme of recent work on the period.[2] It is mistaken to assume that popular political activism in issues linked to foreign policy increased only toward the end of the century. They were seen, for example, with both Genoa in 1746 and the Dutch in 1747.

Turning to the last quarter of the century without necessarily assuming that timing automatically led to a new politics in some form of "Atlantic revolution," both the United States and republican France were born in violence and through war. However, the legacies they variously adopted, adapted, and reacted against (and with significant domestic differences for all three) were very different. In France, the transition was clear as France was already a nation and a state. The revolution both inherited from institutions, military practices, political strategies, and geopolitical issues from the pre-revolutionary ancien régime and released, energized, organized, and directed French resources.

UNITED STATES

In the United States, the transition was more abrupt because the revolution constituted foremost the creation of a new state, although a British organizational structure, albeit a colonial one, was already present in a relatively advanced fashion and could be used by the new government. The seminal moment and document of the new state was a declaration of independence, issued in 1776. As a result, there was the need to conceptualize as well as implement a new strategy and, to employ another word not in use, geopolitics. The novelty of this strategy, indeed, owed much to the geopolitical transformation in North America and the

North Atlantic world from 1758. Up till then, and more particularly in the early 1750s, the British colonies had been threatened and, far more, felt threatened, by the combination of a France that was expanding in the North American interior and its Native American allies. This fear had helped lead to a determination to strengthen trans-Atlantic coop-eration with Britain, a determination that was encouraged by a growing economic interdependence as trade grew. This determination benefited from a major change in British politics from 1754, as the Pelhamite hege-mony was challenged by politicians committed to an imperial policy, notably William Pitt the Elder, who made his political name accordingly, as discussed in chapter 2.

However, the conquest of Canada in 1758–60, a conscious strategic decision by Pitt, transformed the situation, and not least because the French lost Louisiana to Spain in the subsequent peace, which ensured that that colony could not be the basis for a revived North American pol-icy on the part of France. Indeed, in the 1760s, France put more energy into other transoceanic operations—for example, developing the colony of Cayenne in South America as well as into rebuilding the fleet. As Brit-ain's North American colonies moved away from anxiety about France, so they ceased to feel themselves in the front line. This was a point that was fully apparent in 1770–71 when Britain had come close to going to war with France and Spain in the Falkland Islands crisis. At that stage, there was no threat to these colonies.

This situation provided a geopolitical background for rising tensions between Britain and the colonies. However, the eventual outcomes, in the shape, successively, of conflict (1775), struggle for independence (1776), French intervention (1778), and the eventual partition of Brit-ish North America (1783), were all unpredictable, as were their interac-tions. There was a need for the Patriots to create a strategy from the outset of the struggle, a strategy focused on changing British policy. This need was continued thereafter because it was widely believed that the British might attempt to strike back and reverse independence and, linked to this, because the revolutionary war ended not in triumph but in compromise. These points were to be played down in the subsequent memorialization, a situation also seen after the War of 1812. However, the reality was not only independence but also a continued British presence in neighboring Canada as a result of the failure of American invasion. Moreover, this presence was linked to the well-founded belief that this presence encouraged Native American opposition to American expansion, which was very much the case up to 1815 but not thereafter.

The conspectus might appear clear, but strategy was centrally involved, as also in the case of republican France, with a political struggle over the identity of the new state. This struggle encompassed constitutional formulation, political practice, force structure, ideology, and geopolitical alignment. For example, the powerful American ideological-political preference for militia was highly significant. To abstract strategy from this context is not only unhelpful but misleading. In the case of America, the Continental Army, created in 1775 to defend "American liberty," represented a new political identity and social practice. This helped to sustain the cohesion of the army and even the continuation of the revolutionary cause when the war went badly, as in winter 1777–78 when the army camped at Valley Forge.

The formation of the army indeed was a political act: the army, a force that would not dissolve at the end of the year, even if individual terms of service came to an end, symbolized the united nature of the struggle by the thirteen states and thus limited the role of state governments in military decisions. In theory, indeed, creating the Continental Army made the planning of strategy easier, allowing generals to consider clashing demands for action and assistance. In practice, the creation of the army, although essential to the dissemination of a new notion of nationhood, did not free military operations from the view of state governments, nor from the political disputes of the Continental Congress. In June 1775, the Second Continental Congress transformed the New England force outside Boston into a national army. George Washington was selected as commander, and the relationship between Congress and general was defined: Congress was to determine policy and Washington to follow its orders. At the same time, there was to be much tension between the needs of the army and the views of the public, tension that in part focused on the place of the militia. In December 1780, General Nathanael Greene, the new commander of American forces in the South, wrote to a friend, General Henry Knox, who was responsible for the American artillery:

> With the militia, everybody is a general and the powers of government
> are so feeble that it is with the utmost difficulty you can restrain them
> from plundering one another. The people don't want spirit and enterprise
> but they must go to war in their own way or not at all. Nothing can save
> this country but a good permanent army conducted with great prudence
> and caution; for the impatience of the people to drive off the enemy
> would precipitate an officer into a thousand misfortunes, and the mode
> of conducting the war which is most to the liking of the inhabitants is the
> least likely to effect their salvation.

Greene wrote to Governor Lee of Maryland:

> It is unfortunate for the public that the two great departments in which
> they are so deeply interested, Legislation and the Army, cannot be made
> to coincide better, but the pressing wants of the Army cannot admit
> of the slow deliberation of Legislation, without being subject to many
> inconveniences nor can a Legislature with the best intentions always keep
> pace with the emergencies of war: and thus the common interest suffers
> from the different principles which influence and govern the two great
> national concerns.[3]

In running the army, Washington had to confront a marked particu-
larism that revealed itself in hostility to serving in the same unit with
men from another colony, as well as a strong identification between men
and their officers, and opposition to reenlistment among men concerned
about their farmsteads and families.

Appointed general by Congress in June 1775, Charles Lee, a veteran
of the Seven Years' War, in which he had served as a British officer in
North America and Portugal, and as a former major-general in the Polish army when it resisted Russian invasion, advocated radical solutions
amounting to a militarization of society and the creation of a national
army under central control:

> 1st. A solemn league and covenant defensive and offensive to be taken by
> every man in America, particularly by those in or near the seaport towns;
> all those who refuse, to have their estates confiscated for the public use,
> and their persons removed to the interior part of the country with a small
> pension reserved for their subsistence.
>
> 2dly. New York to be well fortified and garrisoned or totally destroyed.
>
> 3dly. No regiments to be raised for any particular local purposes, but
> one general great Continental Army adequate to every purpose. South
> Carolina may be excepted from its distance ...

4thly. The regiments to be exchanged. Those who are raised in one
province to serve in another rather than in their own, viz. the New
Englanders in New York, the New Yorkers in New England, and so on. This
system will undoubtedly make them better soldiers.

5thly. A general militia to be established and the regular regiments to
be formed by drafts from the militia or their substitutes. 6thly. A certain
portion of lands to be assigned to every soldier who serves one campaign, a
double portion who serves two, and so on.[4]

Such notions obviously conflicted with the profoundly local nature of
American political culture, a product of the separate and different governmental, political, social, religious, and demographic development
of the colonies. Lee's ideas also clashed with the respect for the law and
for individuals and property rights that, with the obvious exceptions
of Native and African Americans, was central to this culture and that
compromised any idea of a total mobilization of national resources. Such
a mobilization was not to be achieved by legislation through the developing new political system. In effect, the individual colonies were to
achieve independence first and then to cooperate on their own terms
through a federal structure.

The overthrow of royal authority in 1775 saw large-scale activity by
those not yet in the politico-military system, and this was a key element
of the strategic context, both in so far as those who fought were concerned and more generally.[5] In New York in 1775:

the news of the attack at Boston, reached us on Sunday the 23rd and that
very day the populace seized the City arms and unloaded two vessels
bound with provisions to the troops of Boston. In the course of the week
they formed themselves into companies under officers of their own
choosing, distributed the arms, called a provincial Congress, demanded
the keys of the Custom House and shut up the port, trained their men
publicly, convened the citizens by beat of drum, drew the cannon into the
interior country and formed an association of defence in perfect league
with the rest of the continent.

By June 7, 1775, more than two thousand men were reported to be training daily in New York, and on June 10, it was claimed that "if a stranger
was to land here, he would be at a loss whether to pronounce this a city
immersed in commerce, or a great garrisoned town."[6]

A mixture of popular zeal, the determination of the Revolutionaries, and the weakness of their opponents decided the fate of most of the colonies in late 1775. Intimidation by mob action proved an effective strategy and gave the Patriots strategic depth in subsequent operations. The disorientating experience of the agencies of law and authority being taken over by those who were willing to connive at or support violence affected many who were unhappy about developments. To resist this situation, the royal governors had little to turn to.

In part, there was also the issue of assumptions. First was the British tendency to treat the events in 1775 as a local rebellion, rather than a large-scale event that was a revolutionary civil war. In operational terms, British generals and admirals did not like to disperse their strength, amphibious operations were difficult to execute successfully, and units that were landed might have found it difficult to obtain supplies and would have risked defeat at the hands of larger American forces, with the retreat from Concord being repeated up and down the eastern seaboard. It is, and was, not difficult, however, to feel that the opportunities the British had were missed and that the British failed to make adequate use of their sea power. An anonymous British pamphlet of 1776 complained, with reason, that the Americans had been given "the advantage of gaining time to form a union of counsels, to adjust plans of action, to turn their resources into the most convenient channels, to train their men in regular discipline, and to draw to their camp ammunition and stores, and all the necessary implements of war."[7]

Arguably, the same problems that were to face the British in the South in 1780–81 would have affected earlier operations there: to make a sufficiently widespread impact, it would have been necessary to dispatch substantial forces, but they would not necessarily have been able to dominate the situation and some units could have been defeated. In the event, the widespread activity of the Americans in 1775–56 helped direct the strategic context, even though they failed to do so in Canada where, crucially, the Americans lacked the popular support they could otherwise rely on. The invasion of Canada was seen in Britain as changing the very strategy of the struggle by

> [t]he commencing of an offensive war with the sovereign. . . . Opposition
> to government had hitherto been conducted on the apparent design,

and avowed principle only, of supporting and defending certain rights and immunities of the people, which were supposed, or pretended, to be unjustly invaded. Opposition, or even resistance, in such a case . . . is thought by many to be entirely consistent with the principles of the British constitution.[8]

The invasion of Canada was inconsistent with these principles, however the Glorious Revolution was understood.

In 1776, the declaration of independence reflected the stiffening of American resolve, prefiguring, in a different context, the change in Union strategy during the Civil War toward a harsher conduct of the war and the new goal of slave emancipation. In 1776, Loyalists were harried, as with the disarming of Maryland Loyalists in the spring and the end of the modus vivendi that had enabled British warships off New York to continue to receive provisions.

The new American government slowly became better prepared to wage war, a Board of Ordnance being instituted on June 12, 1776, although this was to prove a considerable hindrance to George Washington. A sense of reaction was important to the politics of strategic preparation. Thus, on December 30, 1776, John Hancock, the president of Congress, announced in a circular that "the strength and progress of the enemy . . . have rendered it not only necessary that the American force should be augmented beyond what Congress had heretofore designed, but that it should be brought into the field with all possible expedition."[9]

Political determination and military preparedness were not well synchronized. This was a repeated problem with revolutions, as in the case of the Dutch in 1787, although also with nonrevolutionary states. Moreover, the military context was scarcely consistent in the case of preparedness. Thus, in the 1700s, the Hungarians rebeling against the Habsburgs/Austria and the Afghans rebeling more successfully against the Safavids/Persia both required different levels of military adaptation to that seen in the case of the Americans. An account from the American headquarters outside Quebec on March 28, 1776, listed

a catalogue of complaints. Indifferent physicians and surgeons . . . a few cannon without any quantity of powder or ball will never take a fortress if by a cannonade it is to be done. . . . Suppose you had a good train of ordinance with plenty of ammunition, we have not an artillery man to

serve them ... a well-furnished military chest [money] is the soul of an
army.... Without it nothing can be done. For want of it, inevitable ruin
must attend us.... The slowness of our operations is one means of a great
backwardness in the Canadians engaging ... we were promised that cash
should be sent after us. None is yet arrived. Without it, recruiting goes
on badly all over the world and particularly in Canada.... Bricks without
straw we cannot make.[10]

The Americans were easily driven from Canada in 1776. Fresh
attempts on Canada were to be suggested and concern was to be
expressed by British generals.[11] However, invasion plans drawn up in
1778, 1780, and 1781 were not followed through for a variety of reasons,
including a lack of French support reflecting strategic priorities in the
West Indies, more pressing opportunities and problems for the Americans in the Thirteen Colonies, and the logistical difficulties of operating
in this largely barren region. Canadian émigrés, such as Moses Hazen,
pressed unsuccessfully for action, but the military task was formidable.
An invasion would have entailed sieges of strong positions by forces
enjoying scant local support and dependent on distant sources of supply.

Ironically, and underlining the problems of judging strategic capability and achievement, the Americans in the long run probably profited
from being driven out of Canada. Such extended lines of communication
and supply and the commitment of manpower required would have bled
the Continental Army dry and might have led to mutinies. Washington,
however, reflected on the failure to take Canada: "hence I shall know the
events of war are exceedingly doubtful, and that capricious fortune often
blasts our most flattering hopes."[12] This indeed was a major blow to what
had at times been a dangerous overconfidence in political circles about
the military challenge posed by Britain. More generally, the situation
deteriorated when a British amphibious force took New York. In addition, acute supply problems were exacerbated by widespread demoraliza-
tion. The Americans were forced to follow a reactive strategy, and low
morale and desertion became major problems.

One of the most insistent themes in the correspondence of the generals on both sides was the weakness of their forces, a theme that was to
grow stronger as the war progressed. This sense of weakness could be
crippling, discouraging generals from acting, even when their opponents

were in no real position to obstruct them. This situation benefited the Americans rather than the British as the latter had to reverse the current situation. General Sir William Howe, the British commander in North America from 1776 to 1778, reflected:

> I do not apprehend a successful termination to the war from the advantages His Majesty's troops can gain while the enemy is able to avoid, or unwilling to hazard a decisive action, which might reduce the leaders in rebellion to make an overture for peace; or, that this is to be expected, unless a respectable addition to the army is sent from Europe to act early in the ensuing year.... If this measure is judged to be inexpedient, or cannot be carried into execution, the event of the war will be very doubtful.
>
> Were any one of the three principal objects, vis New York, Rhode Island or Philadelphia given up to strengthen the defence of the other two, one corps to act offensively might be found, in the meantime such a cession would operate on the minds of the people strongly against His Majesty's interests ... in the apparent temper of the Americans a considerable addition to the present force will be requisite for effecting any essential change in their disposition and the re-establishment of the King's authority.[13]

This letter captured the impact of popular determination as a factor in the war. This determination had been seen earlier in 1777 in the successful American resistance to the British army under General Burgoyne advancing south from Canada. American militia played a major role in the failure of this British force, notably at the battle of Bennington, although units sent from the Continental Army were also important. Burgoyne's surrender at Saratoga enhanced the significance of the popular determination by raising the morale of the Revolutionaries, offsetting the effect of Howe's capture of Philadelphia. So also with the impact on the opinion of the French government. Indeed, in March 1777, Hans Stanley, a government Member of Parliament, had pointed out that "success had always depended much upon opinion."[14]

The role of public opinion gave the Americans a key advantage, one that was not countered by the deficiencies of the American military, even though the latter had clear operational consequences and helped force a reactive character on American strategy. Washington, for example, was not able to prevent Howe from consolidating his position in Philadelphia. The American army was still faced with many of the problems of expiring enlistments and inadequate supplies that had dogged it from the outset.[15] There were also serious command problems and major rivalries. Washington's correspondence was replete with reference to insufficient manpower and supplies. There was also a lack of coherence. For example, Major-General Dickinson ignored Washington's request to bring his militia force from northern New Jersey because he feared that the state would be invaded by the British from Staten Island. Washington had to meet criticism that he was not more active and enterprising as a commander, but his army was in a terrible situation at the end of 1777. At the same time, cautious command combined with the fighting spirit of the troops had helped deny the British the decisive victory that might help convince opinion in America, Britain, and the Continent that Britain was winning and would triumph.

This situation did not preclude choices that can be seen as strategic. For example, Valley Forge was selected as the American wintering position for 1777–78 in order to be able to mount an attack on nearby British-held Philadelphia as well as to shadow any British moves from there. Moreover, Washington hoped that the rich Pennsylvania countryside would provide his men with food and forage because what passed as Continental Army logistics were weak at best, and New Jersey was bare. The decisions taken by the Council of War of the Continental Army provide opportunities for seeing how strategy was discussed. For example, in April 1778, Washington asked his leading officers whether they advised an attack on Philadelphia, an attack on New York, or remaining in camp while the army was prepared for a later confrontation. The response was divided. Anthony Wayne argued that any attack was better than remaining on the defensive and allowing the British to implement their plans, but Washington decided to remain at Valley Forge and to await developments.[16]

These materialized in the shape of British withdrawal from Philadelphia in June 1778, a withdrawal that led to a confused engagement near Monmouth Court House on the June 28. The battle did not work out as Washington had intended, but the ability to provide an attractive gloss reflected the role of war as the source of news to sustain morale: American regulars could be presented as seeing off British regulars and not as retreating in disorder as in previous engagements. More generally, much of the American strategy was affected by their repeatedly proven inability to defend their own fortified positions and by their changing ability to confront the British in defended, fortified positions.

It proved hard to extend his success in the middle colonies to the South where the political context was one in which Loyalism was more prominent. As with Canada, the Americans found offensive operations difficult to sustain. In November 1778, Congress instructed Benjamin Lincoln, the commander in the South, to invade East Florida in order to destroy the threat posed by the British garrison in St. Augustine. Nevertheless, support for this expedition from the states was inadequate and no advance was launched. Moreover, the extension of the war to the South, after a British expeditionary force captured Savannah in December, revealed serious problems in the American army there. Yet again, however, the key element was opinion. Despite the problems faced, there was a growing confidence on the American side about the likely military outcome of the war, a confidence that can be seen in the letters of Delegates to Congress. This confidence owed much to international recognition.[17]

Opinion in the shape of local support became the key element in the war in the South after American defeats there in 1779–80 left Nathanael Greene, the commander there from late 1780, able to carry on only partisan warfare. Daniel Morgan was given command of a section of the army and was sent to "spirit up the people" in upper South Carolina, to hinder the collection of supplies by the British, and to attack their flank or rear if they advanced into North Carolina.[18] In addition, Greene found himself obliged to rely heavily on the activities of partisan bands under such leaders as Thomas Sumter and Francis Marion. The use of partisans was an obvious response to the American defeats at Charleston and Camden, the uncontrollable vastness of the South, and the need to counter Loyalist activity. The consequence was a vicious local war.

This conflict could later be presented as guerrilla warfare and with the implication that such an innovation was a product of a different political culture and one that represented a counter to, and development on, ancien régime professionalism. However, such conflict had already been seen in Europe—for example, being used in Hungary. Rather than being learned from conflict with the Turks or, in North America, as a response to Native Americans, the local environment, or the War of Independence, guerrilla warfare was a sort of instinctive tactics focused on ambushes and based on the weakness of one side and its own knowledge of the ground. Thus, the Piedmontese employed Waldensian militia in small units with remarkable results against the French, especially in the War of the Austrian Succession on the Alpine front in the 1740s, and guerrilla attacks affected French operations by cutting supply lines. The same tactics were applied in the County of Nice by the local population against the occupying French from 1792 to 1796. As a related point, far from "small war" techniques being colonial warfare tactics and spreading from North America to Europe, these techniques were important throughout and not only in the Western world.[19]

Washington and other American commanders were familiar with the European manuals on partisan war. This was an example of a rising power learning from the older powers, America learning from European practice and experience. Thus, there was a combination of forced experience: a knowledge of past practice and adaptation to one's particular circumstances.

The war in the South was to play a major role in the subsequent American understanding and presentation of their success. However, in 1780 and 1781, Washington was far more hopeful of using French forces, land and sea. His initial target was New York. Its fall would be a fateful blow to the British military position in North America and might well lead to the effective end of the war, a step the Americans desperately required. The loss of New York would leave the British without a secure anchorage for their fleet south of Halifax, Nova Scotia, and the Americans could then turn south to besiege Charleston and Savannah, thus reconquering America from north to south. Nevertheless, Washington was sufficiently flexible to appreciate that cooperation with the French came first and that it would be possible to focus on a different target.

After the British defeat at Yorktown in October 1781, the same strategy came to the fore. Washington appreciated that his success there was largely due to French assistance, and he hoped to persuade de Grasse, the French admiral, to cooperate in a speedy attack on Charleston or, failing that, Wilmington, North Carolina. Instead, de Grasse sailed directly from American waters for the Caribbean. In 1782, Washington hoped to combine again with the French, either attacking New York or Charleston. In the event of French support, Washington was interested in an invasion of Canada. A major British naval victory over the French off the Iles des Saintes in the Caribbean on April 12, 1782, ended that possibility, although anyway the French took the view that Washington was not ready for an attack on New York. In the event, the Americans had to wait for the British to evacuate Charleston and New York as part of the peace settlement.

The role of contingency in American strategy emerges clearly both in general terms and in specifics. Following the disasters of 1776, Washington recognized that for many, the Continental Army was the revolution. Thereafter, he did not take risks unless success was all but guaranteed. Had the British been more successful, the Americans might well have resorted to more revolutionary military methods, such as guerrilla warfare and the strategy advocated by Charles Lee. Indeed, Greene succeeded in the South in combining partisan bands with the maneuvers of a field army. Alternatively, and pursuing a very different strategy, the Americans might have continued to rely on field armies, as the French Revolutionaries were to do in the 1790s, but, again as the French Revolutionaries did, those who took power in America could have taken a harsher attitude toward states' rights and private property. The consequence might have been a very different American public culture, one that stressed the national state more than the individual citizen or the individual state, and obligations more than rights.

One part of the strategy for new would-be powers was to secure, if necessary by force, diplomatic recognition. This process entailed not only obtaining legitimacy but also acquiring resources and commercial opportunities. However, there were other goals after independence was recognized in 1783. American concerns drew greatly on colonial culture but also had been fueled by the extent to which the War of Independence had seen conflict with Native Americans[20] as well as British attempts to recruit slave support. Alongside continuing threats after the war from these sources came the other strategic challenge posed by the fact that the closing stages of the conflict, and even more its aftermath, had seen the total dissolution of the pro-American wartime coalition.[21]

This dissolution was fundamental to the geopolitics of the Atlantic world from 1783 until 1812, when in declaring war on Britain, the American government in effect aligned with France, which already ruled, as a result of conquest, the United Provinces and most of Spain. The dissolution of the coalition in 1783 both made Britain more menacing and raised the threat that it might find European allies. For the United States, Canada in British hands underlined past failure and present threat.

More generally, ambition, opportunity, and fear combined to drive forward American anxiety; and this strategic culture was the basis for a number of linked strategies. These included conflict with Native Americans and the organization of trans-Appalachia, which was primarily linked to the Atlantic world by, and through, the United States, a situation secured by the Louisiana Purchase of territories from France in 1803. This conflict appeared necessary and appropriate because stadial models of social development led to the view that Natives, as hunter-gatherers, were at an earlier stage of human development and could only share in the future if they changed. The "merciless Indian savages" of the Declaration of Independence were not only allegedly a tool of British revenge but also apparently an obstacle to America's destiny who had to make way for settlers, a view very much taken by Thomas Jefferson.[22]

Jefferson pursued not only sovereignty but also the acquisition of Native lands and the expulsion of the Native Americans. Whereas during the colonial period, the concept of discovery had not been seen as entailing the transfer of land ownership from the Natives, Jefferson took a very different view. He employed this view to support the exploration of, and beyond, the lands acquired from France in 1803 by the Louisiana Purchase, not least in supporting the Lewis and Clark transcontinental expedition to the Pacific. In 1812, Jefferson observed to John Adams that some Native Americans were becoming agricultural settlers (in his terms), a process he saw as beneficial as far as competition with Britain was concerned:

> On those who have made any progress, English seduction will have no effect. But the backward will yield and be thrown further back. These will relapse into barbarism and misery ... and we shall be obliged to drive them, with the beasts of the forest, into the strong mountains.[23]

Moreover, as another aspect of strategic culture, the very American conception of appropriate governance encouraged expansion. In response to their perception of mistreatment as part of the British Empire, Americans, both before and after independence, pressed for an eventual equality but within a federalism that was seen as the means and ideology necessary to combine liberty with strength and locality with extent. The ideological dimension of government and spatiality was crucial to this strategy of governance and expansionism. The federal approach in practical terms was a way to tackle the bold territorial claims of the preexisting seven colonies that had extensive western lands. Their cessions of these lands to Congress, and the Ordinances of 1784, 1785, and 1787, the last the Northwest Ordinance, ensured a federal goal and means for the organization of trans-Appalachia. In terms of the ideology of the strategy involved, this approach made expansion appear normative without threatening the imperial excess allegedly associated with Rome and Britain. Instead, Americans came to believe not only that their territory must expand but also that the Union had to be dynamic. The new states were to be equal and uniform as far as their government and the federal government were concerned. This solution was regarded as a way to ensure republican ideals, as well as to avoid the divisive characteristics associated with British imperial government and the risk that these territories would become breakaway nations. The equivalent with France in the 1790s was the creation of allied republics, such as the Rauracian, Batavian, Ligurian, Cisalpine, and Helvetic republics and the Republic of the Valais. However, there was no position of equality, the republics were exploited to French ends, and they were all, bar Helvetia, swept aside by Napoleon after he seized power in 1799, as he greatly expanded French territory.

In America, the new system of governance was intended to ensure the rapid development of the economy and the creation of commercial connections that would strengthen the Union and prevent separatism. As later with Revolutionary France, such developmental strategies reflected the concerns of the political nation. There was a need to assert the value and importance of America. In part, this assertion was defensive, notably to disprove the theory of degeneracy advanced by Georges, Count of Buffon, an influential French intellectual, who argued that the climate of the New World naturally resulted in the enfeebling of plants, animals, and people. This view was challenged by the politician intellectuals who were so important in the early American Republic, especially Benjamin Franklin, Alexander Hamilton, and Jefferson in his *Notes on the State of Virginia* (1784).

Washington and Jefferson provided iconic comments for those subsequently seeking to discuss American policy and strategy, comments that reflected an attempt to define a moral space for the new republic and a strategy accordingly. The moral and prudential reasons offered for staying out of the maelstrom of great-power politics were clearly linked to an exceptionalist vision of America as better than, and also separate to, Europe.[24] So also with the determination to dispense with any idea that the universality of a supposed right to happiness proclaimed in the Declaration of Independence carried with it a need to spread this right in foreign countries.

In this respect, there was a clear difference to the situation with Revolutionary France and later, Russia. Aside from moral goals, such a spread appeared to the French Revolutionaries to be the best way to protect their achievement. The Americans had a similar view but were willing to devote less of an emphasis to it and crucially not to persist in the face of opposition, as with the unsuccessful attempt to seize Canada in 1775–76. Depicting individual countries as encapsulating universal necessities lessened the presentation of a restrictive spatial dimension for strategy. However, a tension that was to be seen repeatedly in the geopolitics of strategy, one between realist and idealist conceptions, came to the fore with the United States. Yet again, however, it is appropriate not to push novelty in the eighteenth century too far as similar issues had arisen when discussing the extent of support for confessional themes during the European Wars of Religion.

American strategy was not simply a matter of existential identity and alternatively, the interpretation of American identity and interests in terms of, and in the face of, the existing facts of power and inclination in North America. There were also the problems raised by the extent to which the constitution took time to negotiate, let alone bed down,[25] a process that was even more to be seen in France. As in France, the political settlement was made more necessary by the threatening international situation and the problems of conducting foreign policy.[26] For example, Washington's Neutrality Proclamation of 1793, which annulled the eleventh article of America's treaty with France in 1778, led to a major debate between Alexander Hamilton and James Madison about the roles of the executive and legislature in the conduct of foreign policy.

At the same time, strategy was capability based as well as task orientated and was also affected by the public narratives about goals and means. The new American state was very weak militarily. After independence, its navy was dismantled and its army savagely cut back in response to political views and fiscal needs.[27] The absence, until the Constitution was settled and established, of a well-organized government or a system of direct taxation, was a fundamental limit to military capability. In part, the size of the military reflected an inherent fundamental aspect of any strategic context, and one that underlines the difficulties of separating strategy from policy. In part, these reductions reflected the more contingent financial crisis left by the war, especially heavy debts. Political factors were crucial, including the antiarmy ideology derived from the British background and the colonial experience, the linked support for the militia, and also the extent to which the unsettled governmental situation left any basis for military arrangements unclear, irrespective of the serious political differences and controversies bound up in issues of army purpose, size, and command.

Subsequently but also related to these tensions, the crisis caused in American politics by the growing radicalism of the French Revolution from 1793 ensured that strategy and policy were jumbled together in a mélange that comprised foreign policy, domestic politics, and the nature of the American polity. To many American politicians, the response to the French Revolution had to be vigilance: vigilance against domestic radicals who might support France and be inspired by it and vigilance against French power projection. Linked to this point, American foreign policy was republican, not radical.

Hamilton's sense of a menacing international system and his more specific concerns about France both gave reason to his drive to develop America's public finances and national economy and to his Anglophilia, which resulted in improved relations with Britain. Jay's Treaty of 1794 eased commercial and territorial disputes, while, in turn, the British abandoned the Native Americans, helping the Americans consolidate their position in Ohio, then the key area of conflict with Native Americans. In an approach that presented prudence in ideological terms and ideology as prudential, Hamilton saw Britain as an essentially liberal state and therefore as less of a threat to America and indeed other states than France. He was determined to provide a national bank and a professional army able to unite America against internal subversion and foreign threat. The passage of the Alien and Sedition Acts was regarded as a means to strengthen the government against internal opposition. However, there was widespread hostility to the acts, hostility that took forward the criticism seen earlier in the decade to the assumptions and policies of the Federalists. These assumptions and policies had a counterrevolutionary character insofar as they sought to contain the radical aspects and implications of the American Revolution and the example of its French counterpart.

Differences within America reflected a total lack of unity over political identity and strategic culture. Aside from a major disagreement over the size and organization of the military, a disagreement that arose from contrasting assumptions about the nature of America as a state and about American society, clashing conceptions of the international system were also important. Hamilton advanced a pessimistic interpretation of competing states and of the need, in response, for strategies of governmental and military preparedness on the part of America and also of other powers. In contrast, critics, notably Jefferson, felt that a benign system was possible and/or that America could distance itself from the European powers.[28]

To the Jeffersonians, the struggle that had given rise to the American Revolution in 1775 was being repeated but with the threat now based in America, not Britain, although looking from America to Britain for inspiration and example. Indeed, Hamilton, in Jeffersonian eyes, was another version of George III. More specifically, Jefferson domesticated and politicized the European antiaristocratic discourse and the suspicion of finance and credit, and focused them on the dangers allegedly posed by a European-style army supported by taxation, an approach that also restricted the development of a navy that Hamilton sought.

On the part of the Jeffersonians, there was a profound anxiety about the problems for American public life that would come from the military, irrespective of the intentions of its commanders. In part, this anxiety stemmed from the origins of the American state (the federal entity as well as the individual states), both as a product of British political culture, especially hostility toward a large army, and as a reaction against the supposed authoritarian practices of the British metropole, notably in its use of military force, in its expectations of financial support for the military, and in its readiness to rely on military governance. The issue was exacerbated by the extent to which American assumptions and practices about military goals and activity were militia orientated.[29] The United States thus represented an accentuation of a commonplace reluctance to see regular forces as anything other than supporters of centralization and arbitrary government. In forming this attitude, the acceptance of the theory of natural rights or natural law in the Declaration of Independence questioned the legitimacy of all authority, especially central authority, and the discrediting of executive power was also important.

When conflict with Britain resumed in the War of 1812, this led to a serious crisis in American government. An unwillingness to bear the cost of the conflict, which in part reflected not only political divisions but also the serious limitations of American capital markets, had left the Treasury with insufficient money. As a consequence, government paper bore a significant discount, its own contractors rejected Treasury notes, and the Treasury found it difficult to manage the national debt.

These fiscal problems, which the British understood and which encouraged the strategy of blockade, meant that irrespective of political hopes and claims, large-scale offensive operations by the Americans were no longer a serious prospect in 1815. Had the war continued, with the British able to mount repeated amphibious assaults, the Americans, forced onto the defensive to protect their own areas, would probably have seen a regionalization of the war that would have been pushed further by the crisis in American public finances. They had not thought strategically about how to protect their trade.

While American strategy was therefore circumscribed by resources, debates about strategy were subordinate to political tensions and could not be separated from them. Moreover, these debates drew on a politi-cized historical account or rather, a historicized political account. In this account, strategies appeared directly relevant, more particularly in terms of how best to define the necessary national strategic culture. In part because, other than as British colonies, the independent state lacked a relevant "deep history," ideology was a key element. Thus, Jefferson preferred to rely not on a European-style military but on national unity, which was an example of the comforting illusion that virtue would nec-essarily prevail. This view led Jefferson, in his inaugural address in 1801, to claim that America was the strongest country in the world.

Ironically, virtue was itself to become the key issue of American disunity as it was linked to bitter and potent divisions over the status of slavery in new territories and the value of expansion in order to affect the slavery issue.[30] The lack of a large standing army greatly affected the abil-ity to respond but was also a product of the federal system and culture.

FRANCE

The definition of a virtuous national strategic culture was also an issue with the French Revolution. The rapid speed of changes in France and the absence there of sufficient time, trust, and shared views to permit the development of stable constitutional conventions and techniques of parliamentary management kept the situation unstable and ensured that policy and strategy were jumbled together amid expressions of political opportunity and disagreement. The resolution of the National Assembly on May 22, 1790, after bitter debates at a time of crisis between Britain and France's ally Spain (the Nootka Sound crisis), that the king, Louis XVI, could not declare war without its approval, reflected a pro-found division as to the nature of the political community. This division centered on the struggle between different ideas about the relationship between Crown and nation, with the latter increasingly seen as a more significant and active proposition.[31]

This struggle developed into a clash of royal versus national sover-eignty. Ideological clashes related to content as well as form for the pres-sure for change reflected concern about royal views and the impact of radical writers, such as Rousseau, Mercier de la Rivière, and Condorcet.

They argued that reform required the transfer of control over foreign policy: from essentially bellicose, irrational, and selfish monarchs to the people who, they asserted, would be led by reason and would love peace. Armand-Marc, Comte de Montmorin, the experienced foreign minister (who was to be killed by the Revolutionaries in 1792 during the September Massacres), was convinced that no matter how the revolution turned out, the French ruler would never again exercise the unlimited control over foreign policy that he once had. However, perceptive observers predicted in 1790 that the National Assembly's dismissal of war for the purpose of making conquests would prove only rhetorical and that "democratic" states would be as given to aggression as were "despotic" monarchies.[32] Moreover, Napoleon was to prove Montmorin wrong.

There was praise on moral grounds for the French decision from foreign commentators—for example, in the British press. The *Times* of May 26, 1790, argued that it was clear from history that the most harmful conflicts "originated in the injustice, the animosity, or the capricious passions of individuals," a view that echoed the fashionable distaste for court politics. The more radical *Morning Herald* of May 31, 1790, proclaimed the decrees of the National Assembly as

> the very essence of true philosophy! a death's wound to despotism, arbitrary power, and the false prerogative of ambitious, cruel, bloodthirsty tyrants ... and the total extirpation of that radical disease of the French Cabinet, aspiring to universal dominion! ... may be said to form a new epoch in the annals of the world, tending to spread universal amity.

Thus, a new strategic practice and culture were discerned when in June 1790, Spain submitted a formal demand for French assistance. It was informed that Louis XVI must submit the request to the National Assembly.

More generally, the Nootka Sound crisis of 1790 reflected the difficulty of assessing the strategic context and even more of adopting a clear location in terms of a chronological typology. It was both an aspect of ancien régime confrontation and a foretaste of the post-1815 struggles between imperial powers for transoceanic territory and colonial trading rights. These struggles arose from competing interests rather than ideologies, although the general competitive context itself had an ideological dimension. The interplay of government and public in 1790 was complex,

with Britain, in its relations with Spain, having seen more public engagement in 1739 than in 1790, while France moved in the opposite direction
and Spain revealed scant change. Ideological factors certainly played a
role in 1790. Spanish governmental concern over developments within
France and the possible impact of French revolutionary ideology helped
to induce both hesitation about turning to France and postcrisis interest
in better relations with Britain.

In France, the National Assembly represented a new strategic element. The rapid speed of change in the country and the absence of sufficient time, trust, and shared views to permit the development of stable
constitutional conventions and techniques of parliamentary management both helped to keep the relationship between the royal government and the National Assembly unsettled, as did a crucial lack of trust.
Such a lack of consistency and trust was not an innovation of revolutionary government as the personal diplomacy of ministers also played
a role in states under royal control, such as contemporary Austria and
Prussia.

In France in the early 1790s, the weakness of a state whose governmental system was buckling under pressure, notably a refusal to pay
taxes, combined with changing attitudes. At the same time, as so often
when assessing the impact of revolution on strategic culture, it is possible to detect considerable continuity between the policies of the ancien
régime French state and those of the politicians of 1789–91 and indeed,
although not always in the same fashion, of subsequent years. In a situation that contrasted markedly with Russia but also with Prussia, France
had essentially abandoned an aggressive Continental foreign policy in
midcentury and not in 1789. Its forces had not campaigned in the Low
Countries since 1748, nor had Louis XV or Louis XVI made gains at the
expense of the neighboring Austrian Netherlands (Belgium) and other
territories, other than through small-scale, negotiated border settlements which contrasted greatly with the use by Louis XIV of such issues
in order to pursue major gains. In addition, Lorraine was acquired in
1766 as a result of inheritance in line with a treaty of 1738, while Corsica
was acquired by purchase from Genoa in 1768, although popular resistance in Corsica had to be suppressed. The essential objective of French
foreign policy since 1748, of a stable Europe without aggressive wars,

was at first inherited by the government of Revolutionary France. Thus, revolutionary enthusiasm initially contributed to an established end.

In April 1792, however, France declared war with Austria, beginning a period of war that, with brief interruptions, continued until 1815. The contrast with recent French policy very much indicated the impact of ideology on strategy. France was alone in 1792, bar for the backing of foreign radicals, the extent and effectiveness of which were greatly exaggerated in Paris. Even the republic it had helped from 1778, the United States, remained neutral. Moreover, France was not drawn into war as a result of alliance systems and of the action or problems of an ally, as had been the case for France in going to war in support of Austria against Prussia in 1756. As a consequence, French strategy in 1792 arose largely from domestic circumstances, although these were in part activated by the international situation. In turn, that assessment can be presented differently by noting that the domestic perceptions of this situation were crucial and as instances of a markedly changing strategic culture.

France, moreover, was not the sole player. Indeed, from July 1791, when Emperor Leopold II issued the Padua Circular, an appeal to Europe's rulers for concerted action to restore the liberty of the French royal family, a dynamic had been provided by counterrevolutionary steps. On August 27, 1791, the rulers of Austria and Prussia issued the Declaration of Pillnitz, which sought to give added force to the principles set forth in the Padua Circular.

In part displacing attention from the monarch and providing a focus for the emphasis on the nation, war itself served as a strategy for unity in France or could be rhetorically deployed to that end. The Girondin faction, influential in 1792, saw war as a means to unite the country behind them, with Louis XVI either included in this new unity or clearly identified as its opponent. More generally, politicians were caught up in the dynamic of framing strategy in a volatile context and without stable domestic parameters. Domestic and foreign enemies were allegedly linked, each apparently making action against the other more necessary, so that domestic and foreign regeneration could be aligned.

As so often with strategy, a changing tone, as well as content, was important. In France among the radicals, the determination to secure a transformation contributed to aggressive goals and methods, with compromise not acceptable as a public aim. So also with the response. In 1792, the advancing Prussian commander, Charles, Duke of Brunswick, himself a sovereign ruler, issued a declaration setting out the aims of Francis II of Austria and Frederick William II of Prussia. They claimed to seek the reestablishment of Louis XVI's legislative authority and, to that end, Brunswick warned that Paris would be subject to exemplary vengeance if Louis was harmed, a deterrent threat that totally failed. In this crisis, appeals for zeal in France were matched by paranoia about betrayal, one aided by the surrender of French frontier fortresses to the invading forces.

In response, the strategy proposed for abroad was one of seeking popular support, notably, on November 19, 1792, with the National Convention, the successor to the National Assembly, passing a decree declaring that the French people would extend fraternity and assistance to all peoples seeking to regain their liberty. As a general principle, this was subversive of all international order as well as unrealistic. On December 15, a decree to ensure that the ancien régime be swept away in territories occupied by French forces was promulgated. On February 1, 1793, the National Convention decided unanimously to declare war on Britain and the Dutch, making novel use of the established notion that war was declared on sovereigns and thus arguing that aggression was not being committed against other peoples. More generally, there was a wider struggle between radical and moderate views on the international order, views that helped, both in France and elsewhere, locate both the prospect of peace and the means of waging war.[33]

The mobilization of French society was to be the key strategy adopted at home and one that was made more significant by the failure to win much foreign support. Defeat at the hands of Austria in 1793 led to the army being given new force by the *levée en masse* (conscription), able new commanders, and more effective organization. The armies raised were both larger than those deployed by France hitherto and enabled it to operate effectively on several fronts at once, to sustain casualties, and to match the opposing forces of much of Europe. Moreover, initially at least, Revolutionary enthusiasm was an important element in French capability, one that was helpful in providing the morale required for effective shock action and in particular, for crossing the killing ground produced by opposing firepower. In short, strategic culture and military tactics were closely linked.

In part, strategy was set by ideology and in part, by the very military that had been created. Just as ideology and the mechanism of terror discouraged compromise, so the government, military, and generals required continued warfare, notably operating abroad, in order to fund their activities. By keeping the generals busy, war served to contain their ambitions within France and apparently addressed the issue of betrayal. For the generals, opportunism and the ability to make a new world created a strategic culture focused on aggressive action and on continual activity. Military convenience, lust for loot, the practice of expropriation, ideological conviction, the political advantages of a successful campaign, and campaigning opportunities all contributed to the same end, as with the occupation of Venice in 1797 and the Papal States and Piedmont in 1798, and the invasion of Switzerland in 1798. Force increasingly defined France's response with other powers. Napoleon exemplified this process, and his seizure of power in 1799, initially as one of three consuls, was a culmination, bringing elements of the new strategy to a close and others to the fore.

French success by 1797 and again by 1801 contrasted with a lack of similar Prussian decisive victory, when also up against a powerful coalition, during the Seven Years' War in 1756–63. The contrast reflected resource equations as well as strategic, geopolitical, organizational, and operational factors. Frederick II could deliver major victories but could not spare the time for a lengthy pursuit of a single enemy, given the number of other enemies who threatened him. In addition, not yet organized in divisions or corps, the armies of the time were clumsy instruments, while there were few commanders of detached armies or forces who were psychologically prepared for independent decision making. That Frederick frequently lost more men than his enemies, even in his victories, compounded another organizational issue, namely that his tightly disciplined troops could not be unleashed in a headlong pursuit without the danger of the units becoming less coherent or even disintegrating because of desertion as soon as they were out of sight of their officers. In operational terms, the Prussians were poor in siegework and often lost momentum by getting stuck in front of fortresses and fortress cities.

In teleological terms, Napoleon's seizure of power in 1799 would be an appropriate place to close this chapter and book, one made more so by his significance for later commentators on war, especially Clausewitz and Jomini, and helped by its near coincidence with the end of the century. As with conventional accounts, that approach indeed has value, but it suffers from a number of faults. In particular, the weaknesses of republican strategies attract insufficient attention. Indeed, in 1775–99, it was the fall of republics that was most notable. In 1781, Gustavus III of Sweden, who in 1772 had overthrown the existing Swedish constitution with its system of limited monarchy, pointed out that the art of war of the time, with its large permanent armies and navies, left republics fearful of losing their domestic liberty by these means, such as the United Provinces (Dutch), unable to compete.[34] From 1792, Revolutionary France overran the republics in Western Europe, only to be overthrown itself in 1799. The United Provinces (Dutch) was conquered by France in 1795, while, having been conquered by Napoleon, Venice was transferred to Austria in 1797 in exchange for French rule over the Austrian Netherlands being recognized. By 1810, only Helvetia and Danzig were left as Europe's republics, and both were under Napoleon's control.

In the New World, at the close of the century, the republics of the United States and Saint-Domingue (Haiti), more especially the second, were both in a precarious situation. In the Quasi-War with France that began in 1797, the United States found itself vulnerable to French attacks on its commerce and dependent on British naval strength. At the same time, the new alliance between France and Spain challenged American hopes of breaking through to the Gulf of Mexico. Napoleon's seizure of power was to be followed by his attempt, in 1802–3, to regain control of Saint-Domingue and by the development of a "western design" designed to increase French strength in, and around, the Caribbean. The rush of new republics that was to accompany the overthrow of Spanish rule in Central and South America had not yet occurred. Moreover, the American presidential election of 1800 was accompanied and followed by talk of civil war.

It is this weakness of republican structures that is most notable in the late 1790s. This raises questions about what this weakness meant for strategic cultures and also for ideas of development and modernity.

Turning more specifically to ideas of strategy, there is the possibility that the weakness of republics appeared less significant than the ability of popular movements to see off regular forces in the American and French Revolutions, thus prefiguring the situation with the Spanish revolution against Napoleon in 1808, a revolution staged in the absence of the imprisoned monarch. Clausewitz was influenced by this revolution, seeing it as an example that the Prussians should have followed after their devastating defeat by France in 1806, a defeat of a system.[35] This Spanish resistance offered the possibility of thwarting the victors' ability to translate the output of victory in battle into the outcome of a successful war, thus repeating, as a military means and a moral step, the earlier persistence of both the Americans and the French in the face of defeats.

As so often, the conclusion of republican and popular strength and success indicated the unreliable nature of the evidence that was cited. If the Prussians failed to suppress the French Revolution in 1792, they overthrew the Dutch Patriots in 1787. If the French failed in Spain in 1808–13, their subsequent invasion was crucial to the overthrow of the liberals there in 1823. The British lost when fighting the Americans in 1775–83, but American attacks on Canada were defeated in 1776, 1812, 1813, and 1814, and the British were able to strike at Washington in 1814, even if they failed outside New Orleans the following year. Moreover, that defeat was followed by the opening stages of an expedition to take Mobile, stages that promised a success that was cut short by the end of the war.[36]

The relationship between constitutional form and geopolitical drive was apparent. The geopolitical context, rather than the constitutional form, appears to be dominant. The United States did not create a military able to compete with leading Western powers, whereas republican France did. In the former, threats and opportunities did not prove sufficiently serious to overthrow the decentralized political structure established after the revolution. In the case of France, in contrast, threats and opportunities proved more urgent, but so too did the legacy of a prerevolutionary state that centralized foreign policy and invested in a potent military. The configuration of policy was different to that prior to 1789, but the contrast with the United States was far greater. Looked at in another light, the key element was not republican or monarchical but instead, centralized, as with France, or not, as with the United States.

An emphasis on ideology and/or constitution as key variables, causes, and changes can lead to an underrating of the significance of organizational changes, notably of recruitment practice. This factor was not restricted to republics. Instead, by the late eighteenth century, military entrepreneurship was not as independent in Europe as it had been in the late seventeenth, let alone in the early seventeenth century. As a result, the system did not sap governmental control, both politically and operationally, to the degree that had occurred earlier. This change was crucial to the ability to think and act effectively in strategic terms and to operational ends. This ability was not new, but the increase in discipline, planning, and organizational regularity and predictability that characterized Western armies and navies made it less difficult to implement strategic conceptions. As a result, Western powers could now match the Chinese ability to plan and implement. The greater effectiveness of military forces was widely demonstrated, not least by Russia under and after Peter the Great and by Prussia from 1740. France was able to deploy and sustain significant forces on more than one front, not from the 1790s but in the 1670s, 1690s, 1700s, 1730s, 1740s, and 1750s. This capability, albeit one that faced major difficulties in the 1700s,[37] greatly enhanced the military and political challenge France posed to opposing coalitions and the strategic complexity it represented. France had pursued such activity in the 1550s, 1630s, 1640s, and 1650s but less successfully so in large part due to supply and financial issues.[38] The ability to sustain forces on more than one front focused the strategic issue of prioritization whatever the nature of the governmental system. Conscription took forward the challenge.[39]

Yet, changing ideological factors did have an effect. Pressure for a more rigorous warfare, indeed for what would later be referred to as total warfare, as understood in the terms of the late eighteenth century, was seen both with the French Revolutionary forces and with their opponents. The latter presented the strategy of the former in existential and apocalyptic terms. In 1794, additional instructions were sent to Robert

Liston, the British envoy in Constantinople, to warn the Turkish ministers repeatedly about France:

> those principles aim at nothing less than the subversion of all the
> established religions and forms of government in the whole world, by
> means the most atrocious which the mind of man will ever conceive, by the
> indiscriminate massacre, as practised in their own devoted country, of all
> who were supposed to be averse to their system . . . by sacrilege, plunder
> and devastation of private property.[40]

In August 1792, William, Lord Auckland, formerly William Eden, a
senior British diplomat, urged that the war not be conducted

> with the courtesies of the age . . . the French troops, however despicable
> they may be in point of discipline and command, are earnest in the
> support of the wicked and calamitous cause in which they are engaged. . . .
> I sincerely hope that it may be a plan rigorously observed, to disarm every
> place and district through which the troops may pass, to destroy the arms,
> to dismantle the fortresses, to demolish the cannon, powder mills etc, and
> all forges for arms etc, and to issue a notice that any place or district found
> a second time in arms shall be subject to military execution . . . if neglected,
> there is reason to believe that the impression of the interference will at best
> be transitory.[41]

Such views were also found in military circles. In 1796, Major-
General David Dundas outlined the means that would be pursued if the
French invaded Britain:

> When an enemy lands, all the difficulties of civil government and the
> restraint of forms cease; everything must give way to the supplying and
> strengthening the army, repelling the enemy. . . . The strongest and most
> effectual measures are necessary. . . . The great object must be constantly
> to harass, alarm and fire on an enemy, and to impede his progress till a
> sufficient force assembles to attack him . . . every inch of ground, every field
> may to a degree be disputed, even by inferior numbers. . . . The country
> must be driven, and everything useful within his reach destroyed without
> mercy.[42]

Confronting domestic challenges, real and alleged, was also a key
aspect of the strategy of response to the challenge posed by the French
Revolution. In a handwritten letter sent to Auckland in November 1792,
William, Lord Grenville, the foreign secretary, suggested that there was
"a concerted plan to drive us to extremities, with a view of producing an

impression in the interior of the country."[43] Concern about the situation
in Ireland, notably the threat of alliance between Catholics and radical
Presbyterians, led William Pitt the Younger, the prime minister, to over-
rule the wishes of the Protestant Ascendancy in Ireland and to grant
Catholics the vote there in early 1793. In response to the apparent threat
of insurrection in London, the government in late 1792 moved troops
nearer to London and embodied parts of the militia. A sense of the role of
elements outside the military as an integral part of strategy was captured
by John Hatsell, the clerk of the House of Commons, when referring to
the Association for Preserving Liberty and Property against Republicans
and Levellers, which was launched at a meeting at the Crown and Anchor
tavern in London. He wrote:

> the Society at the Crown and Anchor. This appears to me a better plan than
> trusting to the soldiery and brings the question to its true point—a contest
> between those who have property and those who have none. If this idea
> is followed up generally and with spirit, it may, for a time, secure us peace
> internally.[44]

As part of the process of political mobilization, the British government blocked grain exports to France, introduced an Aliens Bill, and
sought to win over part of the opposition, which strengthened its position in Parliament and thus provided a public show of strength. The
Dutch were encouraged to arm, and Britain sought to define war goals.
These focused not on an attempt at counterrevolution but on the return
of France to its 1789 frontiers, accompanied by a public pledge by France
not to stir up discontent in other states. In return, other powers were to
promise both noninterference and the recognition of the French Republic. In short, the government wanted no war of ideology or any attempt
to revenge losses to France during the War of American Independence,
let alone to make fresh colonial gains. However, the short-term practicality of these goals was undermined by French attitudes, which in turn
sapped British trust in the possibility of compromise. Indeed, the British
considered helping Austria facilitate an insurrection in Belgium in order
to drive French forces out.[45]

In response to the execution of Louis XVI on January 21, 1793, Britain expelled the French envoy and as the two powers rapidly moved
toward war, stepped up both military preparations and steps toward

creating an alliance system. There was still, nevertheless, a reluctance to endorse the cause of counterrevolution. This issue and tension was to be seen in all the ideological struggles of subsequent years, just as it had done during the earlier wars of religion.

The general assumption, one important to strategies and to what can be termed antistrategies, was that domestic and international factors were intertwined. At a time of great instability in France, Grenville observed in 1794:

> nothing but the most absolute and dreadful tyranny can continue those efforts by which alone France triumphs over the rest of Europe, and that this tyranny is incompatible with so insecure and precarious a state as that of the present functions at Paris: whichever of them happens to be the party guillotining for the moment.[46]

At the same time, Grenville's correspondence revealed the problem of coalition warfare: the dependence of strategy on an alliance drawn apart by different interests and concerns and by mutual suspicions: "His Majesty cannot consent to rest the whole system of the combined operations for the next campaign on a foundation so weak and insufficient."[47]

CONCLUSIONS

The French inability in 1802 to translate their success in regaining control of much of Saint-Domingue/Haiti into a suppression of resistance serves to indicate the more general problems of counterrevolutionary strategies. These can be discussed in structural terms, ranging from environmental factors, such as the yellow fever that hit the French there in 1802, and geopolitical, such as the consequences for the French on Saint-Domingue of British naval pressure in 1803, to the more general issues of counterinsurgency warfare. However, there is also need to draw attention to improvements in fighting quality on the part of revolutionaries. This was the case with the revolutions in America, France, and Haiti. Improvement was due not to revolutionary enthusiasm but to the natural trajectories of forces, much of which initially comprised large numbers of civilian officers and men rapidly thrown into war, although in Saint-Domingue, the *bossales*, newly arrived slaves, were experienced in the methods of West African combat, notably ambushes and mass attacks. Troops gained combat and maneuver experience, and learned to respond to their opponents. In aggregate terms, these fed through into the overall result of the war.

At the same time, success could pose major political problems, as was readily apparent in France, where the military became the most important aspect of the revolution and war was hardwired into political culture. Moreover, the conquest and occupation of much of Europe by Napoleon by 1812 created an acute strategic incubus for him. The contrast, that of benign failure, was indicated by the American inability to conquer Canada in 1775–1814. Because of poor leadership, political decentralization, logistical problems, environmental factors, and the strength of the resistance, the Americans were unable to launch a successful offensive against Canada. Both powers, in their wars of 1775–83 and 1812–15, experienced the grave difficulty of inflicting sufficient damage on the other to force them to peace. Combined with war weariness, this led by 1815 to a strategic insight that was of great consequence. The realization that Canada could not be conquered greatly eased subsequent relations with Britain. The comparable process was of much greater difficulty in Europe, due in large part to the attitudes of the Revolutionaries and Napoleon. The net effect was to require the total victories seen in 1814 and 1815 and a postwar settlement accepting occupation and intervention.

It is possible to locate the French trajectory in a teleology that could be extended to comprehend the rise of strategy as a formal concept. Alan Forrest has argued that there was a new "political will to break with tradition and apply scientific knowledge to the needs of the military on a scale that would have been difficult to imagine in the France of Louis XVI."[48] Focusing on changes in intellectual and political culture in late eighteenth century, although not on the rise of strategy, David Bell claimed that

> the intellectual transformations of the Enlightenment, followed by the political fermentation of 1789–92, produced new understandings of war that made possible the cataclysmic intensifications of the fighting over the next twenty-three years. Ever since, the same developments have shaped the way the Western societies have seen and engaged in military conflict.[49]

The basic thesis, however, is highly problematic,[50] while the American comparison indicates the possibility of the Enlightenment playing a role in a different process of learning lessons, as indeed do comparisons with Britain and with Continental ancien régime societies. Moreover, comparisons with non-Western societies suggest that the range of effective strategies, both at the end of the century and during its course, was scarcely to be defined in terms of either French developments in the late eighteenth century or of the subsequent conflicts.

Such comparisons underline the problems of assessing significance and development. Thus, the huge White Lotus rebellion of 1796–1805 in China in the Han River valley and beyond, especially in western Hubei, southern Shaanxi, and northern Sichuan, was in part a millenarian rebellion, but far from that being a "backward" sign compared to France, there were millenarian elements in the effort to create a new religion in France in the 1790s. Moreover, the rebels made extensive use of guerrilla tactics, as with Spanish resistance to Napoleon from 1808. However, there was not a comparable role for nationhood in the Chinese rebels' identity. There was for the Poles in 1794 and the Irish in 1798, but they failed. These failures underline the centrality of political factors in the case of the focus of the counterinsurgent forces as well as resources and location.

The narrative and analysis offered in much of the literature focus on revolutionary movements and associated new methods with strategy located accordingly. Ironically, however, the most significant strategic planning involved the response to these revolutions and notably on the part of Britain which had both to allocate forces across a wide range of commitments and to work out the politics of counterrevolution. British failure was a key element in the success of the American Revolution and British success a key element in the eventual defeat of Napoleon. That is an aspect of the development of strategic thought and practice in this period. The need to respond to revolutionary movements helped drive processes as well as underlining the relevance of strategy. In part, the problems were familiar. Britain had long faced the need to reconcile wide-ranging commitments. Yet there was also a new context, one considered in the next chapter.

NOTES

1. A. Carter, *Neutrality or Commitment: The Evolution of Dutch Foreign Policy, 1667–1795* (London, 1954).

2. J. V. H. Melton, *The Rise of the Public in Enlightenment Europe* (Cambridge, UK, 2001).

3. Greene to Knox, December 7, Greene to Lee, December 31, 1780, Washington, Library of Congress, Department of Manuscripts, Greene Letterbook.

4. L. W. Labaree et al., eds., *The Papers of Benjamin Franklin* (New Haven, CT, 1959–), XXII, 292–93.

5. G. B. Nash, *The Urban Crucible: Social Change, Political Consciousness, and the Origins of the American Revolution* (Cambridge, MA, 1979); H. Ward, *The War for Independence and the Transformation of American Society* (London, 1999).

6. Sheffield, Archives, Wentworth Woodhouse papers, R1–1590, 1575.

7. Anon., *Reflections on the Present State of the American War* (London, 1776): 5.

8. *Annual Register* 19 (1776): 2.

9. Washington, Papers of the Continental Congress, vol. 58.

10. BL. Add. 21687 fol. 245.

11. BL. Add. 34416 fol. 273.

12. *Franklin*: XXII, 438.

13. Howe to Lord George Germain, Secretary of State for America, November 30, 1777, NA. PRO. 30/8/7.

14. HMC, *Lothian*: 300.

15. J. Huston, *Logistics of Liberty. American Services of Supply in the Revolutionary War and After* (Newark, NJ, 1991).

16. P. Nelson, *Anthony Wayne* (Bloomington, IN, 1985): 75–76.

17. P. H. Smith, ed., *Letters of Delegate to Congress, 1774–1789*, vols. 10–11 (Washington, DC, 1983–84).

18. Greene to Morgan, December 16, 1778, T. B. Myers, ed., *Cowpens Papers* (Charleston, SC, 1881): 9–10.

19. S. Wilkinson, *The Defense of Piedmont, 1742–1748: A Prelude to the Study of Napoleon* (Oxford, 1927); P. Bianchi, "La guerra franco-piemontese e le valli valdesi (1792–1779)," in G. P. Romagnani, ed., *La Bibbia, la coccarda e il tricolore. I Valdesi fra due emancipazioni, 1798–1848* (Turin, 2001): 72–117.

20. J. R. Fischer, *A Well-Executed Failure: The Sullivan Campaign against the Iroquois* (Columbia, SC, 1997); M. M. Mintz, *Seeds of Empire: The American Revolutionary Conquest of the Iroquois* (New York, 1999).

21. A. Stockley, *Britain and France at the Birth of America: The European Powers and the Peace Negotiations of 1782–1783* (Exeter, UK, 2001).

22. A. F. C. Wallace, *Jefferson and the Indians: The Tragic Fate of the First Americans* (Cambridge, MA, 1999); P. S. Onuf, *Jefferson's Empire: The Language of American Nationhood* (Charlottesville, VA, 2000): 18–52.

23. Jefferson to Adams, June 11, 1812, L. J. Cappon, ed., *The Adams-Jefferson Letters* (Chapel Hill, NC, 1959): 307–8.

24. P. Onuf and N. Onuf, *Federal Union, Modern World: The Law of Nations in an Age of Revolutions, 1776–1814* (Madison, WI, 1993).

25. W. Holton, *Unruly Americans and the Origins of the Constitution* (New York, 2007).

26. G. S. Rowe and A. W. Knott, "The Longchamps Affair (1784–1786). The Law of Nations, and the Shaping of Early American Foreign Policy," *Diplomatic History* 10 (1986): 199–210.

27. J. B. Hattendorf, "The Formation and the Roles of the Continental Navy, 1775–1785," in Hattendorf, *Talking about Naval History* (Newport, RI, 2011): 200.

28. A. DeConde, *The Quasi-War: The Politics and Diplomacy of the Undeclared*

War with France, 1797–1801 (New York, 1966); B. Perkins, *The Cambridge History of American Foreign Relations. I. The Creation of a Republican Empire, 1776–1865* (Cambridge, UK, 1993): 84.

29. L. D. Cress, *Citizens in Arms: The Army and Militia in American Society to the War of 1812* (Chapel Hill, NC, 1982).

30. D. R. Egerton, "The Empire of Liberty Reconsidered," in J. P. Horn, J. Lewis, and P. S. Onuf, eds., *The Revolution of 1800: Democracy, Race, and the New Republic* (Charlottesville, VA, 2002): 309.

31. D. Bell, *The Cult of the Nation in France, Inventing Nationalism 1680–1800* (Cambridge, MA, 2003).

32. B. Rothaus, "The War and Peace Prerogative as a Constitutional Issue during the First Two Years of the Revolution, 1789–91," *Proceedings of the First Annual Meeting of the Western Society for French History* (1974): 120–38.

33. J. Israel, *A Revolution of the Mind: Radical Enlightenment and the Intellectual Origins of Modern Democracy* (Princeton, NJ, 2010): 129, 150–53.

34. G. von Proschwitz, ed., *Gustave III par ses lettres* (Stockholm, 1986): 213.

35. P. Paret, *The Cognitive Challenge of War: Prussia 1806* (Princeton, NJ, 2009).

36. J. Black, *The War of 1812 in the Age of Napoleon* (Norman, OK, 2009).

37. G. Rowlands, *The Financial Decline of a Great Power: War, Influence, and Money in Louis XIV's France* (Oxford, 2012).

38. G. Hanlon, *Italy 1636. Cemetery of Armies* (Oxford, 2016).

39. D. Stoker, F. C. Schneid, and H. D. Blanton, eds., *Conscription in the Napoleonic Era: A Revolution in Military Affairs?* (Abingdon, UK, 2009).

40. Additional instructions for Liston, February 26, 1794, NA. FO. 78/15 fols. 46–47.

41. Auckland to Morton Eden, August 10, 31, 1792, BL. Add. 24444 fols. 55, 169, 179.

42. Memorandum, October 1796, BL. Add. 59280 fols. 189–90.

43. Grenville to Auckland, November 27, 1792, BL. Add. 34445 fol. 401, 58920 fol. 184.

44. Hatsell to John Ley, November 28, 1792, Exeter, Devon CRO. 63/2/11/1/53.

45. Grenville to Auckland, January 22, 1793, BL. Add. 34447 fol. 186, 58921 fols. 73–74.

46. Grenville to George, 2nd Earl Spencer, envoy in Vienna, September 15, 1794, BL. Althorp Mss, vol. G173.

47. Grenville to Spencer and Thomas Grenville, envoys in Vienna, August 29, 1794, BL. Althorp Mss, vol. G173.

48. A. Forrest, "Enlightenment, Science and Army Reform in Eighteenth-Century France," in M. Crook, W. Doyle, and A. Forrest, eds., *Enlightenment and Revolution: Essays in Honour of Norman Hampson* (Aldershot, UK, 2004): 153.

49. D. A. Bell, *The First Total War: Napoleon's Europe and the Birth of Warfare as We Know It* (Boston, 2007): 9.

50. Review by P. Paret, *American Historical Review*, 112 (2007): 1489–91; J. Black, *War in the Nineteenth Century 1800–1914* (Cambridge, UK, 2009): 7–22; E. C. Kiesling, "'Total War, Total Nonsense' or 'The Military Historian's Fetish," in M. S. Neiberg, ed., *Arms and the Man* (Leiden, the Netherlands, 2011): 223–27.

EIGHT

IMPERIAL IMAGININGS, 1783–1800

> I should think the insurrection, which from its resolution deserves the
> name of rebellion, now in Peru, is an inviting circumstance to tempt us
> to fit out a fleet for the Caraccas, to assist a people that appear so ripe for
> a revolt, to set up themselves independent of the Crown of Spain. This
> perhaps might end not only in the utter ruin of the dominions of that
> haughty court in America, but give such a mortifying blow to the pride and
> ambition of the various branches of the over-grasping House of Bourbon,
> as might have rendered them more tractable and tame in Europe for the
> future.

The anonymous writer in the London opposition newspaper *Old England*
of February 17, 1750, was not original or unique in his optimistic account
about the possible overthrow of the Spanish Empire and of related British
transoceanic force projection. However, these arguments also reflected
a global reach to discussion. This reach accelerated in the second half of
the century, in response to the Seven Years' War, and then to the War of
American Independence.

At the same time, new concepts of strategic interest and concern
developed in the late eighteenth century. In particular, prior to the outbreak of the French Revolution in 1789 and war between Britain and
France in 1793, the British reconceptualized their empire after the "loss
of America," while the French challenged the British over the route to
India,[1] and Russian expansion led to the salience of new geopolitical
issues. Moreover, issues of prioritization and strategy became acute in
the conflicts that engulfed much of the world from Western Europe
to South Asia, beginning in 1787 with the outbreak of what became a
large-scale war between Russia and Turkey.[2] These issues and events

helped lead to the conceptualization of a more geopolitical context for, and idiom of, strategy. These were distinct from earlier dynastic ideas and from the language of both *gloire* and the balance of power, although there were also continuities and overlaps.

In addition, whereas in the 1770s the British had not been able to make a common European imperial cause against the American rebels,[3] in the 1790s, ideological rivalries, notably between revolutionaries and opponents in Europe, and also involving divisions within the United States, helped encourage an ideological dimension in strategy in, at least, part of the world, as well as a determination to extend the latter to include ideological control over European societies. This leads to the question of how far this dimension was different to earlier ideological tensions linked to religious conflict. Alongside these new elements, geopolitical factors repeatedly led to a considerable degree of continuity in strategy and in the political debate over strategy. Thus, for Russia, there was the need to determine between a focus on the Turks and one on the power politics of Germany, a need encouraged by the opportunities of expansionism at the expense of the former and for hopes of such expansionism.

The relationship between opportunities and hopes was often more tenuous than might appear, but both coexisted and interacted. As with strategy and policy, the distinction and also the process of interaction between opportunities and hopes are difficult to assess. However, the assumption, as an explanation and as a basis for judgment, of a high level of rationality related to a supposedly objective reading of resources, needs, and opportunities is misleading.

BRITAIN

To begin with the response to Revolutionary France might appear obvious, both for Britain and for other powers, but to do so is to ignore the number of elements at play in confrontation and warfare in these years. Britain came close to war with pre-Revolutionary France in 1787, with Spain and France in 1790, and with Russia in 1791. Each episode illustrated the variety of factors at play in strategy. Preparing for conflict in each case involved alliance dynamics, and very clearly in 1787 and 1791 as supporting ground action by Prussia was regarded as crucial in each case. In 1787, there was no formal alliance between the two powers, as there was to be in 1791. Paradoxically, the cooperation of the two powers worked in 1787 but not in 1791. In 1790, British naval preparation was the key element, and the role of the Dutch as allies was far less significant for a war that would have been waged solely at, and beyond, the seas. This would not have been a conflict in which Britain needed the support of European land forces. Force structure was thus in a critical dynamic with tasking and alliances, and to prioritize one out of the three elements would be misleading, as would a separation of elements and the designation of only one as strategy, not least of a strategy that was allegedly obvious.

For Britain, by early 1791, the alliance with Prussia negotiated in 1788 had become focused on Eastern Europe and, in particular, on limiting Russian gains at the expense of the Turks with which war had begun in 1787. This conflict had broadened out into a wider international crisis, one that divided both ministry and public opinion in Britain. As so often with strategy, international and domestic factors interacted without any clarity or consistency, there was no segregation, neat or otherwise, of whatever is differentiated as strategy and policy, and issues of operational and political expediency affected goals and tasking. Whereas Prussia could strike at Russia by land across Poland, with which a treaty was signed in 1790, Britain could only act against Russia by the use of naval force. Although the dispatch of a squadron to the Black Sea, where Russian and Turkish fleets had been in conflict for several years, was discussed, this posed formidable logistical problems; also, the Black Sea was unknown to the British navy. The contrast with the dispatch of a large British fleet to the Black Sea in 1854 during the Crimean War (1854–56) with Russia indicated the impact of technological and organizational developments, as well as a very different political context.

In practice, British naval action in 1791 would mean a fleet in the less distant Baltic, but its operation would depend heavily on local bases for replenishment and repair. This made the attitude of local powers, notably Denmark and Sweden, crucial, as again in 1808–12 when there was tacit Swedish assistance for the British naval presence. In 1791, a British fleet in the Baltic would protect the Prussian coast from Russian naval attacks, cover the flank of any Prussian invasion of Livonia, overawe Russia's ally

Denmark, be tangible proof of Britain's commitment to Prussia, and inflict damage on Russia.

Yet strategy was set within multiple contexts, as in August 1790 when Prussia was pressed by its ally Britain, if possible, to "avoid actual measures of force, especially as, in the present advanced season of the year, and in the uncertainty of what may be the issue of his negotiations with Spain, His Majesty [George III] cannot answer for being able actually to send a squadron into the Baltic."[4] The government was reacting to circumstances and necessarily so given the uncertainty about the possibility of hostilities with Spain and France in the Nootka Sound crisis of that year. The extent to which an exhausted Russia would seek to avoid the risk of a broader war was part of the equation.

At the same time, there was concern that Russia would use its capture in 1788 of the major Turkish fortress of Ochakov on the Black Sea—a fortress the British were insisting should be restored to the Turks as a condition of peace. Thomas, 7th Earl of Elgin, the envoy in Vienna and the later acquirer of the Elgin Marbles in the British Museum, warned that the capture might well be followed by that of Constantinople (Istanbul):

> Who could say where the Court of Petersburg would stop if, after forming a solid footing, not only in the Crimea, but in other parts, of the Black Sea, and striking there at the vitals of the Ottoman Porte (and Ochakov alone was perhaps sufficient) she should seize some unlucky moment, when the rest of Europe was unable to assist that country, and erect her standard in Constantinople?[5]

This view was widely taken, and it was argued that in future wars, it would not be necessary for the Russians to be delayed by having to take the fortress as in this and previous wars.[6]

In early 1791, diplomatic support was sought by Britain for pressure on Russia, including from the Netherlands and Sweden. Pressure was to be applied by the Prussians on the German possessions of Denmark and Sweden: "Pomerania must answer for Sweden and Holstein for Denmark."[7] Rumors that the British government would not send the fleet increased tension, while Catherine the Great (II of Russia) rejected the demand that she return all her recent conquests from the Turks. Prussian pressure led to cabinet meetings in London on March 21 and 22, and it was decided in the latter that thirty-nine ships of the line and a proportionate number of frigates were to be sent to the Baltic toward the end of April. This decision was on the supposition that the Danes would not obstruct the passage of the Sound into the Baltic and would permit the use of their ports, notably Copenhagen. Ten or twelve ships of the line were to prepare for the Black Sea, and the support of Sweden, the Netherlands, Poland, and Turkey was to be secured.[8]

Two days later, Joseph Ewart, the bellicose envoy in Berlin, who had attended the cabinet on the March 22, as Sir James Harris, the envoy in The Hague, had done during the Dutch crisis of 1787,[9] wrote:

> The Baltic fleet will consist of 35 sail of the line . . . and the *necessary fireships*, for I have strongly urged the expediency and ease of burning all the B—'s [sic for Bitch, i.e., Catherine II] ships and docks should she be obstinate. I have likewise represented that the moment our fleet has the command of the Gulf of Finland, it would be very easy to transport ten thousand Prussians across and debark them within a few miles of Petersburg, which could thus be taken at once as the Russians would naturally turn all their efforts towards Livonia.[10]

Counting on Russia thereby deploying to prevent a Prussian attack on the Russian frontier province of Livonia (much of modern Latvia), Ewart therefore projected a knockout military blow at the Russian capital, dealing, as a result of Russia's situation, with a crisis in the south by sending a fleet to the north. There were "pull" factors toward the Baltic including, as in 1855–56, threatening Russian power at the center of government and securing naval stores.

In practice, the viability of Ewart's proposition was unclear given the strength of the Russian galley fleet and the lack of a British counter to it, which was a precursor of the situation with the American monitors during the American Civil War. The British navy stepped up recruitment on March 25 while, two days later, Prussia ordered the deployment of 88,000 troops on the Livonian frontier. Turkey was to be offered British naval support. However, in Parliament from March 29, the government faced serious attacks. These included criticism not only of the broader ambit of British policy in the crisis but also of specific details such as the lack of friendly ports in the Baltic, a crucial contrast with the Mediterranean where the British had Gibraltar and later, Malta. Parliamentary criticism exacerbated cabinet division and doubts; and the ministry backed down from the decision to send the fleet. This led Francis, 5th Duke of Leeds, the foreign secretary, to resign and resulted in the collapse of the alliance with Prussia.[11] In the subsequent peace treaty of 1792, Russia gained Ochakov and the territory to the River Dniester.

Strategy was not a word mentioned during the very extensive diplomatic and military discussions and exchanges in 1790–91, but it is difficult to assess the crisis without considering the contemporary use of strategic ideas. The mixture of factors cited reflected not incoherence, whether or not arising from an inability to employ the relevant concept, but instead, the complexity of the situation. On May 24, 1791, John, 2nd Earl of Chatham, the first lord of the Admiralty and the elder brother of William Pitt the Younger, the prime minister, explained to Ewart that the dispatch of a British expedition to the Black Sea was no longer an option:

> the undertaking would be rather an arduous one, the navigation being
> so little known, and the prevalence of particular winds in the summer
> months, rendering the passage up the canal of Constantinople very
> precarious, but these obstacles are to be surmounted, and I should see
> no objection as a military operation to this step, but on the contrary
> considerable advantage, were vigorous measures in question, but . . . this
> plan has not been approved here from the consideration that the sailing of
> a squadron for the Black Sea would be considered as tending to immediate
> hostility, and would renew all those alarms and discussions which have
> to a degree subsided, only from the persuasion that the business was in a
> train of negotiation. It is also feared that it might discourage at present the
> favourable dispositions that seem to manifest themselves in the Court of
> Spain, and the old objection besides of expense recurs.[12]

The settlement between Britain and Spain was part of the equation. For Britain, there was, alongside geopolitical and ideological changes, continuity in the prioritization that was the key issue in the public and governmental politics of strategy. More specifically, for the 1790s, this was the question, as in 1756–63, of a focus on the transoceanic world or one on Europe, a focus that had important implications for the ability to emphasize the navy and for naval dispositions.[13] The related politics were crucial to strategic formulation because the latter was not partly insulated from political pressures and the influence of the commercial interest, by the institutionalization and secrecy that characterized strategic planning in the twentieth century and today.

Furthermore, the politics of strategy helped provide a considerable measure of continuity, with issues and problems interpreted and debated in terms of what was, by 1793, when Britain entered the French Revolutionary War, over a century of experience of conflict with France and also with a long-standing background of conflict with Spain. In each case, experience was perceived through the perspective of collective (and contentious) public myths, such as the hopes invested in "blue water" strategy: naval mastery and the consequent European blockade[14] and transoceanic conquests through amphibious operations. Looked at differently, the reassessment of British strategy in 1791 reflected Russia's ability to see off the threat of war with Britain and Prussia, despite already being involved in a major war with Turkey, a conflict that Austria had abandoned. Russia's strategic capability was the key element in 1791. At the same time, Britain in 1791 was scarcely without strategic commitment, resource, and impact, being also at war with Mysore in southern India.

The established treatment of strategy for the French Revolutionary and Napoleonic Wars period is operational or combat orientated,[15] as well as diplomatic, noting the "jarring interest and intrigues that affected "the course and conduct of the war."[16] It is also necessary to consider the central role of the home front. The struggle with France that began in 1793 was not, simply because of its ideological current, inherently a new type of war. The religious dimension of conflict with Catholic powers had already provided that element. Moreover, strategy, as before, related to two aspects of domestic politics: first, potential supporters of the foreign power and second, conventional high politics. These overlapped, with George III (r. 1760–1820) very concerned about the loyalty of the Whig opposition and the extent to which their attitudes encouraged the French revolutionaries and Napoleon, a position that continued his earlier concern with Whig attitudes during the War of American Independence. Furthermore, George was worried that if the parliamentary opposition gained power, as it eventually did in 1806, Britain's war goals would be jeopardized, if not the war, as it had been in 1782, abandoned. In the event, Napoleon was not really interested in any British peace approach at this juncture.

A key element of the war strategy for the king was therefore the exclusion of the parliamentary opposition from power. This element was very important to George in his negotiations with politicians, as in 1804 when William Pitt the Younger returned to office. Indeed, in 1782, George had considered abdication rather than accepting the loss of America. If this exclusion of the opposition was not quite as central to George in the 1800s as the issue of preventing the extension of equal civil rights to Catholics (Catholic emancipation), it was, nevertheless, of very great importance. This exclusion made greater sense when engaged in conflicts that had an ideological dimension: first, the War of American Independence and second, the French Revolutionary and then Napoleonic Wars. A different continuity in strategy can be seen between wartime planning and discussion over the terms to be offered in peace negotiations, both those in the 1790s and those in 1806. This element is also worth considering for other powers.

Excluding the opposition from power was not the limit of the domestic dimension in Britain. There was also a concern about popular radicalism and the potential it enjoyed, or might enjoy, to recruit support. Such radicalism, and not only in Ireland, was more clearly linked to a fear of treason and its direct military impact than was the case with the opposition. In 1794, Thomas Sunderland reported from Ulverston that "The late successes of the French upon the Rhine has encouraged our Northern Democrats to reassume their mischievous doctrines, and to preach them amongst the mountains of Westmorland."[17]

As a result of this general situation, two major strands of wartime strategy were action against radicals, particularly the trials and changes in the law of the 1790s, and the sponsoring of loyalism. The latter was a spontaneous public movement but also one that was sponsored and sustained by government action. Loyalism, like popular support more generally, had a direct military consequence in the shape of the massive increase in militia and Volunteer forces. These provided a key force for domestic security, notably against any action by radicals (matching the role of the American militia against loyalists during the American War of Independence), and also were intended to strengthen the country against invasion. Of the 162,300 effective rank-and-file troops in Britain in 1798, only 47,700 were regulars: 60,000 were militia and 54,300

Volunteers.[18] As such, the militia and Volunteer forces made it possible to increase the number of regulars who could be sent on expeditions, a situation matching the earlier introduction of the militia in France and Spain and anticipating the role in Britain of the Home Guard in World War II. Thus, loyalism illustrates the multiple overlaps of the domestic and foreign spheres of wartime strategy, overlaps of which contemporaries were well aware. There was a strong emphasis on winning public support.[19]

At the same time, this military need indicated the extent to which strategy was in part a matter of reinterpreting the nuances of domestic power relations. Raising militia and Volunteer forces underlined the need for the state to cooperate with local interests in obtaining resources, which was an aspect of the long-standing balance between the Crown and local interests. For example, militia colonels regarded their regiments as patronage fiefs, immensely valuable to them as county magnates and public men for both patronage and prestige. As a result, important changes in the militia laws had to be negotiated with the colonels, and even the practice of regular drafts into the army was carefully conducted to protect their interests.

As the French were well aware, the domestic dimension was most acute in Ireland, which with increased public criticism of control from London had been seen in and after the War of American Independence as a potential site of rebellion. There was indeed one in 1798 (on a much larger scale than the Easter Rising in 1916), which was followed by a French invasion, although both totally failed. Another far more minor rising in Ireland took place in 1803. Their failure should not direct attention away from the key role of defense in British strategy. This lay behind many military activities, including the construction of fortifications and barracks on the south coast of England in the 1790s and 1800s, and continual naval building.

Domestic strategy was also a matter of national reform and was seen in this light. This was similar to the position abroad—for example, in Prussia after its total defeat by France in 1806—a prime concern of Clausewitz and the emotional fire for, and of, his work. Moreover, this situation was not unprecedented in British history. Aspects of the Revolution Settlement, or governmental and political changes that followed

the Glorious Revolution of 1688–89, owed much to the pressures of war
with France in 1689–97 and 1702–13, not least the establishment of the
Bank of England in 1694 and union with Scotland in 1707. The same was
true in 1793–1815. Similarly, in Britain, the Liberal Unionists of the 1900s
pushed domestic regeneration as an aspect of a strategy of international
confrontation, and the same element was seen with the Labour government's support for social welfare and economic nationalization alongside
confrontation with the Soviet Union in 1945–51. In each case, specific
changes, as well as the process of change as a whole, were regarded as
strengthening Britain, and as key elements of the strategy for keeping the
country resilient and competitive, and of directing the energies of society. As far as naval power was concerned, national strength was clearly
important to an economic strategy of protecting trade and harming that
of opponents because this ensured the financial clout necessary to support operations abroad, both British deployments and the actions of
allied forces.

Important reforms in Britain included the introduction of income
tax, which helped make possible a shift from financing war by borrowing to financing it through taxation and thus tapping different revenue
sources and types of wealth. This shift, from 1798, was a response to the
serious liquidity crisis of 1797 and made it easier to endure setbacks, as
borrowing was very dependent on confidence. A focus on taxation also
fulfilled the vital strategic goal of making public finances far less dependent on the inflow of foreign capital, which had been a key feature of the
borrowing regime. The French occupation of Amsterdam in 1795 had
threatened this flow. The strategy of finance had a key geopolitical character and very much joined domestic and international politics. Another
aspect of this strategy was provided by British concern for the territorial
integrity of Portugal. Alliance with Portugal brought access to gold from
Portugal's colony Brazil, which was the most significant source of gold in
the Western world. Access to bullion also provided a greater opportunity
to raise funds by borrowing.[20]

Parliamentary union with Ireland (1800–1) was regarded as a key
way to reduce the vulnerability represented by Ireland, as it was presented as making the link with Britain acceptable to Irish opinion. The

situation in Ireland, however, remained challenging as a colonel reported in 1807:

> a divided or distracted people like us are not calculated to meet such an invader as [Napoleon] Bonaparte ... the 12th of this month instead of lamenting over the fatal consequences of the battle of Friedland, the Orange Yeomanry of this kingdom were celebrating a battle fought upwards of 100 years ago, with every mark of triumph and exultation as if Ireland had no other enemy than its Catholic inhabitants.

Thus, a Napoleonic victory over Britain's principal ally, Russia, appeared less significant than William III's victory over James II at the battle of the Boyne in 1690.[21] At the same time, the situation in Ireland was manageable. The British containment strategy worked.

There was also a stress on the acquisition of information as a way to strengthen government. The first British national census (1801) was an important instance, not least due to the significance of numbers for recruitment, but more immediate value was gained by detailed mapping by the Board of Ordnance designed to help operationally in the event of a French invasion.[22] Other branches of the military markedly improved their effectiveness, notably for long-range operations.[23]

The focus of major reform initiatives in the late 1790s and early 1800s underlines the value of providing a chronological perspective. The sense of a domestic challenge, and the need for a corresponding strategy, were strongest in the 1790s and, in contrast, less pronounced after victory at Trafalgar over the combined Franco-Spanish fleet in 1805. The radicalism of the late 1800s and early 1810s did not seem revolutionary. Although there was some admiration for Napoleon in the British Isles, his abandonment of republicanism, notably when he became emperor in 1804, greatly tarnished his appeal and that of French political models. There was also a critical response in the United States to Napoleon, although a less marked one. As an instance of the abandonment of radicalism, Napoleon both sought to reimpose slavery and lost interest in the cause of Irish independence, which had always been peripheral to his concerns. Robert Emmet had received a promise of support when he visited Napoleon in 1802, but his preparations for an ultimately unsuccessful rising in Ireland in 1803 were correctly made without any anticipation of French backing.

If the chronological dimension provides an important perspective for the strategy of domestic preparedness, it also offers a crucial one for the very different issue of tasking. The latter might appear readily set: France had to be defeated, and to do so, Britain had to stay in the fight as a credible potential ally. In practice, however, there were two separate but related strands that repay attention. First, there was the issue of what was the goal of the war with France and second, that of the range of opponents and allies, and how this range interacted with the first strand. As far as France was concerned, there was a crucial tension, one fundamental to strategy, between the argument that France had to be defeated in order to contain it, and the far more ambitious approach that containment could only be secured if its political system was transformed, most clearly by a restoration of Bourbon rule or to employ modern language, regime change. This argument was pushed hard by Edmund Burke and by French émigrés. Even before hostilities between Britain and France began in 1793, there was a sense on the part of some ministers and commentators that this was to be a different conflict because of the ideological gulf separating the two sides and that this would require new military measures. In part, this sense reflected the marked attenuation of earlier religious animosity and notably, as a factor in international relations. In part, the novelty of the ideological challenge of the rapidly changing French Revolution was the key element.

British strategy was greatly affected by the presence or absence of the key resources, of domestic stability and alliance partners. These requirements were not eccentric to British (and other) military history but central to it. Tasking was involved and the political strategy crucial in terms of the dynamic and cohesion of coalitions. Military strategy was also dependent on these resources. There was a parallel in India, where the mastery won by Britain depended at least as much on the ability to win allies, ensure stability, and benefit from the mutual enmities of the leading regional powers—Mysore, the Marathas, Hyderabad, Nepal, and the Sikhs—as from success in more conventional "point of conflict" military history. In conflict with Mysore in the 1790s, British forces benefited greatly from the support of Hyderabadi cavalry.[24] The dependence on Indian power politics was also to be crucial in seeing off the challenge of the Indian Mutiny in 1857–58: Britain then benefited greatly from Indian assistance, not least from Hyderabad, Nepal, and the Sikhs.

In Europe, alliance with Austria and/or Prussia made it possible to intervene in the Low Countries and Germany as in 1793 and led to pressure for such action, in particular to ensure the key war aim of an independent Low Countries and to sustain the alliance. Strategy was as one with policy. Conversely, the collapse of such an alliance, as in 1756 and 1797 with Austria and 1762–63 and 1795 with Prussia, removed this option. "Blue water" rhetoric assumed no need for an alliance, but the tradition of the amphibious operation, of seizing particular points, not of engaging an army and defeating it, only worked well in trans-oceanic operations against vulnerable colonies as the Seven Years' War showed. As such, prefiguring conflict with Italy in North and East Africa in 1940–41, the indirect capability was more significant politically, in showing real and potential allies that Britain could and would challenge France on land and would stay in the war, than militarily, in the shape of distracting French forces from fighting the allies. At the same time, the capacity for blockade and amphibious operations could be militarily important, both in seizing colonies and in fighting independent states such as the United States in 1812–15 which saw, on the part of Britain, "the role of an admiral on horseback" and also of a key element of strategy as politics, rhetoric, and contention—namely, the advancing of ideas and plans in order to obtain military resources.[25]

The burgeoning economy of Britain and of the oceanic trading system and the strength of its public finances were crucial to the British war effort and thus helped set the parameters of strategy. It is possible to focus on these parameters and in writing about "strategic policy," to concentrate on "the means available to pursue war, the factors which influenced decision making, and the implementation of policy itself in the light of the actual circumstances,"[26] in sort a functional or applied approach.

Yet these parameters had to be understood by politicians (and in Britain, communicated to Parliament), while, more generally, parameters did not settle the issue of prioritization in tasking. Thus, the politics (both domestic and international) of strategy arise throughout as the key issue. This situation created problems for commanders, but it is all too easy to see these primarily in a negative light and indeed as thwarting efforts and nearly costing victory. From this perspective, bureaucratic inertia, political maneuvering, public opinion, and a hostile press all emerge as grave difficulties. This view can be seen, for example, in Joshua Moon's approach, content, and tone in his study of Wellington's generalship, a study that devoted too much of its focus to Wellington's views rather than those he had to deal with.[27] It is instructive that Moon was a serving officer in the US army at the time of writing the book. His approach failed adequately to capture the perspective of the government, notably the serious and persistent difficulties it faced in balancing commitments and responding to financial constraints and, in both, the difficulties of shaping circumstances. Instead, the friction of which Clausewitz was to write, including the difficulty of gaining sufficient accurate information,[28] was a key element for government.

A RANGE OF POWERS

Similar points can be made for other states. Strategy as politics does not exhaust the subject, but it makes sense of a context in which ministerial contention and even public debate were more potent than institutional continuity. However, in the case of eighteenth-century Britain, the absence of an equivalent, in terms of policy or royal power, to the messianic imperialism of Philip II of Spain (r. 1556–98) or the imperial position of Napoleon and the presence of a developed public sphere resulted in a strategic debate that was readily open to political cross-currents.

Elsewhere, the strategic priorities and means of Britain were important to the imperial activity of the 1790s, but they were scarcely alone in this influence and impact. Indeed, possibly the boldest plan was Napoleon's large-scale expedition to Egypt in 1798, a major strategic gamble.[29] The previous July, the month in which he became foreign minister, Charles-Maurice de Talleyrand had told the Institut de France that the Egyptian expedition would lead to a French conquest of India. This expedition was the first successful amphibious invasion of Egypt since those of the Romans. Napoleon's victories in Egypt and his capture of Alexandria and Cairo, all in 1798, underlined the vulnerability of powerful centers of the Islamic world. Whether this capability contributed to a coherent French strategy was far less clear, but the expedition revealed to those who knew of it a volatility in power politics that suggested new opportunities and needs for strategic insight and planning.

Transoceanic power projection and in terms of capability and plans, both plausible and wilder, was not only restricted to Britain. In terms of capability, in 1796, a Spanish squadron reached Manila, the first major Spanish fleet sent there. In 1800, a naval station in Manila was founded, and in 1802 a shipyard in Cavite was established in order to build and support warships against pirates. Napoleon sought to pursue a "western design," seeking to create a major empire that would include Louisiana, Florida, Cayenne, Martinique, Guadeloupe, and Saint-Domingue, a plan focused on the dispatch of twenty thousand troops to the last in 1802 in order to reestablish control.

The conflicts at the same time in southern and northern India and in Persia indicated the scope of the volatility in power politics. The activities of Agha Muhammad of Persia (r. 1779–97) and of Zaman Shah of Afghanistan (r. 1793–1800) deserve attention because they demonstrate the extent to which the personal and family strategies they pursued, and the tribal contexts in which they operated, were not residual features. In Persia, the late 1780s and early 1790s saw the Qajar tribe under Agha Muhammad take over, destroying the previously dominant Zand. This process was helped by Zand disunity, which, in turn, was accentuated by failure. The capital, Isfahan, was captured in 1785, the cities of Shiraz and Kirman following in 1792 and 1794. Agha Muhammad also sought to reconquer former Persian territories and to assert sovereignty, which he did in Georgia in 1795 and Khurusan (in northeast Persia) in 1796. His threat to Afghanistan in 1799, including backing Zaman's rebellious brothers, a threat encouraged by Britain but not dependent on it, ended the possibility that Zaman Shah would advance across northern India defeating Britain's protégés.[30] Thus, Persia became part of the world of British power politics, not in order to affect Turkey, as in past Western strategic planning, but as part of a wider Indian policy.

To take another ruler of the period who was more successful than Napoleon, Nguyen Anh, from a base around the Mekong delta, conquered all of Vietnam by 1802 and proclaimed himself Emperor Gia-Long, holding the position until his death in 1820 and creating a dynasty that continued until the monarchy came to an end in the mid-twentieth century. Ironically, he had benefited from French help following a treaty in 1787, and however modest, this assistance outlasted the Napoleonic regime. In Siam, Chakri, a general, staged a successful coup in 1782 and became ruler as Rama I, ruling until 1809 and successfully thwarting major attacks by Myanmar. He also established a new dynasty that lasted.

The range of imperial schemes included American expansionism, not that the Americans saw themselves in this light. Although Canada, which was unsuccessfully invaded in 1812, 1813, and 1814, provided the Americans with a clear strategic goal to permit the pursuit of imperial schemes, the Americans were unable to devise an effective means to obtain this goal. The size of Canada (as then under British control) helped to make operational planning difficult for the Americans, as did the characteristics of the environment in the sphere of operations, the nature of contemporary communications, command and control, and also relationships between individual commanders. For these reasons, there was little prospect of coordinated campaigning, which would have been the best way to take advantage of the distribution of American resources. The alternative—their massing in a single concentration of power—was not possible for political reasons, as well as not being feasible in logistical terms. A deficiency in planning, moreover, accompanied the organizational and political limitations affecting the American war effort. The lack of an effective strategy made it difficult to make use of tactical and operational successes: those comprised parts in a whole that was absent. More particularly, multipronged attacks were not coordinated and did not exert simultaneous or sequential pressure on the British. This would have been difficult to execute given the extent of operations, but functional problems alone were not responsible for the American failure of coordination. There were also serious political divisions in America over strategy. There was much support for a focus on the Lake Champlain corridor in order to divide Montreal from Quebec. However, Westerners were opposed to this emphasis and, instead, as part of their expansionism, wanted to prevent British help to the Native Americans. This led them to press for operations farther west, operations that, however, were difficult to support and coordinate.

Jomini chose 1800 as the year in which "the system of modern strategy was fully developed."[31] This description of the Marengo campaign was ironic in light of the more recent stress on improvisation in explaining Napoleon's success, both that year and more generally, and linked to this, on him as an opportunist. Napoleon's opening campaign as First Consul was an invasion of northern Italy boldly begun with a crossing of the Great St. Bernard Pass so that he arrived in the Austrian rear and threatened their line of supply, undercutting the Austrian advance on Lyon. At the subsequent battle of Marengo, however, on June 14, 1800, Napoleon found the Austrians to be a formidable rival, and Napoleon's enforced retreat for much of the battle was only reversed because of a successful counterattack mounted by French reinforcements. Rather than a brilliant "strategic victory," whatever that might mean, Napoleon was driven by the desire to engage and win. By forcing a battle whose shape was unclear, he, like the British admiral Horatio Nelson, placed great reliance on the subsequent mêlée, which rewarded the fighting qualities of individual units, the initiative and skill of subordinates, and in Napoleon's case, the ability to retain reserves until the crucial moment. At Marengo, as elsewhere, Napoleon was also able to dominate the news agenda and present a positive spin on his generalship.[32] This was an important aspect of his modus operandi. It was ironic that Napoleon himself did not employ the term *strategy* until after he was exiled to St. Helena in 1815 and then very infrequently,[33] although, in addition to the usual term of the period, *art of war*, strategy has been a term often applied to him, and that remains the case.

An emphasis on Marengo in 1800 interestingly raises the question of whether there was any strategic purpose to Napoleon's invasion of Egypt in 1798, which was one of the most dramatic episodes in his career. This question emphasizes the issue of "whose strategy?" For Napoleon, concerned to keep his army together as a means of personal power, the expedition fulfilled a key purpose while also enabling him to evade the unwelcome control of the Directory government and to provide him with the opportunity to win fame. That the expedition in practice exposed a portion of the French military to the strength of the British navy, and such that the army, with the navy defeated, was left vulnerable, was unwelcome both militarily and politically. Napoleon himself evaded responsibility for the debacle, which underlines the point about relevant strategic perspective. It is striking that much of the literature of the period discusses what can be seen as strategies although without necessarily using the term.[34]

The focus on Napoleon is ironic as the more impressive strategic achievement was that in countering Napoleon. This was a matter not only of the British naval movements in 1798 and the resistance to Napoleon's siege of Acre in 1799 but also of the concentration of strength in 1801 to support an attack on the French forces in Egypt. This involved operations in the Mediterranean and in the Red Sea, each of which had multiple permutations or knock-on consequences depending on the process one envisages. The combination of "home waters" and the Mediterranean was long established but that with the Indian Ocean was not and had never sought the degree of coordination and planning attempted in 1798–1801. The successful attack on Mysore in 1799 was an aspect of the British strategy. Plans for an expedition from India to Batavia (Djakarta), which was ruled by France's Dutch ally, were abandoned. Instead, Britain moved first ships and then troops to the Red Sea in order to support the main attack from the Mediterranean. Already in 1795, the British had carried out a reconnaissance in order to gain necessary information. A base was established in 1799 on the island of Perim in the Straits of Bab-el-Mandab at the mouth of the Red Sea, but as the island was waterless, it was evacuated. The British plans included seeking to extend influence into the Hijaz in order to thwart any French use of the Red Sea to advance into the Indian Ocean.[35] In the event, British troops, some from India and some from Cape Town, marched from the Red Sea to the Nile.[36] It remains surprising that so much attention is devoted to Napoleon.

JOMINI AND CLAUSEWITZ

Napoleon provided commentators with the need and ambition to explain success in war, and this encouraged a bold attempt to write about a science of command, which became a major route into discussing strategy. Jomini and Clausewitz were to be the major figures.[37] The key rule master proved to be the Swiss-born Antoine-Henri de Jomini (1779–1869).

He served in the French army as chief of staff to Marshal Ney before switching, in 1813, to the Russian army, being made a lieutenant-general by Alexander I. Jomini's influential works, which included *Traité des grands operations militaires* (1805–9) and the *Précis de l'art de la guerre* (which appeared first in 1810 as the conclusion to *Traité*), aimed to find logical principles at work in warfare, which was seen, by Jomini, as having timeless essential characteristics. In particular, Jomini sought to explain the success of Frederick the Great and then of Napoleon, who was treated in his *Vie politique et militaire de Napoléon* (1827).

Jomini, like Clausewitz, wrote in the shadow of Napoleon and had to address the topics of his sweeping success and of his complete failure. Jomini's focus was operational. To him, the crucial military point was the choice of a line of operations that would permit a successful attack. Napoleonic operational art was discussed in terms of envelopment—the use of "exterior lines" and alternatively, the selection of a central position that would permit the defeat in detail (separately) of opposing forces—a position that was described in terms of interior lines. The corps system gave Napoleon a "force multiplier" that greatly increased operational effectiveness. By focusing on decisive battles, Jomini emphasized battle winning as decisive, rather than the wider consequences of social, economic, and technological change.[38] He was, for example, critical of the Spanish guerrilla warfare against French occupation which he himself had witnessed.[39]

Jomini's emphasis continues to be widespread in the discussion of Napoleonic generalship. It can be seen, for example, in the focus on the battle of Waterloo, or the operations of June 15–18, when considering the events of 1815, and not on Napoleon's diplomatic isolation or on his failure to inspire widespread support within and after the battle.

Carl Maria von Clausewitz (1780–1831), in contrast to Jomini, emphasized a broad approach, most notably the inherent political nature of war and, therefore, the balance of political determination. In 1804, he drafted a short work entitled *Strategie* which covered a range of topics. Unpublished, this study emphasized the importance of securing the object of the war and to that end, the value of battle.[40] In his posthumously published account of Napoleon's Russian campaign, Clausewitz presented the policy in 1812 as one of victory in campaign, enabling the dictation of a peace that was to be aided by creating dissension between a weak government and the nobility.[41] The campaigns he took part in influenced his views.[42]

In his work, Clausewitz, who had read extensively in military history and believed in its significance,[43] drew on Machiavelli,[44] but he was not really interested in citing earlier writers, notably if French. In *On War*, he did not cite Saxe, Maïzeroy, or Guibert, while the two references to Lloyd are superficial. The nature of Clausewitz's approach, based as the assessment is largely on this unfinished work, has been subject to a variety of interpretations in a process encouraged by the somewhat opaque nature of much of the text, by his plentiful use of passive tenses and subordinate clauses, and by issues concerning the meanings of particular phrases and words. Clausewitz's early education in philosophy was reflected in his work, but he was not systematic in its argumentation. In that sense, comparison with the development of diplomatic theory—for example, with the work of François de Callières[45]—should not be pushed.

The interplay of passion, reason, and possibility scarcely allowed Clausewitz to be systematic, and it is possible to "re-read Clausewitz in these climatic terms of Romantic self-conception," one in which atmospheric terms best captures the psychological transformation caused by war.[46] Approached somewhat differently, Clausewitz embraced complexity because as a pessimist, he was wary of the idea of simple answers, while he described "a spectrum of war" rather than an inflexible model.[47] He also presented in his book what essentially was a debate about power, one in which the dialectical method of thesis and counterthesis played a central role. Alongside this dialectic, there was that between theory and reality, a dialectic in which Clausewitz was well aware of exceptions to the universal experience of war he propounded. The very educational possibilities of *On War* for the modern audience could be complemented by the stress on the deliberately pedagogic nature of Clausewitz's work as a means to develop the sound intuition necessary for command.[48]

Any translation of Clausewitz represents an interpretation and not least because it is not always clear what the subject is in particular sentences. Differing emphases have been favored in response to current intellectual trends and military exigencies.[49] For example, the commercially highly successful 1976 translation into English, an edition by

Michael Howard and Peter Paret,[50] the third in English, one that was also published in the Everyman's Library in 1993, was initially produced in the context of the Cold War and was republished in the aftermath of the Cold War. This context affected the use and understanding of particular contexts. For example, the 1970s' use of total war had connotations that gave the text meaning; however, in the nineteenth century, there was not a comparable concept of total war.[51] So also with the term *operations.*

The nature of pedagogy was culturally constructed, a factor that helps make it highly problematic to read between periods or to establish supposedly universally laws. For example, the medieval use of Flavius Vegetius's *Epitoma rei militaris*, a work then translated into French, English, Italian, German, and Castilian, rested not on his adages about the practical nature of war but instead, on his argument that the army was for the public service and thus that their moral value explained the need for state-controlled forces.[52] In a very different context, the moral character of military forces was also important for the eighteenth-century commentators and not only those of the American and French Revolutions. Clausewitz can be located in this tradition of assessing the moral character of military activity as an aspect of understanding and placing how war works so that commanders would best be able to evaluate and respond to situations.

THE LANGUAGE AND PRACTICE OF STRATEGY

The works of Jomini and later, Clausewitz, each of which was translated into other languages, were to affect the developing use of the term and concept of strategy. The use of both term and concept spread in the early nineteenth century. For example, in Danish, *strategi*, meaning the preparation and planning for the operations of an army, first appeared (and with a Greek origin mentioned) in a dictionary, namely in Hans Christian Amberg's *Dansk og Tydsk Ordbog* (*Danish and Germany Dictionary*) which was published in Copenhagen in 1810. It also appeared in the *Militairt Conversations-Lexicon* (*Military Encyclopedia*) published in Copenhagen in 1837–43. The adjective *strategisk* (strategical) appeared in the second edition of Jacob Baden's *Ordbog over de af fremmede Sprog laante Ord* (*Dictionary of Words Borrowed from Foreign Languages*), a work published in Copenhagen in 1820. The dictionary mentioned that the word came from German via French and that it was Greek in origin. In contrast, the words do not appear in dictionaries of the medieval, Renaissance, seventeenth-century, and eighteenth-century Danish language.

In Italy, the word *strategia* appeared at least in 1817 and probably came from France, not from Germany. The word and the related adjectives appear to have been used for the first time by Giuseppe Grassi in his *Dizionario militare italiano*, the first edition of which appeared in 1817 in Turin, the capital of Piedmont—earlier Savoy-Piedmont, the kingdom of Sardinia from 1720. Grassi inserted the entry on *strategia* followed by the French word *stratégique*. Grassi began preparing his dictionary in 1814 and finished it in 1816 but did not say from where he took the specific word. However, because he subsequently added the French word, it probably came from France. In the introduction to the second edition, which appeared in Turin in 1833, Grassi wrote that in 1814–16, he had taken some French works and translated their words into Italian, although he had also used a lot of Italian sources. In the Neapolitan edition published in 1835, Grassi mentioned strategy in the body of the entries on *arte militaire* (p. 63), *operazione* (p. 349), *ricognizione* (p. 359), *stato maggiore* (p. 433), and *strategia* (p. 438). Grassi quoted some letters Pietro Colletta, a Neapolitan general, had addressed to him in 1828. Colletta had used the word *strategia* in the *Memoria militare sulla campagna d'Italia dell'anno 1815*, an undated work which was left unpublished at his death in 1831. Colletta, who started his military career in 1792 in the artillery of Naples, subsequently served both the French rulers of Naples, Joseph Bonaparte and Murat, before serving the Neapolitan Bourbons anew in 1815. The word *strategic* appeared for the first time in Italian in the second chapter of *Opera inedite o rare di Pietro Colletta*, published in Naples in 1861. This work includes a letter to Grassi about the *Dizionario militare italiano* he had just read in the second half of 1828 in which Colletta said that the word *strategia* was a recent one.[53]

Another source was the Italian translation in 1818 of the Archduke Charles's *Grundsätze der Strategie erläutert durch die Darstellung des Feldzugs 1796* (1814). In 1854, Mariano d'Ayala, in his *Bibliografia militare italiana antica e moderna* (1855) referred to the 1818 translation as the first work published in Italian using the then-current meaning of strategy. The 1833 edition of Grassi's *Dizionario* quoted both Colletta and Charles in its entry on *strategia*. Archduke Charles (1771–1841) was the most effective Austrian opponent of the French in the 1790s and the 1800s.[54]

Grimm's *Woerterbuch* gives *Strategie* as first used in German in 1813, although it was written about by Clausewitz in 1804 and employed in the title of an 1805 book by Adam Heinrich Dietrich von Bülow. There was no mention of the word in Johann Christoph Adelung's *Wörterbuch Hochdeutschen Mundart* (1793), a dictionary of the language.

In Russian, the linkage with Greek ensured that the term had been present for a long time but that it reflected Byzantine usage, as in *strategos* or stratagem. In addition, *stratig* (military leader) was long-standing. The modern sense of *strategy* was acquired at the end of the eighteenth century, and the Napoleonic Wars helped Russians to get a better sense of the term. By the 1820s, it was well established and was mentioned in the popular periodical press. The first dictionary to mention *strategiia* was the Academy dictionary of 1847.

Although the word was coming into use, many commanders did not do so. Thus, Blücher understood the concept of strategy but without using the word. The term *strategy* was not employed in British official or private correspondence of the period when referring to strategic concepts, thinking and intentions. In 1808, Wellington used the word to refer probably to what is today understood as tactics or organization. John Wilson Croker, a pro-government MP who handled for Wellington (then Sir Arthur Wellesley) the latter's business as chief secretary for Ireland, recorded of a discussion that the general said, "Why to say the truth, I am thinking of the French that I am going to fight. . . . They have besides, it seems, a new system of strategy, which has out-manoeuvred and overwhelmed all the armies of Europe."[55] It is not certain that this memorandum was written at the time.[56] At any rate, it is unclear whether the reference is to the French corps system or the use of infantry columns, or effective combined arms.

Government policy or plans were often cited when referring to what we would term strategy. Prospects or plans with respect to Spain, Austria, or other powers was another term. *Arrangements with nations* was also an often-used phrase. It was chiefly the employment of the word *government* that was used to signify a strategic concept. The *art of war* was another commonplace term. Nevertheless, Wellington's 1806 memorandum on British plans for South America and his 1809 memorandum on the defense of Portugal articulated the concept of strategy. In 1806, Wellington scotched a plan to deploy forces simultaneously on the east and west coasts of South America, while in 1809 he clearly explained how the British army should be used to defend Lisbon, how this would facilitate the defense of Portugal, and how it might even enable the British to go on the offensive in Spain. The means to accomplish this were thirty thousand to forty thousand British troops, the retraining of the Portuguese army, and the construction of the Lines of Torres Vedras.[57] In 1819, Wellington presented a plan for the defense of Canada to Henry, 3rd Earl Bathurst, the secretary for war and the colonies. He identified the keys of Canada as Quebec, Montreal, and Kingston and in an interesting guide to strategic assumptions and the idea of a center of power, emphasized lines of communication from the Atlantic access in Nova Scotia, rather than troops and fortifications. With reason, Wellington argued that the existing lines, the marine routes along the St. Lawrence and the Great Lakes, were overly exposed to American attack, a view supported by American plans in the War of 1812. Instead, he proposed a new line of communications, one, farther from America, that benefited from rivers and canals. As another key instance of what he regarded as significant in strategic terms, Wellington emphasized the importance of the local population remaining loyal, not least as this would provide militia to support the regulars.[58]

However, as with many other commanders, Wellington was less keen on grand strategy when it clashed with his interests. For example, he did not appreciate that his reiterated calls during the Peninsular War for resources, both military and naval, had to align with other governmental concerns. In particular, Wellington's demands for naval support were inappropriate. Strategy as a term was employed in a military context from the 1810s and was employed in a broader political context by the 1840s. Nevertheless, in many books there was no mention of the term. For example, an online search of *An Impartial History of the Naval, Military, and Political Events in Europe, from the Commencement of the French Revolution* (1815, 2nd ed. 1816), by Hewson Clarke, a Cambridge-educated London writer, reveals no references to the word.

In Spain, the first definition of the term *strategy* was recorded in 1822 in the sixth edition of the *Diccionario de la lengua castellana de la Academia Española* (*Dictionary of the Castilian Language of the Spanish Academy*). The definition was "science of the general of the army."[59] During earlier periods, generals had understood the concept but employed other terms. For example, when they formulated the strategy to follow during the seventeenth century, they used terms such as *the policy to follow, the requirements of Your Majesty, the needs of the monarchy,* and *to maintain the reputation.* As the language became more modern, the semantics changed. In the Netherlands, the 1820s saw the term first used, while Jomini was published in The Hague in a Dutch translation in 1830: *Inleiding tot de groote strategische en tactische operatien.*

In the case of Portugal, the key year was 1837 when Major (later General) Fortunato José Barreiros published the first book on strategy, a work on the general principles of strategy and grand tactics that drew on Jomini's *Traité des grands operations militaires* and on the work of Napoleon's most impressive Austrian opponent, Archduke Charles. Barreiros defined strategy as the art of leading troops to the key points of the area of operations and tactics as the art of leading those troops in battle.

Clausewitz therefore wrote at a time of changes in the terminology used to comment on war. He addressed the issue of the nature of war in history, focusing on the problem of the significance of change during his military career and on the question of whether there was going to be more change. The validity of both offense and defense was one dichotomy changing in time that concerned him. His use of strategy was primarily in terms of how battle was employed for the purpose of war, a question at once operational and political. The context and content of strategy in part depended on the nature of the opponent. Aside from the contradictions in the revised as well as unrevised parts of his work, Clausewitz did not really address the questions of the mechanisms for elucidating strategy as a concept and practice or how militaries explained their strategic relevance to policymakers. That is not a criticism, because these were not his intentions, but it is pertinent to note the consequences of the disjunctions because Clausewitz's understanding of his subject, as well as the misreading of Clausewitz, have both guided modern consideration of strategy to a disproportionate extent and continue to do so.

NOTES

1. F. Charles-Roux, *Le projet français de conquête de l'Égypte sous le règne de Louis XVI* (Cairo, 1929).

2. B. Stone, *The Genesis of the French Revolution: A Global-Historical Interpretation* (Cambridge, UK, 1994).

3. S. Conway, "'Founded in Lasting Interests': British Projects for European Imperial Collaboration in the Age of the American Revolution," *International History Review* 37 (2015): 22–40.

4. Francis, 5th Duke of Leeds, Foreign Secretary, to Joseph Ewart, Envoy in Berlin, August 14, 1790, NA. FO. 64/18 fols. 216–17.

5. Elgin to William Pitt the Younger, First Lord of the Treasury, December 20, 1790, NA. PRO. 30/8/132 fol. 158.

6. Leeds to Francis Jackson, temporarily in charge of British representation in Berlin, January 8, 1791, NA. FO. 64/20 fols. 21–23.

7. Leeds to Jackson, January 8, 1791, NA. FO. 64/20 fols. 16–19.

8. Cabinet Minute, March 22, 1791, A. Aspinall, ed., *The Later Correspondence of George III* I (Cambridge, UK, 1962), no. 663; O. Browning, ed., *The Political Memoranda of Francis, Fifth Duke of Leeds* . . . (London, 1884): 150–52.

9. Third Earl of Malmesbury, ed., *Diaries and Correspondence of James Harris, First Earl of Malmesbury* (4 vols., London, 1844), II, 303–7.

10. Ewart to Jackson, March 22, 24, 25, 27, 1791, Williamwood, Ewart papers.

11. Black, *Parliament and Foreign Policy*: 119–23.

12. Chatham to Ewart, May 24, 1791, Williamwood, Ewart papers. For the poor quality of naval advice, see R. Knight, *Britain against Napoleon: The Organisation of Victory, 1793–1815* (London, 2013): 19.

13. P. Mackesy, *War without Victory: The Downfall of Pitt, 1799–1802* (Oxford, 1984).

14. Richmond to Harris, May 13, 1788, Winchester, Hampshire CRO. Malmesbury papers, vol. 180.

15. Mackesy, "Strategic Problems of the British War Effort," in H. T. Dickinson, ed., *Britain and the French Revolution 1789–1815* (Basingstoke, UK, 1989): 147–64.

16. Auckland (formerly William Eden) to James Bland Burges, Under Secretary at the Foreign Office, May 6, 1793, Bod. Bland Burges papers, vol. 31 fol. 18.

17. Sunderland to "Mylord," February 1, 1794, Preston, Lancashire Record Office, Cavendish of Holker papers, DD ca22/9/14.

18. State of Forces in Great Britain, February 1798, BL. Add. 59281 fol. 15.

19. Thomas, Lord Pelham, "Further Considerations on the Plan for a General Enrolment of the People," July 2, 1803, BL. Add. 33120 fol. 135.

20. M. Robson, *Britain, Portugal and South America in the Napoleonic Wars: Alliances and Diplomacy in Economic Maritime Conflict* (London, 2010).

21. Colonel Hawthorne to Henry Addington, July 17, 1807, Exeter, Devon Record Office, 152 M/C 1807/018.

22. W. Seymour, ed., *A History of the Ordnance Survey* (Folkestone, UK, 1980): 21–31; W. Ravenhill, "The South West in the Eighteenth-Century Re-Mapping of England," in K. Barker and R. J. P. Kain, eds., *Maps and History in South-West England* (Exeter, UK, 1991): 20–21.

23. R. Knight and M. Wilcox, *Sustaining the Fleet, 1793–1815: War, the British Navy and the Contractor State* (Woodbridge, UK, 2010); G. Cole, *Arming the Royal Navy, 1793–1815: The Office of Ordnance and the State* (London, 2012); M. Wilcox, "'This Great Complex Concern': Victualling the Royal Navy on the East Indies Station, 1780–1815," *Mariner's Mirror* 97 (2011): 32–49; M. Robson, "'A Considerable Portion of the Defence of the Empire': Lisbon and Victualling the Royal Navy during the French Revolutionary War, 1793–1802," *Historical Research* 87 (2014): 466–90.

24. G. J. Bryant, *The Emergence of British Power in India, 1600–1784: A Grand Strategic Interpretation* (Woodbridge, UK, 2013).

25. C. J. Bartlett, "Gentlemen versus Democrats: Cultural Prejudice and Military Strategy in Britain in the War of 1812," *War in History* 1 (1994): 153.

26. C. D. Hall, *British Strategy in the Napoleonic War 1803–15* (Manchester, UK, 1992): xi.

27. J. Moon, *Wellington's Two-Front War: The Peninsular Campaigns, at Home and Abroad, 1808–1814* (Norman, OK, 2011).

28. On this, see also R. Muir, *Wellington: Waterloo and the Fortunes of Peace, 1814–1852* (New Haven, CT, 2015): 38.

29. F. Charles-Roux, *Les origines de l'expédition d'Égypte* (Paris, 1910).

30. H. Fas'i, *History of Persia under Qajar Rule* (New York, 1972): 52–54.

31. A.-H. Jomini, *Summary of the Art of War* (Philadelphia, 1862): 137.

32. O. Connelly, *Blundering to Glory: Napoleon's Military Campaigns* (2nd ed., Wilmington, DE, 1999); C. J. Esdaile, "De-Constructing the French Wars: Napoleon as Anti-Strategist," *Journal of Strategic Studies* 31 (2008): 515–52.

33. Napoleon, *De la guerre*, edited by B. Colson (Paris, 2012): 147–49.

34. F. C. Schneid, ed., *European Armies of the French Revolution 1789–1802* (Norman, OK, 2015).

35. E. Ingram, *Commitment to Empire: Prophecies of the Great Game in Asia, 1797–1800* (Oxford, 1981) and *The British Empire as a World Power* (London, 2001): 178–83; R. W. Beachey, *A History of East Africa, 1592–1902* (London, 1996): 14–15.

36. P. Mackesy, *British Victory in Egypt, 1801* (London, 1995).

37. For comparisons, see M. Handel, *Masters of War: Sun Tzu, Clausewitz and Jomini* (London, 1990).

38. A.-J. Rapin, *Jomini et la stratégie: Une approche historique de l'oeuvre* (Lausanne, Switzerland, 2002); L. M. Crowell, "The Illusion of the Decisive Napoleonic Victory," *Defense Analysis* 4 (1988): 329–46.

39. B. Heuser, "Lessons Learnt? Cultural Transfer and Revolutionary Wars, 1775–1831," *Small Wars and Insurgencies* 25 (2014): 864.

40. C. von Clausewitz, *Strategie: aus dem Jahr 1804, mit Zusätzen von 1808*

und 1809, edited by E. Kessel (Hamburg, 1937): 37–82.

41. Clausewitz, *The Campaign of 1812 in Russia* (London: Greenhill Books, 1992): 253.

42. D. Stoker, "Clausewitz's Lost Battle: Sehestedt 10 December 1813," *Military History Monthly* 68 (May 2016): 40–46.

43. P. Paret, "*On War* Then and Now," *Journal of Military History* 80 (2016): 481–82.

44. P. Paret, "Machiavelli, Fichte, and Clausewitz in the Labyrinth of German Idealism," *Ethics and Politics* 17 (2015): 78–95.

45. K. W. Schweizer, "Clausewitz Revisited," *The European Legacy* 14 (2009): 461n9, 461n14.

46. Thomas Ford, "Narrative and Atmosphere: War by Other Media in Wilkie, Clausewitz and Turner," in Neil Ramsey and Gillian Russell, eds., *Tracing War in British Enlightenment and Romantic Culture* (Basingstoke, UK, 2015): 182–84, quote 184.

47. C. Bassford, "John Keegan and the Grand Tradition of Trashing Clausewitz: A Polemic," *War in History* 1 (1994): 325.

48. J. T. Sumida, "The Relationship of History and Theory in *On War*: The Clausewitzian Ideal and Its Implications," *Journal of Military History* 65 (2001): 333–54 and *Decoding Clausewitz: A New Approach to "On War"* (Lawrence, KS, 2008).

49. A. Gat, *The Development of Military Thought: The Nineteenth Century* (Oxford, 1993); H. Strachan, *The Direction of War: Contemporary Strategy in Historical Perspective* (Cambridge, UK,

2013): 46–63. Important recent works include B. Heuser, *Reading Clausewitz* (London, 2002); A. J. Echevarria, *Clausewitz and Contemporary War* (Oxford, 2007); A. Herberg-Rothe, "Primacy of 'Politics' or 'Culture' over War in a Modern World: Clausewitz Needs a Sophisticated Interpretation," *Defense Analysis* 17 (2001): 175–86 and *Clausewitz's Puzzle: The Political Theory of War* (Oxford, 2007); Strachan, *Clausewitz's* On War: *A Biography* (New York, 2007); P. Paret, *Clausewitz and the State: The Man, His Theories and His Times* (2nd ed., Princeton, NJ, 2007); D. Stoker, *Clausewitz: His Life and Work* (Oxford, 2014).

50. C. von Clausewitz, *On War*, edited by M. Howard and P. Paret (Princeton, NJ, 1976).

51. For the issues and problems of definition, see J. Black, *The Age of Total War, 1860–1945* (Westport, CT, 2006).

52. C. T. Allmand, *The "De Re Militari" of Vegetius: The Reception, Transmission and Legacy of a Roman Text in the Middle Ages* (Cambridge, UK, 2011).

53. *Opera inedited o rare di Pietro Colletta* (Naples, 1861): 55, 196, 306, 392, 509.

54. G. E. Rothenberg, *Napoleon's Great Adversaries: The Archduke Charles and the Austrian army, 1792–1814* (Bloomington, IN, 1982); A. Gat, *The Origins of Military Thought from the Enlightenment to Clausewitz* (Oxford, 1989): 95–105.

55. Croker's memorandum, June 14, 1808, *Memoirs, Diaries and Correspondence of the Right Hon. John Wilson Croker*, edited by Louis Jennings (3 vols., London, 1884): I, 12–13.

56. See commentary at http://www.lifeofwellington.co.uk/commentary/chapter-fourteen-dublin-and-westminster-october-1807-july-1808#sthash.pylldowVD.dpuf, accessed April 17, 2016.

57. Second Duke of Wellington, ed., *Supplementary Despatches . . . of Duke of Wellington* (15 vols., London, 1858–72), VI, 35; Colonel John Gurwood, ed., *The Dispatches of . . . Wellington* (8 vols., London, 1844), IV, 261–63; M. Robson,

"Sir Arthur Wellesley as a Special Advisor, 1806–1808," in C. M. Woolgar, ed., *Wellington Studies V* (Southampton, UK, 2012): 38–60, esp. 39–54.

58. *Despatches, Correspondence, and Memoranda of Field Marshal, Arthur, Duke of Wellington*, edited by his son, the Second Duke (8 vols., London, 1857–80): I, 36–44.

59. *Diccionario de la lengua castellana* (6th ed., Madrid, 1822): 368.

NINE

CONCLUSIONS

SUDDENLY, STRATEGY, THE LOST ART, BECAME A CENTER OF
attention in the 2010s, as indeed did geopolitics.[1] The year 2013 saw the
appearance both of Lawrence Freedman's much reviewed work, *Strategy:
A History*, and of Hew Strachan's *The Direction of War: Contemporary
Strategy in Historical Perspective*. Considering the two, each important
and impressive, tells us much about the subject today, its strengths, and
its limitations, at least in the Anglophone world. If what follows is critical, that should not distract attention from the seminal significance of
both books and particularly the welcome ambition of the Freedman
volume. First, it is readily apparent that strategy attracts both the energy
of skilled, fluent, and important scholars and the commitment of pub-
lishers. The latter commitment owes much to the interest of the public.

It is also clear from these two volumes that there is no agreed definition of strategy or its implementation, and that in the Anglophone world,
let alone the rest of the world. In part, this problem reflects the question
of change, a specialty of historians. Take two successive sentences by
Mackubin Owens, an American commentator, writing in 2014:

> Strategy is designed to secure national interests and to attain the objectives
> of national policy by the application of force or threat of force. Strategy is
> dynamic, changing as the factors that influence it change.[2]

This dynamism clearly extends to the definition and use of strategy. In
a book at once accessible and scholarly, Freedman offered a very wide
account, including both "Strategy from Below," an introduction to radical thought, as well, separately, as business strategies, which indeed
offered a central and growing usage for the term. In 2016, there were more

than 56,000 entries on Amazon.com for strategy under "Business and Money." Indeed, strategy is a buzzword in the field of management and economics, one frequently employed alongside terms such as *managing* and *directing.*

Freedman helpfully began with the ubiquity of strategy, his preface opening with a quote from the prominent American boxer Mike Tyson. Similarly, Alan Downie has profitably used the concept of "polemical strategy."[3] However, Freedman's preference, certainly prior to 1800, was for the strategy of military thinkers, and not the strategy of military actors, let alone political actors, which is indeed a general choice, albeit a misleading one. Freedman had sections on Weber, Tolstoy, Gramsci, and Alinsky, but no well-informed account of what strategy meant in the Middle Ages or the early-modern period, to Süleyman the Magnificent or to Aurangzeb, to Louis XIV or to the Qianlong emperor.

Strachan, in contrast to Freedman, was very circumscribed in his definition and account of strategy. He was austere and critical, self-consciously so, and notably of "politicians," whom, to him, seem only to live in the present without anything more than a romanticized and self-serving sense of the past.[4] Strachan argued that "we have so stretched our understanding of the term that it is in danger of losing its usefulness. In particular, we have conflated it with policy."[5] The approach offered by Strachan was clear:

> Strategy is a profoundly pragmatic business: it is about doing things, about applying means to ends. It is an attempt to make concrete a set of objectives through the application of military force to a particular case.... If war is an instrument of policy, strategy is the tool that enables us to understand it and gives us our best chance of managing and directing it.[6]

This was an attempt to end confusion by applying reason, but one that did not match the inherent complexity of situations, not least the integral role of both politics and emotions. Indeed, in 1745, René-Louis, Marquis d'Argenson, France's wartime foreign minister, argued (wrongly) that the death of Charles Albert of Bavaria, the Emperor Charles VII, would only bring more confusion to the international situation by multiplying "les passions, les interêts, et les efforts" of the warring powers.[7]

Strachan's book in practice derived from thirteen pieces already published elsewhere, in some cases more than once, but all revised in order to update them, to remove duplication, and to add fresh material. The pieces were first published between 2005 and 2012, having in most cases been delivered as lectures between 2003 and 2011. This academic archaeology, an approach also very useful with Clausewitz and Jomini, tells us much about the volume. It was written with the clarity and directness that makes for a good lecture, and in many cases, as a linked point, for a military audience. However, there was very little of the internal debate, if not equivocation and ambiguity, that is seen in much academic prose. Instead, *The Direction of War* was almost a users' (intellectual) manual, a manual in particular for the military, as much as for academics.

Again, the intellectual archaeology offered by the book, notably the preface, was clear. Strachan obviously spent much time with the senior military, and they would have found much of the book welcoming, as would their junior counterparts. Particular ire was directed by Strachan at politicians, and there is real anger in his book toward Bush, Blair, Obama, and the conduct of the wars in Afghanistan and Iraq in 2001–11. The sidelining of the military in the United States and Britain came in for criticism, as did the loss of control of strategy by soldiers. Indeed, there was an attack on the armed forces remaining silent on the issue, a theme Strachan also advanced elsewhere.

Strachan was far from alone in this approach. It is most common with the military, and can be seen in subsequent discussion of the US chiefs of staff over the Vietnam War[8] and with Colin Powell's arguments as head of the Joint Chiefs of Staff in the United States. This approach was also very frequent with civilians, notably if pro-military. Academic historians can also make similar comments. For example, Peter Heather, in his discussion of frontier defense and the later Roman Empire, wrote, "politicians' egos and internal political agendas have long interfered with rational military planning, and it should come as no great surprise that this was also true in the ancient world."[9] This is amusing in its location of egotism, which can in practice be found with both politicians and the military, as well as with historians.

Indeed, the isolation of military planning as a rational pursuit supposedly unrelated to political agendas is unhelpful and an illusion. To identify, for example, the "correct balance," whether between assets and on the other hand, roles and commitments, or between other factors, in practice, too readily presupposes that these ideas are not value-free. In fact, ideas are not, and strategy can be readily approached from this perspective. This is so whether strategy is presented as rhetorical or as pragmatic.

Strachan's tone was frequently angry, notably in the references to what he termed historical illiteracy and to those presented as the lazy, a group partly defined for him by an inability to read Clausewitz at length and to understand the development of Clausewitz's thought.[10] There was also urgency as in, "Until we wake up. . . ."[11] There was the criticism, moreover, of intellectual fashion, practice, and language, notably with an attack on the concept of strategic culture and of the alleged confusion between strategy and policy. Political scientists were held up as foolish by Strachan: "They use case studies all the time, but they tend to choose those topics which prove or disprove a thesis, not subjects which are to be studied in their own historical contexts."[12]

Like other writers on strategy, including myself, Strachan produced a historical document as much as a work of scholarship. His history and polemical analysis were written in the shadow of unsuccessful interventionist wars in which much of the British military felt betrayed by the civilian politicians, while senior figures faced criticism from one another and from junior ranks. As such, the book took forward the collection *British Generals in Blair's Wars* (2013) that Strachan coedited.

This approach helped give the book energy and intellectual thrust, as well as a somewhat polemical demand for a reassessment of the relation between politicians and the military, but it is deeply worrying that so much of the world was left out, other than as a sphere for Western operations. With a few exceptions, and those Western, Strachan, indeed, wrote a book only about the United States and Britain. In short, his was not about contemporary strategy or the direction of war but rather, about these in a highly circumscribed fashion. The question of the strategic thought of other societies was rather ignored. This approach was, and is, highly disappointing, as such a coverage would have permitted a valuable comparative context, not least in terms of making strategy work, and of the dynamic aspects of the context. Similarly, although far less narrow than Strachan, Freedman focused largely on Western thinking. There was a major failure on his part to engage with China other than Sun Tzu and Mao, or with India.

So also with other works. For example, the major collection on strategy in the ancient world, that edited by Victor Davis Hanson, reflected the editor's powerful commitment to his views of the pedigree of modern warfare, notably as a project of virtuous citizen republics, and thus focused on classical Greece and Rome and, through their perspectives, also covered some of their opponents. As a result, however, this is not a collection on the ancient world itself, and China, India, and much else, are missed out completely. Even within the world as more narrowly defined by Hanson, there is a serious failure to engage fully with other states such as Carthage.[13]

Strachan and Hanson were far from alone in their geographical and conceptual limitations. Clausewitz himself did not properly engage with sea power and the many and important issues of trade, resourcing, and geographical range it raised. Indeed, this omission is a problem with most accounts of strategy that are based on land warfare.

Geographical scope was not the sole problem with Strachan's work, and here, there was a contrast with Freedman. Strachan was only interested in societies in which the term *strategy* exists and could be very cutting on the point:

> Gray [Colin Gray, author of Modern Strategy (1999)] rides roughshod over
> change across time and assumes that there can be a concept of strategy,
> and a practice derived from it, for epochs and civilisations which had
> no word for it. His hero, Clausewitz, knowing that strategy was a recent
> phenomenon, did not.[14]

This was a key point. Strachan was only really happy with precision, but strategy as practice has existed for far longer.[15] The last point emerges from Freedman, from Heuser, and from much of the literature on the topic. My shelves are full of instructive works that fall foul of Strachan's approach, such as J. P. LeDonne's *The Grand Strategy of the Russian Empire, 1650–1831* (Oxford, 2004).[16] There are also valuable collections on the history of strategy that in their chronological coverage span the actual introduction of the term in the late eighteenth century and find no difficulty of discussing strategy both before and after that. Moreover, alongside Strachan's remark about Gray, place, for example, Williamson

Murray's blunt but informed description of the chronologically limiting approach as "nonsense."[17]

The idea and practice of strategy certainly predated the vocabulary. And the same is true of many other terms, such as *geopolitics*. Like certain other scholars, Strachan did not adequately address this point. Indeed, to a degree, he avoided it by criticizing the concept of strategic culture, a concept that had been advanced in part as a description of an important aspect of the situation and in part in order to deal with the problem of strategy without the term. The concept is employed to discuss the context within which military tasks were/are shaped. General beliefs, attitudes, and behavior patterns were integral to the politics of power, rather than being dependent on the policy circumstances of a particular conjuncture.

The result, in Strachan's case, was a rather disturbing weakness in chronological and geographical perspective. In practice, strategy in Strachan's terms—the implementation of policy through force and the related understanding of war, the application of means to ends—was (and is) scarcely new and certainly did not require that particular term. Nor is the key element of prioritization between options and tasks new. The language, texts, and mechanisms that Strachan focused on scarcely exhaust the subject nor indeed his discussion of it in terms of "the art of the commander."[18]

In addition, the distinction between policy and strategy is not, and was not, as clear as Strachan or Gray proposed. There appears to be a clear distinction, with policy setting the ends, and strategy tackling the art and science of doing so, both deploying tools and analyzing means. In this perspective, strategy is about action and reaction, and thereby offers an emphasis on dynamism as it entails imposing one's will on events. However, both in the past and in the present, policy and strategy frequently do not admit of this clear separation.

Moreover, in a key aspect of the often partisan nature of discussion, the attempt to argue for a distinction is not inherently value-free. This is not least because this distinction is commonly employed to treat the former as inherently political and rhetorical, and strategy as, in some way, more professional, military, and precise. The distinction may be aimed for in certain contexts, notably modern academe, with its preference for terminological exactitude and organizational precision as a basis for analysis. However, it is unclear that this distinction describes most states across time and space. This, in addition, offers an instructive comment on some of the content of military education and in particular of the way in which strategy is sometimes taught. Similar comments can be made about the treatment of military ethics.

Rather than restricting strategy, chronologically, geographically, or conceptually, there is need for a total view of strategy. Such a view was present in the early debates over strategic culture in the 1970s–1980s when there was an existential threat and thus a clear context that could be explained in terms of such a culture. However, this total view had to be defined anew in the wake of the wars from 2001. Encompassing domestic and international issues, it is necessary to offer such a total view in order to make the best sense of war preparation and war-making. Domestic politics were, and are, an integrated part of this strategy and were understood in this light. This tendency is encouraged by pragmatic considerations, as, for example, assuaging domestic grievances or apparent grievances makes it easier to ensure support for foreign war or for military preparations. Governmental backing for Civil Rights in America in the 1950s can in part be located in this context by noting concern about the possibility that the Soviet Union would take advantage of African-American discontent.[19] There is also support for the integration of the domestic and international dimensions of strategy from those who endorse organic theories of country, nation, and state.

Moreover, strategies emerge in part as the product of coalitions of interest, both domestic and international, coalitions at once explicit and implicit. The terms by which these coalitions are formed and reformed become important to the process by which strategies are advanced, debated, and reformulated. Indeed, the ability to keep such coalitions going is a key element of strategic activity and a central link between war-making and domestic policies and politics. The changes in this relationship are a central dynamic element in the strategic equation. Again, this is a point that is valid for the past as well as for the present. The maintenance of support, both domestic and international, was a major goal and means of strategy. Linked to this, operations that showed the weaknesses of opponents, as well as one's own strength, were important to fulfilling these objectives.[20] This theme was captured in 1758 by George Ross, the London agent of the Scottish royal burghs and of many military figures. He wrote to Brigadier John Forbes about a British attack on the French coast that "it cannot do much mischief, though those repeated insults must make France low in the opinion of mankind, as well as in that of Europe."[21]

The wide-ranging use of the term *strategy* in the policy debate around the Middle East in the mid-2010s might have offended those seeking ever greater terminological precision, but in practice, this usage captured the extent to which policy, the idea treated as coterminous with strategy, encompassed a range of means and responses. Focusing only on those seen as military, in terms of the delivery of force, appeared in practice "unstrategic" in that force was widely treated as likely to be effective only if as part of a wider series of moves. Moreover, the very interpretation of force was presented as resting on a context framed by this series. The frequent use of the word *strategy* helped make it normative in public discussion. The use of *strategy* as noun, adjective, and adverb is now a common currency with an assumed meaning, but that poses a serious problem. For example, on the BBC Radio Four discussion program *Any Questions?* on November 28, 2015, a program devoted in large part to the security crisis in the aftermath of terrorist attacks in Paris, Charles Clarke, the former Labour home secretary (minister of the interior in most states), referred to "a strategy to achieve what you are going to do," while the highly experienced chairman, Jonathan Dimbleby, commented on what he termed "a strategic point."

Returning to the eighteenth century, it is pertinent in the conclusions to consider how far changes in warfare and international relations led to a new strategic environment and thus, to a new language about war. The progressive, developmental, and teleological model would argue that that was indeed the case. The explanation might vary, with differing emphases placed on the rise of public politics, or of global power projection, or of the new politics of revolution. So also with the weight placed on classification and categorization, and thus on the scientific revolution and Enlightenment as applied to war. In part, this serves as a parallel with the varied accounts offered for other eighteenth-century developments, whether described in terms of Enlightenment or the age of revolutions.

It is also pertinent to draw attention to the rise in military preparedness as a consequence of the development of productive capacity and
organizational methods. It was possible to equip large armies and navies.
Large quantities of powder and shot were available for operations. Mass
itself provided a strategic resource. A British memorandum of February
1798 noted the scale of the Royal Navy, including 85 ships of the line,
23 sixty-four gunners, 13 fifty gunners, and 136 frigates, as well as their
global range. Alongside 116 out of the 257 warships above being in home
waters in the Channel, the North Sea, and Ireland, there were large and
potent forces elsewhere, including 39 in the Mediterranean, 42 in the
West Indies, and 24 in the Cape and East Indies.[22]

There are, however, shared problems for the various narratives of
change in the eighteenth century mentioned above. Notable problems
include an unwanted degree of westernization, the shaping of variety
into a misleading degree of clarity, and the mistaking of language and
concepts for reality. In short, this issue, like so many others, returns us to
perennial questions of conceptualization, methodology, and historiography in historical scholarship and indeed to the values and deficiencies
of such scholarship as an account of the past.

In practice, despite the growing importance of bases in and on the
route to the Indian Ocean,[23] change in the eighteenth century was not
transformative, and there were no significant developments in the tactical, operational, technological, and geopolitical spheres and certainly
none to match those in the nineteenth century. Similarly, as far as Western navies were concerned, there was remarkably little change in the
eighteenth century, in contrast to the expansion of professional navies
and specialized fighting ships and the development of line-ahead tactics.
As there is scant sign of novelty being seen as the solution, the emphasis
instead on both land and sea was placed on command skills and character. These were particularly significant because commanders operated in
a context of only limited information.[24] The tools to obtain and process
information about the enemy do not seem to have been very well developed. The terms *spion* (spy) and *kundschafter* (social) appeared rarely in
Clausewitz's *On War.*

Westernization is a valid charge against much of the discussion of
eighteenth-century warfare because what is decried as a Western-centric

view can lead to a failure to appreciate the extent to which other cultures were also well capable of strategic analysis and practice. This is the case whether these are conceived in the shape of narrow, more operational, military criteria or with reference to the broader approach offered in this book. Caveats can be readily offered in the shape of a lack of activity by Japan and of external warfare by China for most of the period 1770–1835.[25] However, even if weight is placed on these arguments, they scarcely address the questions of developments in India or southwest Asia, or indeed of Chinese policy prior to 1770.

This, then, leads to the question of whether there was indeed strategic innovation outside the West, or whether it was simply the Western powers that saw such innovation. The difficulties of studying this issue for non-Western states are apparent, but there are many signs of flexibility by such states in response to the challenges of the period. This description presents the situation in a somewhat mechanistic action-reaction fashion, which is less than a complete account. Nevertheless, that element is apparent—for example, with rapid and substantial developments in Maratha war-making in India late in the century, in part developments in response to British military capability and activity.[26]

When conflict between Western and non-Western states is considered, it is apparent that strategy embraced a range of factors. For example, in India, Britain's ability to benefit from divisions, between and within regional powers, involved military, political, and financial factors. Key structural advantages for British strategy included the institutional continuity of the East India Company, the world's leading corporation, and the ability of the most profitable global trading system, that of maritime Britain, to generate profits and provide credit that would enable both company and state to wage sustained, large-scale conflict. Funds helped ensure success in the crucial military labor market.[27] Operational factors, notably the improved logistics that underwrote mobility, were crucial, as were command skills, contingency, and political factors. To abstract one of these factors and label it strategy is, at best, unhelpful.

Strategy was a fully fledged process and habit of thought prior to the widespread use of the concept with that term in the nineteenth century. Strategy was employed to assess state interest, to further it, and to expound it. This understanding and practice of strategy was both a traditional usage but also in part one related, at least in its presentation, to the development of the idea of the state and thus to political modernization. In particular, strategy rested, at least in part, on a capacity for abstraction and on the conviction that planning was necessary. In 1758, Holdernesse responded to a point made by Frederick II to the British envoys and presented strategy as a key way to gain the initiative:

> The remark that was made to you, that our enemies acted upon a systematical plan, and guided their operations to the execution of it, is certainly a very true one, and if there is no fixed system, or particular plan of operations, settled between His Majesty and the King of Prussia, it has not arisen either from neglect, or want of good-will, on this side, but, from the nature and circumstances of the war . . . all that could be thought of was how to make head against so many enemies.[28]

Pitt the Elder pointed out the need in Germany to base strategy on the moves of opponents.[29]

Strategy, in its conceptual development in eighteenth-century Europe, drew on the measurement of factors and calibration of concerns linked to the mathematization related to the scientific revolution. For example, in early 1748, as diplomats negotiated an end to the War of the Austrian Succession, Giuseppe Ossorio, the experienced Sardinian envoy in London, who was to go on to be an effective foreign minister, mentioned the possibility of the Dutch being ceded all of Austrian Brabant (part of modern Belgium) north of a line from Antwerp to Maastricht to serve as a better barrier to French expansionism, adding that it would mean that this loss would ensure that Britain had to satisfy Austrian interests in Italy.[30] That would be unacceptable to Charles Emmanuel III of Sardinia, who was threatened by Austrian power there. This possibility, which was not in fact pursued, was a classic instance of the equivalence that was significant for diplomatic negotiations. Both these equivalents and the negotiations involved another aspect of strategy, one not only closely linked to preparations for renewed conflict but also capturing the unfixed nature of the possible battlefield, of the sides involved and of their determination.

Ideas of strategy in the eighteenth century were in part linked to the categorization of knowledge and means of expressing opinion. These ideas, however, also had a degree of imprecision that reflected both the difficulties of definitions and, separately, the range of political cultures, their disparate views, and the more general lack of distinction between public and private life, not least due to the importance of connections and networks. Indeed, the very imprecision of strategy as a concept and practice in the period helps ensure that it is both more nebulous and yet also more useful as a subsequent analytical approach. That provides a way to consider the background to Clausewitz. Rather than reacting to a well-established literature on war and practice of strategy, he, a military practitioner first and foremost, was responding to a situation that appeared singularly unfixed and therefore threatening as well as ripe with possibilities, notably in the example of popular resistance to Napoleon offered by Spain.[31] Instability, threat, and the need for analysis were all linked.

Moreover, the situation would have appeared even more unfixed had Clausewitz been aware of the position around the world. From that perspective, Clausewitz's background was unfortunate as he had no direct experience of conflict with non-Western forces and/or in non-Western environments. In that, Clausewitz was very different not only to the British military but also to many of their Russian and Austrian counterparts, as well as some of the French ones. The capacity for reflecting on strategic cultures and parameters in this widest sense was more present for a Wellington than for a Clausewitz, although the latter was interested in and interesting on the dynamic of insurgency and counterinsurgency warfare.[32] Wellington himself was extremely well read in military matters but more significantly, had held senior command positions in India as well as in Europe.[33]

Any emphasis on Wellington underlines the point that it was Britain (and Russia), and not France, that was victorious in the long eighteenth century and therefore, that any concentration on the latter is misplaced. This is even more the case if due weight is devoted to the significance of strategy for naval power and vice versa. The political and organizational revolutions that underlay the development and sustaining of British naval power were more significant for the pursuit of strategy on a global scale than the French Revolution. So also with the geopolitics and strategic thinking that led Charles, 3rd Duke of Richmond, to comment on France in 1785: "Instead of drawing her off from the continent [Europe] to the ocean, we [Britain] want some power to draw her attention from the ocean to the continent."[34]

The standard focus on Clausewitz is an instance of the unfortunate dominance of the study of war not only by Western commentators but also by commentators whose willingness to engage with other traditions and with their implications was limited, which underlines the problems posed by his recent and current influence.[35] To work today, military analysis has to apply to Madagascar and Paraguay, as well as to European powers. The same was true of the past. This book serves to indicate the variety of circumstances and developments that commentators could draw on and therefore, the difficulties of generalizing or indeed of discerning a crucial identity to war and an inherent set of practices. The challenge looking forward is to produce a global account of strategy.

The limited use of the term *strategy* in the early decades of the period when, because it had been advanced, it could have been employed is instructive about the contemporary need for such a term. This limited use can be presented as a failure or alternatively, the lack of a need can be suggested. For example, Charles Ingrao's analysis of Austrian policy is based on the thesis that the government sought to create and maintain secure and stable buffer zones, rather than pursuing extensive conquests in any specific direction. Ingrao continued by arguing that immediate needs dominated the situation and proposed the existence of strategy without the term:

> To be sure, there seems to be no evidence that the Emperor and
> his ministers ever conceived or clearly elucidated a strategy for the
> maintenance of secure buffers beyond the monarchy's borders. Nor are
> there more than a few instances when they expressed an appreciation
> of the multiple strategic difficulties that were occasioned by Austria's
> exposed position in the heart of East Central Europe. The state and extent
> of their awareness, however, cannot confute the course of their actions,
> nor the compelling strategic structures that predetermined the path they
> chose. Rather like actors reading a new script for the first time, they simply
> stumbled through their lines without benefiting from the perspective that
> comes with familiarity with the plot.[36]

This account finds strategy in geopolitical needs, with a response similar to that which the stadial writers of the eighteenth century discerned in the case of nomadic peoples. That account has some merit, but strategic cultures, however, entailed a more active contribution from the assumptions and views of contemporaries, and these assumptions and views cannot be traced solely to geopolitics.

These cultures, as discussed in this book, focused on the political contexts, causes, and purposes of the use of power rather than the military choices that related to implementation. The use of strategy in the eighteenth century was somewhat different from the popular understanding of it that was to follow. It is instructive, for example, to note the definition in *The Compact Encyclopedia*, a British work of 1927 based on *The New Gresham Encyclopedia* (1921–24). This definition drew on Jomini, as reflected by Sir Edward Hamley's *Operations of War Explained and Illustrated* (3rd ed., Edinburgh, 1872) and Lieutenant-Colonel Walter James's *Modern Strategy: An Outline of the Principles which Guide the Conduct of Campaigns* (2nd edition, Edinburgh, 1904):

> Strategy is the art of war which deals with the movement of troops within the theatre of war, or, alternatively, the art by which a commander or other responsible authority is enabled to formulate his plan of campaign. Tactics, on the other hand, is the art of moving troops in the presence of the enemy, or of carrying out the movements and operations necessary to bring the strategical plan to a successful conclusion. The two words are therefore complementary, and strategy depends more or less for its success on the tactical handling of troops by subordinate commanders. The aim of military strategy is the ultimate destruction of the enemy forces.[37]

This account, however, was of only limited applicability for the 1920s, let alone the eighteenth century. It assumed a form of decisive victory that was frequently, in practice, neither viable nor sought and underplayed the political dimension. The latter factor in particular arose when an operational definition of strategy was advanced, as in this encyclopedia. This operational definition reflected a militarization of strategy that was not only not appropriate for the eighteenth century but that also helped to lead Germany to total failure in World War I.[38] In practice, the German military became too powerful and too focused on the concept and pursuit of decisive victory through attack, as in Moltke the Elder's *Instruction for Large Unit Commands* (1869).[39]

This situation ensured that the earlier one, in which institutional practice and political assumptions rested on important political and social configurations reflecting linked constituencies of support, was superseded by one far more focused on the military high command. Ironically but possibly not surprisingly,[40] this development and indeed the general staff, the body entrusted with strategic planning, were not capable of the strategic acuity that was required. In part, this failure reflected a difficulty in moving from a linear pattern of strategy consideration in which outcomes were planned and secured to one in which strategy was relative as well as contextual, such that the enemy gets his say, and it was necessary to adapt plans accordingly and in a perceptive fashion. This Germany failed to do in either world war.

NOTES

1. H. Sicherman, "The Revival of Geopolitics," *Intercollegiate Review* (2002): 16–23; L. Simón and J. Rogers, "The Return of European Geopolitics," *RUSI Journal* 155, no. 3 (2010): 58–64.

2. M. T. Owens, "Editor's Corner," *Orbis* 58 (2014): 162.

3. J. A. Downie, "Polemical Strategy and Swift's *The Conduct of the Allies*," *Prose Studies* 4 (1981): 134–45.

4. Strachan, *Direction of War*: 2.

5. Strachan, *Direction of War*: 3.

6. Strachan, *Direction of War*: 12, 23.

7. Instructions for Fournier, sent on mission to London, April 18, 1745, AE. CP. Ang. 421 fol. 14. For the role of Argenson and of François de Bussy, former envoy in London, P. Vaucher, ed., *Recueil des instructions données aux ambassadeurs et ministers de France, vol. 25, pt. 2, Angleterre vol. 3* (Paris, 1965): 321.

8. R. A. Gabriel and P. L. Savage, *Crisis in Command: Mismanagement in the Army* (New York, 1978); Lieutenant-General H. R. McMaster, *Dereliction of Duty: Lyndon Johnson, Robert McNamara, the Joint Chiefs of Staff, and the Lies that Led to Vietnam* (New York, 1997).

9. Peter J. Heather, "Holding the Line: Frontier Defense and the Later Roman Empire," in Victor D. Hanson, ed., *Makers of Ancient Strategy* (Princeton, NJ, 2010): 228.

10. For similar criticism directed at the American military, W. J. Astore, "Loving the German War Machine: America's Infatuation with Blitzkrieg, Warfighters, and Militarism," in M. Neiberg, ed., *Arms and the Man*: 14–15.

11. Strachan, *Direction of War*: 252.

12. Strachan, *Direction of War*: 253.

13. Victor D. Hanson, ed., *Makers of Ancient Strategy* (Princeton, NJ, 2010). The focus on Europe is seen, for example, in Beatrice Heuser's interesting "Betrachtungen zum Krieg im Zeitalter der Aufklärung," in S. Stockhorst, ed., *Krieg und Frieden im 18 Jahrhundert. Kulturgeschichtliche Studien* (Hannover, Germany, 2015): 349–73, and in the volume as a whole.

14. Strachan, *Direction of War*: 256.

15. For Gray's comment on Strachan, C. S. Gray, *The Strategy Bridge: Theory for Practice* (Oxford, 2010): 10n10.

16. For Great Power strategies, P. Lindström and S. Norrhem, *Flattering Alliances: Scandinavia, Diplomacy, and the Austrian-French Balance of Power, 1648–1740* (Lund, Sweden, 2013).

17. W. Murray, "Thoughts on Grand Strategy," in R. H. Murray and J. Lacey Sinnreich, eds., *The Shaping of Grand Strategy: Policy, Diplomacy, and War* (Cambridge, UK, 2011): 6n17.

18. Strachan, *Direction of War*: 11.

19. J. A. Delton, *Rethinking the 1950s: How Anticommunism and the Cold War Made America Liberal* (Cambridge, UK, 2013).

20. *Payne's Universal Chronicle*, August 19 and 26, September 9, 1758.

21. Ross to Forbes, September 15, 1758, Edinburgh, Scottish Record Office, GD 45/2/20/13.

22. BL. Add. 59281 fol. 13.

23. J. Black, *British Foreign Policy in an Age of Revolutions, 1783–1793* (Cambridge, UK, 1994): 34–50.

24. With regard to the fortifications of Dömitz and its capacity to provide a supply base, Richelieu to Champeaux, Envoy in Hamburg, September 6, 1757, Paris, Bibliothèque Victor Cousin, Fonds Richelieu, vol. 58.

25. T. Andrade, *The Gunpowder Age: China, Military Innovation, and the Rise of the West in World History* (Princeton, NJ, 2016).

26. S. Gordon, *Marathas, Marauders and State Formation in Eighteenth-Century India* (Delhi, 1994).

27. R. G. S. Cooper, *The Anglo-Maratha Campaign and the Contest for India: The Struggle for Control of the South Asian Military Economy* (Cambridge, UK, 2003).

28. Holdernesse to Yorke, May 11, 1758, NA. SP. 90/71.

29. Viry to Charles Emmanuel III, September 27, 1758, AST. LM. Ing. 63.

30. Ossorio to Charles Emmanuel III, January 19, 1748, AST. LM. Ing. 54.

31. C. Daase and J. W. Davis, eds., *Clausewitz on Small War* (Oxford, 2015).

32. P. D. Hughes, *Small Wars, or Peace Enforcement According to Clausewitz* (Carlisle Barracks, PA, 1996); C. Daase, "Clausewitz and Small Wars," in Strachan and A. Herberg-Rothe, eds., *Clausewitz in the Twenty-First Century* (Oxford, 2007): 182–95; B. Heuser, "Small Wars in the Age of Clausewitz: The Watershed between Partisan War and People's War," *Journal of Strategic Studies* 33 (2010): 147–59.

33. It is also worth comparing Napoleon and Wellington, in light of Clausewitz's reflections on command ability, indeed genius: see C. J. Rogers, "Clausewitz, Genius, and the Rules," *Journal of Military History* 66 (2002): 1167–76.

34. Richmond to Carmarthen, December 30, 1785, NA. PRO. 30/8/322 fol. 24.

35. J. Achenbach, "War and the Cult of Clausewitz: How a Long-Dead Prussian Shaped U. S. Thinking on the Persian Gulf," *Washington Post*, December 6, 1990, Style, D1, 4.

36. Ingrao, "Strategy and Geopolitics": 63.

37. *The Compact Encyclopedia* (6 vols., London, 1927), VI: 158–89.

38. A. Mombauer, *Helmuth von Moltke and the Origins of the First World War* (Cambridge, UK, 2001); D. E. Showalter, "German Grand Strategy: A Contradiction in Terms?"

Militägeschichtliche Mitteilungen 58 (1960): 65–102.

39. D. J. Hughes, ed., *Moltke on the Art of War* (Novato, CA, 1993).

40. N. Dixon, *On the Psychology of Military Incompetence* (London, 1976).

TEN

POSTSCRIPT: STRATEGY
AND MILITARY HISTORY

THE CONCLUSIONS OF THIS BOOK ARE READILY APPARENT. Strategy precedes the term, and unsurprisingly so. Moreover, the very imprecision and development of both term and concept reflects the protean nature of war and also its many interrelationships with other aspects of human activity. To focus on the eighteenth century, when the term was developed, it is possible to point to a range of new circumstances and requirements and to suggest that these made possible, indeed necessary, a new terminology. Such an approach might well center on the new languages of classification and analysis associated with the Enlightenment, or on the greater global range of power projection of the leading European powers, or on the need in Europe to adapt to the new geopolitics created by the rise of Russia and Prussia.

Alternatively, the focus could be narrower, notably on the combination of the crisis in French power and self-confidence following the Seven Years' War with the attempts of French commentators to offer solutions. These attempts included looking back to classical comparisons as part of an attempt to derive a general typology. This reading can then be taken forward to find this Enlightenment ferment helping shape the novelties of French Revolutionary warfare, and then its Napoleonic development. In turn, the assessment of the latter and the need to respond to it, both at the time and subsequently, are given explanatory power when both nineteenth-century strategy and Clausewitz are rolled forward for consideration.

So far, so good, but as this book also suggests, there are significant cross-currents, other narratives, and different analyses. Here, it is appropriate to pause and to reflect on the subject as currently discussed. In general, military history appears to encapsulate many of the faults of history as a subject, both academic and nonacademic. There is a tendency to provide overarching interpretations, to argue for significance, and to claim definitive status. Authors rarely say they work on interesting subjects and produce accounts and interpretations that are defensible. Instead, their topics are apparently of fundamental significance and their accounts are definitive. In short, we have the classic role of what are termed alpha males. Indeed, one of the authors cited in this book has referred to "penis envy." Readers might like to guess which one. Christopher Bassford described John Keegan, who referred to his "life cast among warriors," as "a moonstruck romantic about soldiers."[1] Possibly, military history proved especially attractive to "alpha males," however defined, while the exigencies of the publishing industry do not help. At any rate, a whole series of highly questionable works and interpretations have been launched and trumpeted accordingly—for example, those of the putative early-modern military revolution or of the allegedly transformative character of the French Revolution for warfare.

It would be wrong to make these points and then argue for an interpretation of my own as if it is some fashion was definitive. That would be mistaken because as is apparent from this book, any account based on Western developments has only so much to offer as a global history. Indeed, military history as a subject has benefited enormously over the last thirty years from a determined engagement with non-Western perspectives, perspectives that are no longer restricted to area studies. As a consequence, the subject is being rewritten. Second, modern strategic concerns have since the 1990s increasingly focused on non-Western topics, notably in East Asia and the Islamic world.

In comparison, some of the theoretical writing on strategy appears somewhat stale, not least in deploying a familiar cast of subjects and themes. Instead, there is much to be said for starting afresh, not least because much that is presented as the fundamentals of strategy are, in practice, culturally located and conditioned, rather than the universals they are suggested to be.

Moreover, turning solely to the West, it is more appropriate to be suggestive about links and influences, let alone causes, than to adopt the argument of assertion. The chronological context for the development of strategy is interesting, but the term could have been first advanced a century earlier or indeed later. The influence of this term can also be questioned and certainly prior to the need for a language to help justify the development of general staff systems. Fitness for purpose ensured that there was no particular need to use a new term during the Enlightenment or during the French Revolutionary/Napoleonic period.

This point returns us to the questions of the significance of the half century, ca. 1765–ca. 1815, or incorporating the consequences of the Seven Years' War and the American Independence, French Revolutionary, and Napoleonic Wars, together covering the period ca. 1760–ca. 1835. More specifically, how far does a reading of the warfare of the period encourage the idea that the development of strategy as a term was more than coincidental, and what about the added dimension of the renewal of military theory associated with Jomini and Clausewitz? The development of the term can more particularly be associated with the aftermath of the Seven Years' War, and the renewal of theory with Napoleon or rather, the response to him.

However, the idea of a causal link is less well established. Possibility, probability, coincident, and linkage and variables thereof offer an appropriate vocabulary and not, instead, cause or result. In contrast, in much social science work, there is the tendency to deploy past examples as if, far from their being problematic, indeed complex, there is no doubt about what they indicate. If strategy is intended to meet the challenge of uncertainty about the future, and thus to face conditions that are inherently unpredictable,[2] the nature of the context, within which change is being changed and the future considered, is far from constant. Moreover, individual conflicts emerged from particular circumstances. They did not set unprecedented strategic tasks, not least because the relationship between external and domestic challenges was far from new.

Within Europe, this relationship had been seen, in particular, with the "wars of religion" that followed the Protestant Reformation. Indeed, there was a somewhat circular pattern in Europe with the second cycle of conflicts ending in the restoration of the ancien régime in 1814–15, as the first cycle had led in 1648–67 to a series of peaces between states and to a consolidation of authority within them. Only in the New World was that course and chronology different, but ironically, the revolutions there between 1775 and 1825 neither set the theme for a new language of strategy nor proved the prime topic for commentators, as arguably, they should have done. That a misleading series of priorities and set of assumptions dominated the work of commentators possibly however should not surprise us.

Military history as a subject is made more significant because of its use in the discussion of modern military affairs. The assumptions that guide the former influence the latter, and vice versa. That, indeed, helps explain the context, if not relevance, of this book. The discussion of strategy at present, both in the public and by the military, tends to reflect the suspicion of politics and politicians that is an aspect of current discussion in at least part of the West. The content and tone but also confusion entailed can be gauged from a comment by Andrew Roberts, a leading British popular military historian and conservative commentator who also has influence in the United States. In 2016, he claimed, "Political considerations ought to play a minimal role in the formulation of strategy, though of course wars are ultimately fought for political reasons."[3] This approach is similar to that of Strachan. In seeking a space for military direction, a space presented as strategy, and defined by means of a strategy/policy dichotomy, Roberts, Strachan, and others are, explicitly or implicitly, criticizing the political dimension. Indeed, this dimension is frequently presented as incapacitating the military. The charge relates not simply to the supposed failure of strategy due to political direction but also to issues of resourcing, procurement, doctrine, and social engineering.

All these points are long-standing. Complaint about politicians was found from the Patriots during the American War of Independence, from British commanders during the Napoleonic Wars, and in many other instances. Such complaining reflects not simply debates about strategy, debates that generally involve criticism of those holding opposing views, but a more general situation of differentiation within governmental systems. This differentiation entailed political differences and social tensions, as well as institutional rivalries. The combination of these with the rise of the public sphere in the eighteenth and, even more, nineteenth centuries entailed issues and practices of accountability and would-be accountability. Wars encouraged this process, and notably if there were difficulties and failures.[4] In the nineteenth century, this was especially seen with the Crimean War for Britain (1854–56) and with the American Civil War (1861–65).

Civilian criticisms of military negligence were particularly apparent in both of these conflicts, but they were matched by military claims of civilian failures. The same was to be the pattern in the twentieth century, but this remark covers a number of different tendencies including significant crosscurrents. The emphasis varies by country, period, individual war, and specific service. Particular bitterness attached to the conduct of World War I, and notably from the 1930s. It was argued that the generals had devised unrealistic prewar plans and then pursued attritional strategies that both caused high casualties and lacked success. Indeed, the historical discussion of strategy in part became a retrospective about that conflict. This was not only the case in Britain and France. For example, the long and ultimately rather self-defeating debate on Frederick the Great's strategy, centering on the question of whether he survived the Seven Years' War by waging decisive war or a war of attrition, in part reflected the German preoccupation with their defeat in World War I, although the debate had begun before 1914.

World War II brought aspects of the same situation. British commanders took much of the blame for repeated initial defeats at the hands of Germany and Japan in 1940–42, as well as for a more general lack of preparedness. The American equivalent was subsequent blame for failure in the Vietnam War and in particular, criticism of the area commander, General William Westmoreland, and of the Joint Chiefs of Staff.[5]

In each case, there were responses from the military that both countered specific criticisms and found responsibility for failure primarily in the field of political direction and intervention, as well as in prewar circumstances stemming from political control, notably an alleged lack of expenditure. The range of factors included, in World War I, the anger by British generals focused on the Western Front about attempts to direct military resources elsewhere, a strategic debate sometimes summarized in terms of "Westerners" versus "Easterners." There was also criticism of direction by Lloyd George in World War I and by Churchill in both.

Moreover, for the Vietnam War, there was the repeated claim that the prospects for victory were compromised by limits on American strategy set by politicians and as a result of political considerations.

The emphasis on a nonpolitical strategy, therefore, was in part located in the realm of counterfactuals or might-have-beens and, in particular, in terms of arguments that more favorable outcomes were possible and would have been pursued but for political interference. This thesis drew part of its force from revisionist work emphasizing the success of British and American forces in the world wars and, in particular, the stress, among specialists, on the marked improvements in British fighting quality and method in 1916–18 and the consequent ability to win victory over Germany on the Western Front in 1918.[6]

Moving the focus in explanations of Allied victory in both world wars from superior resources to campaigning ability was significant as it fostered the view that the military dimension had been underrated and, instead, led to a concern with distinctive features of this dimension. Much of the discussion was in terms of "face of battle" considerations, notably unit cohesion and tactical skill, but strategy appeared the key element that could be isolated as providing an explanation of and from command skill. Setting up strategy as an area of rivalry between military and politicians therefore helped account for military failure and also established an analysis within which accountability to political direction and public scrutiny could and should be constrained.

This has been the pattern for post-1945 discussion and became more significant when the end of the Cold War led to a marked revival in warmaking by both the United States and Britain. Political interference was held responsible for strategic, operational, and tactical limitations and failures, and most notably in the American failure to use the Iraqi defeat in Kuwait in 1991 to ensure the overthrow of Saddam Hussein, in the unwillingness in 2003 to plan for the aftermath of his overthrow, and in the British decision to send insufficient forces to Afghanistan in the late 2000s.

The specifics of these charges repay examination, but so, too, do the misleading tendency to treat military and civilians as automatically opposed abstractions and the latter as generally wrong. For example, in 2003 in contrast to this view, the US State Department followed a different policy to that of the Department of Defense, a policy that was more alive to circumstances in Iraq. Moreover, the military leadership was scarcely unwilling to take part in expeditionary warfare. There is room for different assessments of the conflicts of the last quarter century. More relevant for this book is the suggestion that these conflicts have influenced the historical discussion of strategy, overly so, and indeed, that such discussion is generally affected by current and recent circumstances.

The dependence on circumstances is readily apparent on the international scale. For example, in the Middle East, the modernization of armed forces in the 1920s and 1930s, notably in Egypt, Iran, Iraq, and Turkey, and the opening to foreign influences led to the use of the word *al-stratijiah*, a term derived from the Western world. There was not a word drawn from classical Arabic that could be used, and the idea would therefore have been previously conveyed as a phrase, notably planning and military leadership. In the modern Middle East, *al-stratijiah* has become a very common term, one applied to economic programs as well as military.

Arguing for contextualization, and for variations and contention accordingly, does not address the issue of how best to discern any consistent elements, but it does explain why particular interpretations should be treated as emerging from specific circumstances. As this book has suggested, the value of these interpretations as global models can be questioned. This is notably so if attention moves from technology to its impact in particular contexts, and also if stadial interpretations of development, with their emphasis on common trends, albeit at a different pace, are replaced by more culturally specific accounts.

The book began with a discussion of the concept of strategic culture; and consideration of the situation not only in the eighteenth century but also more generally leads to an underlining of the value of this concept which is loose enough to permit consideration not only of the context and contents of strategy but also of its means. Therefore, rather than assuming a somehow "pure" or "essential" character of strategy, however defined and whatever the authorities cited, it is better to put that approach to one side as inherently unable to cope with the temporal, spatial, ideological, and organizational range of relevant human experience and with the key role of context in helping establish analytical concepts and their validity. Thus, for example, Sun Tzu is best approached through the perspective of Daoist philosophy.[7]

As long as cultures are not unduly reified, the understanding of such a range of experience is provided by the concept of strategic cultures. That concept does not mean a lack of disagreement about specific strategies, but it presents such disagreements as occurring in very different contexts, each molded by specific circumstances, whether human, environmental, or geopolitical. Taking this further, the contextual and relative nature of strategy both reflects and helps ensure that actions affect the situation.

This approach suggests that a looser definition of strategy is both valuable but also beside the point as it is necessary to do the hard work of assessing specific strategic cultures. This assessment has to take note of change through time, and it is possible to shape the account of change in order to suggest a general trend setting new strategic parameters. That approach has been employed, most prominently with attempts to find global meaning in the "gunpowder revolution." That is clearly an approach that has some value, but it needs to be matched by an awareness not only of the deficiencies of the theory, but also of the vitality and significance of difference in past circumstances.[8]

No one branch of scholarship owns the past, and much of value can be gained from the questions raised by a range of specialists. However, for the answers to be valid, it is appropriate to note the complexities of the past and the changes within it. These are best approached through archival work, the close scrutiny and careful contextualization of texts, and an understanding of a broad range of scholarship. The label of the scholar involved does not matter. They do not need to call themselves historians, but they do need to appreciate and deploy historical sources in order to understand the past, as opposed to rushing at it with the issues and values of the present. The latter is a challenge for all of us, but some are better at appreciating the resulting need for caution in exposition. Strategy is an aspect of this more general analytical tension and not an element outside it. This was the case in the eighteenth century, and it remains so today.

NOTES

1. C. Bassford, "John Keegan and the Grand Tradition of Trashing Clausewitz: A Polemic," *War in History* 1 (1994): 334.

2. C. S. Gray, *Strategy and Defence Planning: Meeting the Challenge of Uncertainty* (Oxford, 2014).

3. A. Roberts, *Elegy: The First Day on the Somme* (London, 2016): 35.

4. B. H. Reid, "Rationality and Irrationality in Union Strategy, April 1861–March 1862," *War in History* 1 (1994): 20–21.

5. Lieutenant-General H. R. McMaster, *Dereliction of Duty: Lyndon Johnson, Robert McNamara, the Joint Chiefs of Staff, and the Lies that Led to Vietnam* (New York, 1997).

6. J. Black, *The Great War and the Making of the Modern World* (London, 2011).

7. D. M. C. Yuen, *Deciphering Sun Tzu: How to Read the Art of War* (London, 2014).

8. J. Black, *Beyond the Military Revolution: War in the Seventeenth-Century World* (Basingstoke, UK, 2011).

SELECTED FURTHER READING

Barfield, Thomas J. *The Perilous Frontier: Nomadic Empires and China, 221 BC to AD 1757.* Cambridge, UK: Basil Blackwell, 1989.

Baugh, Daniel A. *The Global Seven Years War, 1754–1763.* Harlow, UK: Longman, 2011.

Chickering, Roger, and S. Förster, eds. *War in an Age of Revolution, 1775–1815.* Cambridge, UK: Cambridge University Press, 2010.

Dai, Yingcong. *The Sichuan Frontier and Tibet: Imperial Strategy in the Early Qing.* Seattle: University of Washington Press, 2009.

Glete, Jan. *Navies and Nations: Warships, Navies, State-Building, 1500–1860.* Stockholm: Almqvist and Wiksell, 1993.

Gommans, Jos. *The Rise of the Indo-Afghan Empire, c. 1710–1780.* Leiden, the Netherlands: Brill, 1995.

Harding, Richard. *Seapower and Naval Warfare, 1650–1830.* Abingdon, UK: Routledge, 1999.

Ostwald, J. *Vauban under Siege: Engineering, Efficiency and Martial Vigor in the War of the Spanish Succession.* Leiden, the Netherlands: Brill, 2007.

Perdue, Peter. *China Marches West: The Qing Conquest of Central Eurasia, 1600–1800.* Cambridge, MA: Harvard University Press, 2005.

Rodger, Nicholas. *The Command of the Ocean: A Naval History of Britain, 1649–1815.* London: Allen Lane, 2004.

Starkey, Armstrong. *European and Native American Warfare, 1676–1815.* Abingdon, UK: Routledge, 1998.

Storrs, Christopher, ed. *The Fiscal-Military State in Eighteenth Century Europe.* Farnham, UK: Ashgate, 2009.

Tallett, Frank, and Trim, David, eds. *European Warfare, 1350–1750.* Cambridge, UK: Cambridge University Press, 2010.

Waley-Cohen, Joanna. *The Culture of War in China: Empire and the Military under the Qing Dynasty.* London: I. B. Tauris, 2006.

INDEX

JEREMY BLACK is a British historian and professor of history at the University of Exeter. He is author of more than one hundred books including *Fighting for America: The Struggle for Mastery in North America, 1519–1871* and is a recipient of the Samuel Eliot Morison Prize from the Society for Military History.